NAMIBIA

by

COLIN O'BRIEN WINTER

LUTTERWORTH PRESS
GUILDFORD AND LONDON

First published in Great Britain 1977
Lutterworth Press
Guildford & London
ISBN 0-7188-2325-7

255 Jefferson Ave. S E, Grand Rapids, Mich. 49503

Printed in the United States of America

To
HERMAN JA TOIVO
a Namibian patriot
who has been on this mountain before us

Contents

Chapter One

The Removal of Undesirables

The car pulled into the driveway of our home in Windhoek, and two members of the Secret Police got out. This time they were coming for me. My wife Mary was chatting to Erica Murray, a young visitor from Cape Town who had come to us to lead a conference aimed at examining racism in our Church.

"No fuss," I thought. "I must not be arrested with the kids around." I quickly got up and, without looking at the women, walked towards the front door. I could take them into my study, then we could leave by the back door with no scene. My mind felt very clear, and though in my ministry in South Africa I had often experienced fear of one sort or another, I was not afraid now. I just wanted to get the whole thing over with.

"Good afternoon, Captain," I said. "Please come in." Captain Thomasse of the Security Branch stood there in front of me clutching a piece of white paper against the breast of his blue shirt. We shook hands. His assistant, whose nickname was "Kalahari," shook hands also. In Southern Africa we always observe the old world courtesies, if nothing else. I moved aside for them to enter the small hallway and noticed that they too looked awkward.

"Do you mind coming through to my office? It's at the back of the house. We have a guest." My eyes were riveted to the paper that the captain was holding.

Then he began, "Bishop, I'm very sorry to have to do this to you . . . I . . . er . . . that is, we both want you to know that there is nothing personal in it." Now he was stammering and looking apologetically at me. This was the same man who had watched me in the Magistrate's Court week after week while the black leaders of the Ovambo contract workers' strike were standing trial; he had politely arranged for me to see the Ovambo accused. He moved the sheet of paper until it rested against his tie so that the print was towards him. It was impossible to read what was on it.

Now the strain was mounting. I just wanted to grab at the paper. What was it to be: house arrest, 180 days solitary confinement, or hours of questioning down at Special Branch Headquarters?

We stopped for a moment while I replied, "Please don't apologize, Captain. I don't hold you personally responsible. I fully understand that you have your orders and that you must do what you have come to do." It was then that I remembered that my tiny study was in utter chaos, with papers lying scattered all over the floor. I stood by the long table which the Africans had made for me from kiaat wood at our mission in Odibo. As Mary was within hearing distance, I just stood helplessly, and then, since there was nowhere else to go, I asked them to sit. I gripped the edge of the thick table top and looked the captain in the face, noting that he too was pale and nervous. He licked his lips and said, "I have now to caution you." ("That thou doest, do quickly.") I nodded and said nothing.

"Are you the Right Reverend Colin O'Brien Winter, Bishop of Damaraland?"

"I am."

In retrospect, I felt that I should have attempted to say something impressive, something that might have strengthened me as I uttered it. There was nothing to say. For thirteen years, I had waited for this moment, and I knew that it could have come at any time.

It might have been as I handed out soup to old black people in the shanty town of Windhoek's Old Location. I might have received it after the Synod of our Church dared to raise its voice and call apartheid "repugnant to the Christian conscience." It could have happened any time in a thousand different situations. Somehow, I had never thought of receiving it in the privacy of my own home.

Then came the legal jargon. He let the paper drop from where it nestled against his chest, cleared his throat, and began to read in a voice that was quiet and restrained, with strong Afrikaans overtones to his English.

"Whereas the Administrator in Executive Committee has, in terms of Section I (I) of the Undesirables Removal Proclamation, 1920 (Proclamation No. 50 of 1920) as amended, directed me to issue an order to you The Right Reverend Colin O'Brien Winter, Bishop of the Diocese of Damaraland, 5 Braams Street, Box 57, Windhoek, to leave the territory of South West Africa before 12 noon on the fourth day of March 1972. . . ."

"Thank God, it's deportation, thank God, thank God," I thought. I heard no more, but I kept staring at him. "Thank you, Captain," I said when he stopped reading. "I have understood what you have said." He handed me the paper; I took it and read it through until my eyes rested for a moment on the words at the bottom. It was written on ordinary official administration paper, and printed at the foot of the page was this advice: "Avoid delay, please quote above mentioned reference number." I was tempted to smile.

What followed was a simple piece of etiquette. I looked at him and said, "No, I don't hold you responsible. Please pray for me and I shall pray for you."

They rose to leave and the Captain stumbled over my Boxer dog. I showed the men out and then walked back to join the women, now sitting in silence in the other room.

Erica was the first to speak. "Why was that man crying?" she asked me. "He was crying, wasn't he? What's the matter with him?"

I looked past her towards Mary, who had sensed, the moment that I had left the room in silence, that the police had come for me.

"We've been deported," I said, fighting back the tears. "They've given us a week to get out." After thirteen years in South Africa, we were now homeless. Mary burst into tears.

A deportation order had also been made out against David de Beer, my young South African assistant. A few days later one would be given also to Father Stephen Hayes and Toni Halberstadt, a teacher in our high school at Odibo.

Dave strode into the house, pale but as determined as ever. "The two Branch men were waiting outside the office and they handed it to me as I was helping Ed. D'you see what they did? They tampered with the law to get us out. They had to tamper with the law. They couldn't do it any other way. It makes you sick as hell. But, it doesn't say that we are to leave South Africa."

As he was speaking, an old, beat-up Peugeot station wagon rolled into the driveway. It had been fondly named Musrum, after a mythical mouse. The staff of the diocese had come to stand by me. They had driven over from our embattled diocesan office, where crisis after crisis had hit us. Into that office, telephone calls had come from England, America, and South Africa as people tried to find out about the Ovambo strike and wanted information about the freedom struggle. Here came diplomats from all parts of the world, as well as African chiefs, black miners, students, writers, journalists. We had attempted to focus the attention of the outside world on this arid, suffering territory and to be the mouthpiece of the oppressed. We had refused to be silenced.

Ed Morrow, a builder from South Africa, had come to the diocese after withdrawing from a South African company in protest against the poor wages it paid its blacks. He ran a multiracial cooperative building team for me. He now sat on the couch opposite me and then moved quietly round the room handing out cool drinks. He and his wife Laureen lived in the flat beneath us. She worked with Coloured and African people in the local TB sanatorium.

Father Hayes came in and said: "You can tell our bishop's a Commie, 'cause he wears blerrie red shirts." Everyone laughed and the tension eased a bit. We had all known that tribulation was bound to come, yet all were shattered when it did. Marge Schmidt, my American secretary, wept and then calmly helped to serve drinks to the others as they arrived. Everyone seemed determined to avoid brooding, self-pity. They grieved and then got over it.

Suddenly, tiredness hit me. Great black thunderclouds were gathering overhead. The heat was oppressive, and even though the doors and windows of the house were wide open, there was no air. I told everyone that I was going to lie down and excused myself.

Once, Catherine, my youngest, had asked me in her direct way: "What would you do if they put you in jail, Dad?" I had laughed, thought for a moment, and then replied, "Well, I'd read my Bible a lot."

"Do they allow you a Bible, then?" she asked, shoving a piece of meat into the dog's mouth. Then, looking at me again, she added thoughtfully, "I should think it would be very boring just reading an old Bible all day and night long in prison, wouldn't you, Sheba?" The dog tried to bite her nose.

"Fat lot of sympathy you get from your kids," I thought.

"Go and get ready for ballet, darling," Mary interjected.

"I'm not going." Without any warning, Catherine suddenly burst into tears. Mary rushed after her into the bedroom, and I listened wretchedly to this conversation:

"Why not? What have they been saying to you?"

"Nothing."

"Tell me. Who's been saying things to you . . . have they been saying nasty things about Daddy? Tell me, darling."

"I won't tell you and I won't go. I'm never going there again." Catherine seemed determined not to add to my burdens, so we never found out what had been said. Her mother took her out to buy a new pair of shoes. She came back bouncing, grabbed the dog around its neck and rolled with it to the floor. "Dad, can you teach dogs to do ballet?"

Now the dog lay at my feet on the bed, made a few circles, sighed and dropped down again with a flop. I hadn't the energy to move her off the covers.

I opened my eyes and looked towards the ceiling to where one of the top drawers of the cupboard was open. An old radio, which had belonged to Bishop Mize, my American predecessor, lay inside it covered in dust. A pair of candlesticks, which he had used when he said Mass for the African contract workers in their shanty churches lay lopsided next to it. I put both my hands behind my neck, lifted my feet onto the dog's back, and closed my eyes.

My mind raced back and forth and I tried to think about the past years in Namibia. It had been thirteen years to the day since we came to South Africa. I'd been in Windhoek seven years. Catherine was just over two when we came here. Bob Mize was deported four years ago. I had been his dean for four years. His picture hung next to my bed. Much in the room belonged to him. He'd taken nothing away with him when he left us, just a small suitcase containing his cassock and vestments. Mary now came into the room and lay on the bed next to me.

"Have they all gone?" I asked her.

"Yes, they are such pets. They say you have to fight it. They think you should appeal to the High Court, that you mustn't give in; they are all right behind you. The government couldn't bring anything that would stand up in a court of law, so they had to alter the law to get you out. This 1920 law says you can't do that to a British citizen."

"You sound like Disraeli. Do you want Ted Heath to send in gunboats?"

"Will you fight it?" she turned to me appealingly.

"Not right at this moment, I won't; I'm sleeping." I wasn't. I was thinking of Bob Mize again.

They had said that he was promoting terrorism by corresponding with expatriate Namibian blacks in Dar es Salaam. I could hear him telling about his own deportation: "I offered to show them the letters, but they just said that they had opened all my letters and knew what I'd said. Shucks, it just makes you mad as crazy when they say things like that. They know that I am a pacifist and don't hold with violence."

Yes, Bishop, they knew; indeed, they knew. They had watched your every movement, tapped your phone, planted spies and informers on you, stalked you as you traveled, asked black students in Ovamboland to report back on your trips there, visited your parishioners when you left them and asked for a report on your conversations. Oh, they knew you all right.

Then they deported him. They couldn't tolerate his honesty, so they just had to get rid of him. I remember clearly the day he left. The waiting room at Windhoek airport was crowded with white people, sitting around; some of the white women wore expensive Karakul furs. African porters carried the luggage of departing passengers. The loudspeakers called for passengers to board the plane for Cape Town. Then, suddenly kneeling at my feet was my bishop asking me, in his rich Kansas drawl, for a blessing. I stammered one out, holding back the tears and then he got up; hunching his shoulders, he was gone.

Mary's arm reached out to me. "Why don't you sleep?" she asked. "You'll feel better for it later. Try and relax; forget everything."

"I can't seem to drop off. My mind keeps racing from one thing to another. I was just thinking about Bob Mize, and Catherine . . . and it's so hot. Why couldn't they have chucked us out in July? What am I supposed to say to the blacks in Katutura tomorrow? I just don't want to go and face them. Why don't we send Captain Thomasse to tell them?"

I got up and showered. The cool water had a calming effect and I returned to the bedroom. I didn't want to see anyone or go anywhere. I just wanted to hide.

Mary came into the room. "Catherine's back."

"Have you told her?"

"Yes."

"What did she say?"

"Well, she cried, and asked if we could take the dog to England with us. She's fine again and has gone to the drive-in with the Morrows. Dave is here and I've asked him to stay for supper. Someone phoned him at the cathedral to 'congratulate' you all on being deported. He said it was too good for you; hanging would have been better." Our well-wisher was the son of a previous dean of a cathedral in South Africa.

Chapter Two

Diocese in a Desert

I was given a week to get out of Namibia or be arrested. During the last few days there, I celebrated Mass with a few friends around the kitchen table in the bishop's house. I thought it would have been wrong to worship in the cathedral, a place where I felt I was no longer wanted or welcome. To my staff and me it seemed that the whites there had made their stand with the oppressor. The new dean did nothing to enlighten them. I felt this was a sellout of everything I'd stood for. When Bishop Mize was deported, the white churchwardens, though distressed, were prepared to do nothing to protest his removal. I fared no better. "We will sign no petitions," they told me flatly. At a time of mental stress, the cathedral might have been the place I would have gone to find peace; but, under these circumstances, it was the last place I would set foot in.

St. George's Cathedral, Windhoek, was the seat of seven successive bishops of Damaraland. It is a small stone building with a green, corrugated iron roof, and like so many other Anglican churches in Southern Africa, it made a poor attempt at capturing the style of an English village church. Begun in the early 1920's, it had never been completed. The obvious intention from the beginning, it seemed to me, was to cater to the needs of the small, white, English-speaking community of Windhoek. That their cathedral should ever minister to blacks had never been in their minds; they concentrated their attention on the local white settler community and government officials. These latter had been sent out from South Africa to replace the German colonial government after the League of Nations, in 1919, had declared them no longer fit to exercise colonial rule in the territory. So this cathedral congregation of expatriate South Africans had never grown into a lively Christian community solely because its horizons were too narrow; it was concerned simply with its own needs. In a word, it preferred to remain exclusively and monotonously white and so had never grown because it had never wanted to, remaining all the time a white religious club.

Nonetheless, this unpretentious brown stone building had a vital place in my own life. When I was in Windhoek, my day began inside its walls when, with my staff, I spent about two hours at worship and prayer there. I knew most of its people intimately and tried hard to be both their pastor and their friend. Yet, this little church became a center of conflict, a rock of offense to Windhoek's white community. Certain whites sneered at it, calling it "that kaffir church." For them, integrated worship was a threat to what they termed "the traditional white South African way of life." If I had found peace in meditation and prayer there, I had also experienced the pain of bitter struggle. After two years of patient ministry to the whites, I made the calculated decision that the time had come to integrate the services in the cathedral. All my preaching and teaching had been aimed at removing white prejudice. To achieve this integration, I used to drive out to the black quarters and "bus" people in for Sunday services, usually collecting them in a ton-and-a-half Chevrolet truck. The white settler community reacted immediately; all their values were being threatened. My two churchwardens found occasion to quarrel with me and both resigned. People stayed away from church; members of our women's group became quarrelsome towards my wife and me. A few did remain faithful, but they too came under constant pressure from colleagues at work and from their neighbors; from time to time, some of them were actually visited by the Special Branch. A white, adult member of my confirmation class was visited one night by the Branch and commanded to produce the minutes of the church vestry meeting he had just attended; he was then warned that notice was being taken that he was mixing with "blerrie Communists." He got the message, and we never saw him in church again.

It was in the grounds of this same cathedral that my staff and I had been jeered at and pelted by Windhoek's whites when we stood in silence to protest the detention without trial of Dean ffrench-Beytagh in Johannesburg. Of course, there were happier memories too, and these can never be eroded. Into that cathedral on Sunday evenings, my children would tiptoe in their night clothes to sleep on their mommy's lap or to play through my sermons. This was the place also where as a priest I had shared the joys and sorrows of my people, baptizing and marrying them and comforting those broken-hearted in bereavement.

It still seems to me today almost an absurdity, a freak of history, that this tiny church could ever have been a threat to anybody. Yet it was, because the state in Southern Africa will not tolerate the slightest deviation from the monolithic design of apartheid. The Security Police kept it under constant surveillance and on the day before I left descended in force to photograph the entire congregation at an ordination service, desisting only when, from the pulpit, I ordered them to stop. One scripture text could summarize what many of my congregation and I wanted to attain: "My house shall be called the house of prayer for all people."

People were not the only thing one had to battle in Namibia; the climate and terrain themselves were a constant challenge. My family and I realized this as soon as we set foot in the territory. It is 300 miles from the Orange River to the first town of any size, Keetmanshoop, which is a center for the thriving karakul industry. As my car sped along the unmade roads from the mountains of the Orange River through the desert in the southern part of the country, dawn was just breaking. Never has there been such a magnificent beginning to a new day; the colors were indescribably lovely. As my children awoke from their sleep, and peered out of the dust-encrusted windows of the car, they, too, were captivated at the sunrise. They gazed in astonishment at the rock-littered landscape around them. Paul, my eldest son, pointed to a sandstorm in the distance and to thermals which were rising high over the desert, but his smile soon vanished as that same storm caught us seconds later. The car shook and zig-zagged crazily from side to side as the wind batted against it. I could see nothing ahead of me at all, and I brought the car to a stop, happy that we had not gone into a skid and rolled over. I got out and surveyed the now speckled windshield, which was sandblasted so that it looked like frosted glass. I could just see out of it and so I climbed back into the car again, yearning for a cold shower, limbs aching, nerves stretched to the breaking point, with the sheer physical strain of trying to keep the vehicle from swerving off the sandy road. It suddenly struck me that it was in conditions such as these that the first Afrikaner voortrekkers had died in this country from the most frightful thirst. I relaxed as the wheels of my car touched the tar-covered road on the outskirts of Keetmanshoop.

At the most southwesterly tip of Namibia, where the waters of the Orange River meet the Atlantic Ocean, is one of the world's richest diamond mines. If it was the lust for colonies that brought the Germans to this country in the mid-19th century, so it is the lust for diamonds, uranium, and copper that keeps the whites there today. If the natural wealth of Namibia could ever be equitably distributed, it could provide my liberated countrymen with a per capita income that would place them among the richest people in Africa.

To reach the diamond fields of the Orange River, one can travel by road through the deserts of the south or arrive there by air from Windhoek. A protective fence, many hundreds of miles long, guards the diamond area, which is patrolled by helicopters, armed police in Land Rovers during the day, and, in its closer precincts, by guard dogs day and night. Yet, the company loses every year a staggering number of diamonds which people still manage to smuggle out. In fact, illicit diamond buying and selling has almost become a national sport in Namibia. The cost in human suffering to mine these stones is enormous. Thousands of contract Ovambo laborers have to be brought in every year to wrest them from desert sands which cover the diamond-bearing alluvial rock to heights of up to fifty feet. Deprived of their wives and their children, these blacks are paid a pittance in return for their labor. They live in carefully segregated areas, euphemistically termed by the company, "single quarters." Their white overalls are smartly laundered and, by Namibian standards, their food is among the best that is offered to blacks on contract. But their sporting facilities are rudimentary, to say the least, and they are mostly left to fend for themselves.

By startling contrast, whites in Oranjemund live pampered lives. Their neat bungalow homes are surrounded by gardens; the company has provided them with a yacht basin, a golf course which is irrigated daily, tennis and squash courts, plus all the amenities for outdoor sporting activities. The children of these same whites are flown out at company expense, to schools elsewhere in Namibia or in South Africa. The furniture and fittings of their homes, as well as the cars they use in the diamond area itself, are provided free by the Anglo-American Corporation, and all this for people who are, in fact, among the highest paid white workers in Namibia. A look around the Anglo-American complex, or any other industrial plant in Namibia, is enough to establish what apartheid is all about: the exploitation of the black man for profit by the whites.

The whole western seaboard of Namibia is called the Skeleton Coast, forming part of the Namib Desert. It is one of the two deserts in the world whose sands stretch right to an ocean, the other being the Spanish Sahara. The rusty wrecks of ships can still be seen engulfed by the desert sands. About two hundred miles to the north of Oranjemund lies the crumbling heap of a town called Lüderitzbucht; into its craggy harbor the first ships of the German colonizers stole warily in

1884. Now fishing boats unload their catches here. The first German settlers found diamonds among the alluvial rocks upon which the town was built, but today these diamond diggings have run out and the town is literally falling apart. Ghost-like, it lies dripping wet in the mist produced by the Atlantic rollers. Many of its old German-style houses, built on outcrops of rock, stand empty; shutters hang limply from broken windows, and the town's rusty power station, with most of its windows caved in, looks as though it has been the victim of a recent bomb attack. The white burghers of Lüderitz are constantly badgering their counterparts in Windhoek's administration for more assistance, including loans, to keep their town alive. It has little to attract tourists, and the roads which intertwine through the deserts and mountains make it one of the most inaccessible places in the south of Namibia. Close to it lies the Fish River Canyon, with its breathtaking scenic beauty, similar to America's Grand Canyon, though, of course, far less known. Further up the coast, settled among the lofty sand dunes of the Namib Desert, is the town of Walvis Bay, which provides the only viable port in the entire territory. Ships from America, Japan, Russia, South Africa, England and Norway visit it. Here it is that our church ran the only truly interracial community in the entire territory. I felt proud of this, for our Mission to Seamen's Institute offered a haven of rest and a caring service to 60,000 sailors a year. These sailors, coming from many different lands, would never have tolerated a segregated form of hospitality. Father Peter Banyard, at one time chaplain of the mission, told me how important this rejection of apartheid was to him personally. He carries in his memory the picture of a black American sailor buying a coke for a white South African conscripted soldier in the mission canteen; this memory has become for him a vivid reminder that apartheid had to be enforced by South Africa for it to have lasted a quarter of a century in Namibia.

It rarely ever rains in Walvis Bay, which enjoys a mild climate by comparison to the rest of the territory. It is cooled by the waters of the Atlantic Ocean. When a factual, nonracial history of Namibia is finally written, Walvis Bay will be remembered as the place which gave birth to the 1971 general strike of contract laborers, which single act heralded the rejection of apartheid by the black workers of our country.

A tarred road and a single-gauge railway line link Walvis Bay to the capital city of Windhoek, which lies inland some 250 miles away. The road and railway track go right through the heart of the Namib Desert, after which Namibia is named. The first stop on the railway is the seaside resort of Swakopmund. This town is pervaded by the nostalgia of the late 19th century—its old German houses seem to have been imported lock, stock, and barrel from the Rhineland. Many of their high-gabled houses have lookout windows from which their occupants could sight approaching vessels bringing goods and news from Bismarck's Germany. In the middle of the town's sandy, untarred road is a war memorial, a gingoistic offering to the German dead who launched a campaign of genocide against the Herero people.

Swakopmund offers the visitor two reminders of German inventiveness and ingenuity. The first is a method of surfacing their roads by pouring sea water over them, rolling them with old-fashioned steam rollers and then allowing the surface to dry in the hot desert sun. Using salt gleaned from the salt pans in the Namib Desert produced a gray surface similar to macadam, which was almost as durable and vastly cheaper. Their other experiment was not so successful. A small steam engine with caterpillar tracks was brought by sea from Germany to be used against the Hereros in the war of 1904. It was suitably received by frock-coated Swakopmund townspeople, who watched it roll triumphantly out of town. Once off the road, however, its pace slackened, and it sank deeper and deeper into the hot, fine sands of the Namib Desert, much to the confusion and consternation of the assembled crowd. Today, its rusty skeleton offers a sad reproach to the might of Western imperialism. Travelling inland from Walvis Bay through the intense heat of the Namib Desert, one has to climb to a height of 6,000 feet to enter the capital of Windhoek through the various mountain ranges which surround it. In every sense, the capital is a boom city which had almost doubled its size in the six years I was there. Today, it has an estimated population of some 90,000 people. The white group comprises Afrikaners, Germans, and English-speaking South Africans. The black group which lives in enforced segregated housing at the outside of the city comprises Damaras, Hereros, Namas, Ovambos, and a small number of Coloureds. Old German shops and buildings still give character to the city's streets, which include such names as Kaiserstrasse, Goering, Haydn, Bismarck, Beethovenstrasse. The limits of the city were once set at the Ausspanplatz, so named as the place where the oxen were untethered from farm, commercial, and military vehicles. The German brewery provides the fine beer much sought after in Southern Africa and consumed in vast quantities during Windhoek's annual Oktoberfest.

Four generations of Germans live in Windhoek. I met an erstwhile aristocrat who had fought in the German army in the 1914-18 war and prior to that had attended a military college for officers in Paris. He was forced to live in a stable and was cared for by an old African woman. I was amazed that he was still able to converse and write in impeccable French. I was soon to learn that Windhoek was a refuge for Germans of a different sort from this gentle, charming old man. They were the men who were still bewitched by the magic and vision of a discarded Fuehrer. As they reminisced about their war experiences, they would assert in confidence that the Western allies had fought against the wrong side and that the real enemy all along had been Stalin and not Hitler. Sometimes they would take a photograph down from the wall and proudly show themselves in their Nazi uniforms. It astonished me to learn from a German pastor, who later resigned in disgust, that during a confirmation service, photographs of Adolf Hitler had been handed out to some German children.

Though German was recognized, along with Afrikaans and English, as one of the official languages of Namibia, many among the German community regarded the ruling Afrikaners with contempt as being uncouth. They sneered at their Calvinism and mocked their sexual hangups where Black women were concerned. Though the German regime in Namibia had fought the most ruthless war of any colonial power in Africa, the presence in the country of some 30,000 people of mixed descent is a constant reminder that the mighty German overlords had never been averse to receiving comfort from African women.

Scattered throughout the southern part of Namibia are tiny dorps, hamlets which consist of a garage, a store, and a single unkempt hotel. The only other town of real importance is the American-owned mining town of Tsumeb which nestles in the hills some 285 miles north of Windhoek. The town owes its existence to the vast seams of copper which have provided the American Metal Climax Company and its partners with an annual average profit of 17 million dollars over the past ten tears. AMAX bought the mine for the ridiculously low figure of just under three million dollars from the expropriated German company which had been its previous owner.

The new American owners apparently covered their costs in the first year by reprocessing the ore waste which had been only hastily treated by the Germans. Today, the Tsumeb Corporation is the largest single employer of black contract labor in Namibia, offers wages which grievously exploit its African labor force, is totally committed to the Vorster regime for obvious economic advantage, and is a scandal to the name of America.

Some sixty miles north of Tsumeb is the fence which marks the boundary of Ovamboland, the sandy wastes where half the country's present population is hemmed in. The fence prevents the free passage of the Ovambo people southward and has been moved several times to take away from them more of their land. Entry into Ovamboland is confined to a check point at a police post called Oshivelo. The fence is Namibia's Berlin Wall. Whites must apply for passes to be allowed into Ovamboland, and even when these are issued, they are given on condition that no social contact be made with Africans and that whites do not enter African homes. White women are forbidden to wear such articles of clothing as mini skirts in Ovamboland. Most of Namibia's black labor force is recruited from this territory.

Life is tough in Ovamboland, and the people for the most part are poor. If they wish to obtain education for their children or want to supplement their basic diet of millet porridge or provide amenities for their families and meet the tax that South Africa puts on each adult male, the men are forced to move south to work as contract laborers.

South of Ovamboland, and on the eastern side of the territory, along the fringe of the Kalahari Desert, are two reserves set aside for the Herero people. The first is called Epicuro, and 150 miles to the south of it is Aminuis.

From the fence at Oshivelo to the southernmost boundary of the Orange River, a distance of almost a thousand miles, lies what is called the Police Zone. This part of the country was so named because during German colonial days it was the section which had been policed by the German invaders.

Near to every town, but segregated from it, is a "location," a ghetto where blacks are forcibly segregated from whites. In Windhoek, this separation has been taken to the limits of absurdity, for blacks are even segregated from each other. Windhoek's location is subdivided into an Ovambo section, a Damara section, a Nama section, and so on. The Old Location, which was a freehold piece of ground at the edge of Windhoek, knew no such divisions, and there blacks co-existed with each other. But with the forcible implementation of apartheid, the white government officials scrupulously followed Pretoria's policies and segregated blacks into their ethnic or tribal groupings; even in the misery of a ghetto, black unity could not be tolerated.

Our church had arrived comparatively late on the scene. Already working in the South were the Rhenish Mission and the Evangelical Lutheran Church. In the North, the Finnish Mission concentrated its work in Ovamboland, and the Roman Catholics had two dioceses in the South in the Police Zone. The work of the Methodists was confined to whites and Coloureds. The Dutch Reformed Church was strongly established and concentrated on whites in the main towns of the South. The arrival of the Anglican Church in Namibia was fortuitous. A priest named Nelson Fogarty, from Kimberley, had followed the soldiers of Smuts in an expeditionary force which annexed the territory for South Africa in 1917. This army chaplain returned first as archdeacon and was later made bishop. His task was to cater to the small groups of white Anglicans on farms and in small dorps. The main business of evangelizing the Ovambos was undertaken by an outstanding and remarkable missionary named George Tobias, who later became bishop.

Unfortunately, the missionaries also played their part in the process of subjugation. One thinks of Hugo Hahn, the first missionary to the Hereros. Though he had worked among the Hereros for fifteen years, he had not made a single convert. It was he who wrote to Bismarck, afraid for his own safety and that of his children during the war between the Hereros and the Namas. After the Battle of Otjimbingwe in 1863, Bismarck finally answered his request, and a German expeditionary force arrived on the 6th of June in 1884 in Lüderitzbucht. Only when the Hereros had been broken in battle did Hahn succeed in converting them to Christianity.

Not only did the first missionaries bring in their wake the guns of the German colonists; it seems from their writing and conduct that they exhibited scant disapproval of the destructive forces which were assaulting the conquered black races. When the war of genocide against the Hereros was over, they were robbed of their cattle, and chain-ganged to a system of indentured labor. Dr. H. Vedder, Praeses of the Rhenish Mission in Damaraland, offers the black people very little in the way of sympathy as he writes:

> The Hereros have yet to realize that there are other nationalities with rights in South West Africa besides themselves who have a right to existence. But if the Hereros haughtily decline the opportunities offered them for developing and working themselves up and persist in wishing to live an isolated life, according to their own ideas, there are distinct signs that brutalisation, degeneration, childlessness, rapidly increasing sexual diseases, bodily debilitation, in consequence of spirituous native drinks, will end in their digging their own national grave.

Elsewhere Dr. Vedder comments,

> Being used to subservience, the Berg Damara is happiest when under a firm hand, which rules his daily conduct, and nips sudden desires for insubordination and impertinence in the bud. . . . [He] may be regarded as an important economic factor in the economic life of South West.

These comments by the Praeses are a sad reflection on the church's failure to respond to the black man's cries for liberty. From the start, there have been so few missionaries who have been able to see things from the black man's point of view. Time and time again, churches have stood silent and acquiescent when hundreds of racist laws have robbed the black man of his human dignity in Namibia. Nevertheless, some members of the church have been faithful to the demands of the gospel. What follows is a document prepared for the 1971 Synod of my church which lists those deported from Namibia. Some other churches will have similar documents. I present them for two reasons: first, so that history will know that there were a few whites willing to stand up and be counted, and second to show the continual harassment the church experienced when it did finally identify with the oppressed.

DIOCESE OF DAMARALAND

Action taken by S.A. Government against Church workers since July 1968

Date	*Names*	*Country of Origin*	*Action taken*
July 1968	Bishop Mize	U.S.A.	Residence permit not renewed.
Jan 1969	D.E. de Beer	R.S.A.	Ovamboland permit withdrawn.
Feb 1969	Mr. & Mrs. Whitford	R.S.A.	Ovamboland permit refused.
Mar 1969	V. Spencer	U.K.	Ovamboland permit withdrawn.
Feb 1970	Miss Sally Camp	U.S.A.	Ovamboland permit not renewed.
Feb 1970	Miss M. Kelly	Australia	Ovamboland permit not renewed.
Nov 1970	L. Weeks	U.S.A.	Residence permit withdrawn.
Apr 1971	S.T. Hayes (priest)	R.S.A.	Ovitoto permit refused.
Sept 1971	C. O'Brien Winter (Bishop)	U.K.	Kaokoveld permit refused.
Sept 1971	D.E. de Beer	R.S.A.	Ovamboland permit refused.
Oct 1971	Miss A. Halberstadt	R.S.A.	Ovamboland permit withdrawn.
Oct 1971	S. Singleton	U.K.	Ovamboland permit refused.

Delays

Sept 1970	Enid Green	U.K.	Ovamboland permit delayed 2 months.
	Margaret Read	U.K.	Ovamboland permit delayed 1 year.

Aug 1971	Barbara Wilden	U.K.	Ovamboland permit delayed 1 month (renewal).

In addition to the above, there have been delays to permits for visitors, often with the result that the visitor concerned has not been able to visit certain parts of the Diocese. It is also interesting to note that of S.A. born church workers, 5 out of 7 have had their work interfered with by official action.

Diocese of Damaraland
P.O. Box 57,
Windhoek, S.W.A.

20th October 1971.

Chapter Three

Into Africa

I was born in Stoke-on-Trent, a smoky industrial city in England, in 1928, the youngest child in a family of four children. My father, a hosier, had grown up in Liverpool and was the son of an Irish immigrant mother who at the age of twenty-three had been left a widow with two small children when her husband was drowned at sea. My father had little time for organized religion, thought that the church lived off the backs of people, but never forgot the love and kindness that the Little Sisters of the Poor had shown him when he had been hungry as a child or the help that the Salvation Army had given him when he fought in the trenches in the First World War. To the end of his life, he always gave generously to these two organizations, but to little else; so he was not particularly charmed at two of his sons becoming Anglican priests. When I confided to him my intention of being ordained, he muttered with a fair degree of agitation, "Good God, what have I done to deserve this?"

We were a poor family and my early childhood was spent in the back streets of a tough, working-class area in the Potteries, which is where I received my early education. These were the days of the Depression. I remember at the age of seven going to a new school and having to fight every boy in my class just to establish at what level they were prepared to admit me into their tight hierarchy.

I list three strong influences during my formative years. The first was my mother, a person of immense humor and a woman of compassion whom I loved deeply and to whom I was devoted. Although she had trained as a nurse, she was not well educated and caused me endless embarrassment at being unable to write letters or to be at ease in the company of schoolteachers, parsons, or any whom she considered to be her social superiors. But she did have a truly profound love for people, especially young children, which she kept to the end of her life. I think I derive my love for and identification with the poor from her. One of my earliest and abiding childhood memories is of watching her bathe the feet of an old Welsh miner who was wandering around the streets of our town and who had knocked at our door asking for a cup of tea. She treated him with tenderness as she gently washed his feet and bathed them in calamine lotion and then, having shared our evening meal with him, sent him away wearing my father's best shoes.

The second influence was that exerted by the Christian brothers in the local Roman Catholic High School. They implanted in me a deep sense of God, and from their teaching and example I absorbed more than mere dogma. At ten I was read the life story of the leper saint Father Damien of Molokai, and I knew then that I wanted to be a priest. I knew too that being a Christian entailed total surrender to Christ and the possibility of suffering.

The strongest influence of all, however, was my older brother Tom, today an Anglican priest in Cape Town. He nurtured in me a love of English literature, particularly the writings of T.S. Eliot, D.H. Lawrence, and James Joyce, together with the poetry of Hopkins and Donne. He shared with me, too, his love of Bach. But best of all, he coaxed me into the fold of the Anglican Church when I was hovering on the brink of atheism. It was through his influence too that I became a pacifist and conceived an understanding of nonviolence. I listened to him, read everything he suggested, and trusted his judgment implicitly. Most of what he taught me, I still retain today.

From 1946 to 1948 I trained in athletics and gymnastics at Loughborough College, and it was here, at the age of nineteen, that I began to attend daily Mass. I was a sprinter on the college athletic team, rode to dances in an old beat-up Velocette motor bike, enjoyed the greater freedom the college allowed me, fell in love with every girl I met, and at the end of my training there, shyly let it be known that I wanted to be a priest. My family were naturally suspicious and my mother giggled, "They'll never take you seriously, you fool."

In the final term at Loughborough, I had to register for conscription in one of the armed forces. I decided to face a legal tribunal as a conscientious objector. I remember walking into the local labor bureau to register and meeting, head-on, the rage of the clerk to whom I announced that I would not fight for king or country. I spent the next eighteen months working as a farm laborer, digging ditches, draining boggy fields, and cutting sugar beets.

During this period, I lived in a hostel with other agricultural workers in what had once been a stately home called Teddesley Hall. It was being systematically torn apart by the migrant laborers from

Ireland, Scotland, and Wales who had been billeted there. Many of these men were illiterate and had come to England to find work. After sending a few pounds out of their weekly wages home, they would use the rest to get drunk on weekends. I was trying to get a place at Oxford and was learning New Testament Greek with my grammar book propped up at the side of the ditch as I dug out the clay. Week after week, I watched men fight each other, even try to kill each other: I was witnessing the frightful effects of loneliness. I saw these men wantonly destroy property. No one cared a damn for them, and they, in turn, respected no one and nothing. I spent six weeks in a Nissen hut alone with a mental patient who had been released from the Stafford asylum to see if he could be further rehabilitated by working as a farm laborer. I watched him disintegrate until he went mad again, driven back to the mental home by the loneliness and isolation of that camp. From time to time, men would come to my hut at night after supper and ask if I would read the Bible to them and explain what it meant.

I was freed from this work in 1950, when I obtained a place at Lincoln College, Oxford, to read theology. I could never have achieved this without the constant guidance of my brother, who was already in his second year at Wadham College. It was in my second year at Oxford that I met and subsequently married my wife Mary, who was working as a maternity sister in a hospital in Bradford. My training for the priesthood was done at Ely, a theological college near Cambridge; after completing my studies there, I was ordained a deacon by Bishop George Bell in his cathedral in Chichester in 1956. Years later, in my first charge to my diocese, I used George Bell as an example of what it cost to be a Christian prophet. Many felt that he was the leading contender for the position of Primate of All England, but because he had made a passionate speech in the House of Lords in which he had condemned the indiscriminate bombing of defenseless and nonmilitary cities in Germany, he was passed over. George Bell ordained me priest in 1957.

Mary and the children and I moved to a working-class parish in Eastbourne, and it was to here that Joost de Blank wrote in 1959 inviting me to become rector in Simonstown in Cape Province, South Africa. Again, I had my brother to thank for preparing the way for me. Joost de Blank was a courageous and outspoken critic of apartheid, but it was proving difficult for him to find priests to come to South Africa at this time. We did not hesitate and were released within a matter of two months, arriving in Cape Town by ship.

I knew little about South Africa, and before leaving I had gone to see Father Trevor Huddleston CR, who, along with Father Michael Scott, was my particular hero. I remember how nervous I was at being ushered into Huddleston's presence when he was working in a predominantly black area in Notting Hill in London. He discussed the South African situation with me at length. Time and again in my life I have reached back to his classic *Naught for your Comfort* to take courage from the man and from his vision. I had once heard Michael Scott speak in Birmingham, had read his book *A Time to Speak*, and felt I simply wanted to go out to South Africa and make the same stand that these men had made. For me they were the giants of the Church of England, priests who were totally identified with the oppressed and refused cheap sellouts or soft options. Of course, at this time, I had no real idea of the personal suffering that their prophetic witness had cost them. I was to learn that in an apprenticeship period of some fourteen years in Southern Africa. Today, I still hold them both as dear and respected friends, men whom I would still be prepared to follow and for whom I have the deepest admiration. Would to God that our church in South Africa had produced many more like them.

Few people, I suppose, could have been less prepared for a ministry in South Africa. Mary and I had only one thing going for us: we loved people. The rest we had to learn the hard way—mostly from our mistakes. But we had excellent teachers in the Cape Coloured people themselves. The Coloured community of Simonstown took us all to their hearts. It was their custom to flock to church on Sundays, their children neatly dressed, the girls wearing clothes of flaming multicolors. Their worship, their music, their dancing and laughter all enthralled us: they were so easy to love. Archbishop de Blank had called our parish the most integrated in his diocese, and if that was so, it was because the Coloured people themselves wanted it and made it possible. Even though in their daily lives they were humiliated and rejected by the whites, they themselves had not rejected white people. St. John of the Cross said, "Where there is no Love, put Love and you will draw Love out." We saw that happening, time and time again, in Simonstown. I have tried to recapture the spirit of the place and the many characters who made up my congregation there in a little book called *Just People*. My family and I lived from 1959 to 1964 in a lovely old stone rectory overlooking the harbor and the Indian Ocean.

If, as I firmly believe, it is the people who make the priest, then what Simonstown gave me was an even more passionate concern for justice and social righteousness. I had entrée into every single Coloured home, and I knew and loved the people I'd been called to serve. I taught in their church school, I drove their sick to the hospital, I knelt by their dying in smoke-filled pondokies. They made me a part of their daily lives. It was to me that they turned when they needed someone to speak for them in the Magistrate's Court. My very first job on becoming their parish priest was to raise £100 to brief a lawyer who would fight the dreadful consequences of the Group Areas Act. Though the Coloured people had lived in Simonstown peacefully and happily for over two centuries, this Act sought forcibly to remove them from their homes and dump them in the sandy wastes of a scrub area in the bush some fifteen miles away. I became their spokesman because they turned to me naturally and spontaneously; they sought my help because there was no one else to whom they could go. My ministry here was a vital training ground for my future work in Namibia. I went to Simonstown knowing little of apartheid, but came away totally convinced that it was a demonic evil. I saw the misery and suffering that it caused people and families. I watched the young people fall in love and then shared their anguish when they realized that they could never marry, because a scrap of paper declared one to be white and the other Coloured. I saw the daily injustices and insults that apartheid heaps on the people. When black priests visited my home, we broke the law if we went for a swim together in one of the loveliest oceans of the world. We could never sit down to a cup of tea or a Coke together in the local café. I saw the poverty of the people's homes and the hunger and disease that wracked them, all due to the appallingly low wages which an affluent white society paid them. Apartheid has been called by many different names: separate development, multi-nationalism and so forth; but for me it can only ever have one name: it is naked racism in its ugliest form and it destroys people.

Martin Luther King, Jr., defined racism as genocide, and my thirteen years in Southern Africa, including the six I spent in Simonstown, convinced me of the truth of that statement. The dignity of a people is stripped from them, their self-pride is assaulted; call them trash, second-rate citizens, and some of them believe it. My time in Simonstown also showed me that the Christian ethic of Love can work, if only the church has the courage to witness to its convictions. This witness is a costly one, but in Simonstown the church proved that black and white can be united in Christ and live in peace with dignity together. Simonstown was a microcosm of what the rest of South Africa could be: black and white worked together because they worshipped together. We had a mixed Sunday School, a mixed youth group, a mixed men's group, and a mixed women's group. Black and white crowded into the same buses to go on parish outings to beauty spots around the Cape Peninsula. Our youth went on annual camps together as did our choir boys and servers. As a parish we followed a definite policy of breaking down all that separated man from man, whether it be race, class, or money. Each Wednesday evening men from the Simonstown dockyard met in our church for Mass, shared in the readings of lessons and prayers, and sat down to dinner in each other's homes; this was done in the teeth of a fanatical government's policy which heaped law upon law in the statute book to prevent the coming together of the races. St. Francis' Church was, in fact, a living reproach to all that South Africa's Nationalist government stood for.

The enthusiasm of the Coloured people for their church knew no bounds. They shared generously with any who needed help. In 1964, in response to an appeal from Robert Mize, our parish got together bundles of blankets and clothes and wished to present these and a check to the bishop for the poor of his diocese. The people loved Bob Mize and responded to his relaxed and friendly approach. There was not a trace of snobbery about him and people felt very much at ease in his presence. They recognized him also as a man of prayer. As a parish we wanted to send a multiracial working party to build a school or clinic for him in Ovamboland, and he had come to the parish to receive the gifts of the people and to discuss this project with us.

As he sat at supper, our children were intrigued with this charming American who would pour hugh dollops of tomato ketchup over most of the food on his plate. They laughed at his stories, and we were all delighted to have him in our home. When dinner was over and we were about to leave the table, he caught me completely off guard when he suddenly said, "I want you to be dean of my cathedral in South West Africa." I blocked the request immediately and felt threatened by his continual probing. South West Africa was a desert—its heat was frightful. Also, it was a thousand miles away from Cape Town. If I went there to work for him, it would mean inevitably that I would lose my children, who would have to come to school in Cape Town. I didn't want to lose them and I didn't want to go to such an isolated country. I loved Simonstown, although admittedly I had begun to wonder whether it might be time for me to leave. Bob Mize continued to pressure. He began to describe the job and said that he wanted me to do there exactly what I had done in Simonstown. Above all, he wanted an integrated cathedral and a parish priest who would visit his people and would have a caring ministry for them.

Yet, I still didn't want to go. I had a foreboding about the place. I kept asking myself, How could I exist in a desert when I found the summer climate in the Cape oppressive? The children would have to be shuttled backwards and forwards eight thousand miles a year to school. The whole idea seemed absurd, and I told Mary so. "It's like sending your children to school from London to Eastern Poland," I said and wanted to leave the matter there. But the bishop had already won her over. "Well, the least you can do is go up and see the place," Mary coaxed, and so I agreed to visit Windhoek the week after Easter.

Mary and I were met at the Windhoek airport by the bishop. He did everything to make our visit as happy as possible, but what I saw of the white community in Windhoek and of their callous treatment of the black people appalled me. We were entering a very strange society indeed.

Bob Mize had wonderful pastoral gifts and these, together with the modesty and generosity of the man, penetrated even the whites in Windhoek cathedral. But there were some who took me aside and warned me that though he was a good and kindly man, he just didn't understand the problems of South West Africa. They showed hostility to the fact that he kept his home open to all races; they noted that neighbors complained of blacks roaming all around their streets on Sunday afternoon as they came to call on their bishop. This gave the area a bad name, and if he continued to be "soft on blacks," he would soon be kicked out of the country. The wealthiest members of the congregation were embarrassed that he welcomed all people into his house and thought it was a quirk of a religious crank. So whites in Namibia either hated him or made excuses for him—they certainly were not prepared to follow his example.

I spent a long weekend in the Windhoek Cathedral parish meeting the people and was entertained by them at dinners and cocktail parties. Their hospitality knew no limits, and they were extremely friendly to Mary and me and kept letting us know that they hoped I would come to be their priest. Given the way I observed them treating their servants and the way they gossiped about their bishop, I had the gravest doubts about coming and confessed them to Mary as we sat in our bedroom in the bishop's house. "They'll eat us alive in this place. Most of them are unashamedly Nationalists who really want apartheid. A couple of them are snobs who just want an Oxford man here so they can put the degree on the parish stationery. We all get along famously now, but once I start to integrate their cathedral, they will begin to hate me." I could sense that violence lurked under the surface. I saw it in the faces of whites when they spoke to me about their bishop. Mary listened to all this and, despite my doubts, said all along that I should accept. The more she did so, however, the more I backed away.

The bishop had asked me to preach the sermon in the cathedral at Sunday Evensong and also wanted to know my decision before I left the next day. I had already made up my mind; my frank reaction was that I was too young and too inexperienced for martyrdom. No one could move that parish from the path of apartheid.

After the evening service, I went to the bishop's study and found him sitting in shirtsleeves dealing with a massive pile of correspondence on his desk. He looked up at me as I entered, and for a split second I caught the look of anxiety in his eye. Mary's final comment to me had been, "He desperately needs you here." It was the look that did it. Without waiting for him to say anything, I said quietly, "Bishop, I've decided to come."

I felt wretched.

We returned to Simonstown and released the news of our imminent departure to our beloved people at St. Francis' Church. They gave us a tumultuous sendoff and showed characteristic charm by boasting to all and sundry that "Father's going to be a dean." "Dean of what?" I wondered.

Leaving Simonstown in July 1964, we travelled through the barren, yet beautiful, wilderness of Northern Namaqualand, crossed the flimsy bridge over the Orange River, and plunged right into the desert of South West Africa. The impact was like an uppercut. The car never recovered from the battering it took on that thousand-mile trip from Simonstown to Windhoek. Never in our lives had we seen roads or landscapes like those that lay ahead of us. It was impossible to tell which was the road and which was the rest of the desert. One simply kept up a speed of seventy miles an hour, chose a certain track, and fought to keep the wheels in it as one sped along. If the speed dropped below fifty miles an hour, the car would dance wildly from side to side, flung about by the corrugations. The idea was to hit those corrugations as fast as possible and so avoid being dragged down by them. This was a highly dangerous affair, especially when travelling through narrow cattle gates which divided farm from farm, on roads which were strewn with rocks and boulders. The car would plunge down into dry river beds, over ruts, and through sand dunes which the wind had swept across the road. Dust poured in under every door and through closed windows; it clung to our faces, clothing, and hair until we could hardly breathe. We were fighting heat and fatigue every mile of that journey.

Another abiding memory of that journey is of white communities huddled together, surrounded by a vast, arid wilderness. Often they were separated by hundreds of miles from their next white neighbors. All of these white communities had one thing in common: they totally rejected and were rigidly segregated from their black neighbors. Even in a howling wilderness, white men and women preferred the pains of loneliness and almost total isolation to making any loving contact with blacks.

Finally, as the car reached the foothills of Windhoek, we saw the white roofs of the city's houses shining in the distance. The town looked small and insignificant surrounded by drought-blasted brown scrubland. The contrast between Simonstown could not have been worse. Rachel, one of my younger daughters, woke up, looked at the city we were approaching, and said incredulously, "Gosh, is that supposed to be the capital? . . . *Ag sis*" (an Afrikaans expression of contempt). We walked up the steps which led to our new home, and I caught a glimpse of myself reflected in the window panes of the front room. I was covered from head to foot with fine, grey mica dust, and my hair was clotted and stood out like the braided locks of a rag doll.

I had laid plans carefully before I began my ministry in Windhoek and realized that if there was any hope of winning over the whites so that they would accept blacks at their worship, this could be done only if they loved and trusted me. In Anglican tradition, a cathedral, besides being the seat of the bishop, is also the mother church of all Christians in the diocese. In the Diocese of Damaraland, 85 percent of the people were black, and it seemed to me both logical and natural that they should feel themselves welcome in its daily and weekly worship. We had managed to integrate the church in Simonstown with a pastoral ministry of love and service; I wanted to do just the same in Windhoek. To have attempted to do this immediately would have frightened off the whites, so I gave myself over to a caring ministry and week by week, through patient teaching, tried to lead the people out of their ghetto of white isolationism into a concept of being a full catholic church. Two years, I thought, would be sufficient to calm their fears and eliminate their prejudices. They could meet blacks in my home, and I hoped that before too long the whites would accept them as fellow Christians. So I threw myself into my work and set myself the task of visiting the homes of all the Anglicans in the white community. I paid daily visits to the hospitals, taught five days a week in the church school, visited the state high school and got to know the students there, sought out the business community, and tried to make contact and establish friendly relations with as wide a cross section of people as possible. I managed to acquire a ton-and-a-half Chevrolet truck from a local Jewish garage owner who was kind enough to let me pay off the cost over several years. On weekends I drove young people to outlying farms and explored the country that I was beginning to love. I was working a fourteen-hour day but was loving it, and the white people seemed to be coming along.

I do have to admit that the tensions of such a racially restricted ministry were painful. It was physically impossible not to make contact with Africans and Coloureds in day-to-day life, and so I found it increasingly difficult to restrict my ministry to whites only. The needs of the blacks, their poverty and isolation, forced me to respond. The African who pumped my petrol or sold me a newspaper in the street would turn out to be a practicing Christian from our mission in Ovamboland. Such men besieged me with requests for Prayer Books or for Bibles. Elderly African men sitting on the pavement during lunchtime would shyly tell me that they were learning to read or write by themselves and then would ask if I could provide them with a Standard III textbook or an exercise book. I want to stress that I was not initiating a ministry to the blacks, but was merely responding to their human needs as they daily pressed upon me. I could otherwise never have lived with myself. As a result I began literacy classes every Sunday afternoon in the cathedral hall. Africans flocked to these, and the hall was packed with men learning to read and write. After Sunday lunch my children would join Mary and me at tables to help coach men in their English grammar exercises.

From a safe and respectable distance, the cathedral congregation observed, talked behind my back about these classes, and then began to quarrel with me over them. "They have their own church in the Location, so why must they come to ours?" The Ladies' Guild which met once a month in the cathedral for a social gathering disapproved; in a meeting with me they became very angry and through their leader complained that these blacks were drinking coffee from their cups which had been bought with their money. I continued teaching the Africans, and the resistance of the whites mounted. Over the four-year period that the classes were held, only two people from the cathedral congregation ever came forward to help me: one was an Afrikaner, the other an American.

One day I drove an old African priest home to the Old Location and saw for the first time its appalling slums, the crowds of hungry, black children, and the helpless plight of its sick and aged people. When I looked into the faces of these hungry children and old people,

I knew that their needs could not wait the two years for white people to respond. So I began to carry food into the Old Location each week. At the same time, I continued the faithful round of visiting and teaching in the cathedral. But my ministry was widening through the daily contacts I had with blacks wherever I found them—on the street, in the shops or garages, and in the Old Location.

Chapter Four

A Bishop and Apartheid

Lazarus Haihambo is a gentle man. He is an old man now and can be seen at meetings quietly listening, sometimes dozing, and often puffing away at an old pipe. He has a natural smile, moves quietly, and when he speaks, uses gentle words. He came into my room at the deanery in Windhoek as the appointed spokesman for his people; he had something confidential to discuss with me. The afternoon air was dry and burned one's throat, and when he sat down in my study, I got us both some orange juice as I waited for him to tell me the reason for his visit.

There were no preliminaries. He got to the point straightaway. Bob Mize had been deported, and the clergy and people in Ovamboland wanted me to be their next bishop. My reaction to the request was immediate: I rejected it outright. When Bob was deported, I witnessed the dreadful spectacle of whites just backing away from him, leaving him to face strain totally alone. I was angry and deeply hurt and had the abiding feeling that our whole ministry to the whites had failed. I just wanted to leave Windhoek and offer myself to work in another part of Africa.

I thanked Canon Haihambo for coming and assured him that notwithstanding my refusal I was grateful and flattered that he and his people should think me a suitable person to be bishop. He left without protest as quietly as he had entered, thanking me for the orange juice. The Africans were not to be deterred and pressed ahead with my nomination.

The Elective Assembly met in the tiny cathedral in Windhoek on 12 October 1968. About eighty delegates, both clergy and lay people, attended it. They came from all over the diocese, with Ovamboland—because over 85 percent of our church's strength was there—having the greatest number of delegates. After a brief period when, as senior priest in the diocese, I chaired the proceedings, my candidacy came up for discussion and I relinquished the chair and left the chamber. I came back for the voting.

Mary was walking along the path from the cathedral hall, carrying the tea dishes, and Catherine, our six-year-old daughter, was running alongside her. One of her helpers, Jessica Bassingthwaite, heard clapping in the cathedral followed by me speaking. Lazarus Haihambo's wish had been granted: I had been elected bishop through the determination of the African delegates from Ovamboland.

"Who is it?" Mary asked Jessica.

"It's the dean," came the reply. Mary went white with shock.

I was consecrated on the 17th of November, 1968, in St. Paul's Church, Durban, with the first bishop of Swaziland, Anthony Hunter, and the suffragan bishop of Johannesburg, John Carter. The night before the service, the cistern above our bedroom in the house in which we were staying began to leak, and Mary and I spent several hours on our knees mopping up the bedroom floor. The children remember the house more than any other they have ever stayed in. There were several pairs of false teeth scattered throughout the drawers of dressing tables and they had a riotous time trying them on.

Christians believe that the church can never go under because the hand of God sustains it, but its work can be hindered by inadequate finances or manpower or by a shortage of essential equipment. Damaraland faced crisis after crisis due to a lack of regular funding. It seemed an impossible situation. You met one need, and a hundred more occurred. We were broke and I had just over a month in which to raise the salaries of my clergy and lay workers. The problem was that we did not have sufficient assets or investments, nor did we have any strong outside financial backing. We had been quietly pushed into independence as a diocese by the rest of the church in South Africa and left virtually to go it alone. We received very little financial support from the South African church by comparison to the cost of the overall operation; in fact, we were hopelessly underfinanced. Bishop Mize had led the church in a great surge forward, had brought several American priests to the diocese, had ordained more Africans than ever before in our history, had opened schools and churches, and had finally succeeded in effecting the necessary legislation to give us our own democratic synod. He had done more than any single person before him to put life into us and to give us a far greater outreach. No man could have worked harder or achieved more. Unfortunately, when he left, funds trickled to a halt. By removing him the South African government had aimed a mortal blow at the diocese which could have set back our work for years.

So when I returned from the consecration ceremony in Durban, I faced the frightening spectacle of a diocese on the verge of bankruptcy, with no resources or contacts in my own background and with no experience in fund-raising on a large scale. My first task was to try to keep the diocese solvent. Our African congregations, huge by any standards, could give church collections only in corn and grain.

My second task was to keep the diocese united. If the church had a reconciling role in Namibian society, it would have been sheer foolhardiness to have split off the North from the rest and particularly at that time. Because we had such strong attachments and contact with Ovamboland, we were a constant threat to the state. We were the one informed source who could tell the outside world what was going on in Ovamboland. The state knew this, feared us, and therefore was determined to see us removed. Arguments about the diocese being unwieldy were secondary as we faced this particular crisis.

Many of our adult members had been deprived of formal education. It was not enough merely to teach them the basics of reading and writing; we felt that it was our task to show them what their rights were and what the Christian gospel had to say about such things as injustice, oppression, and freedom. They needed a gospel which spoke to them about their own situation. A committed staff was required to do this, and so my third task was to obtain such dedicated people. They were not hard to come by. A number of such people—mainly students—rallied to what we were doing.

My fourth task was to lead the church in an attempt to break out from the laager of silence and complicity in which it was hiding from a state which had forced it to retreat, and from which it occasionally peeped out nervously, cowering as the state ran rampant through the country arresting, deporting, and intimidating at whim any who had the temerity to oppose it.

My address to my first synod stressed the abiding truth that the church of God is one entity and can never be split into ethnic groups. From this single premise, every action that we took on behalf of the oppressed followed. I felt it right to hammer home this one fact which was being violated daily in Namibia and South Africa.

Two years later, as I prepared to face my second diocesan synod, which met from the 1st to the 3rd of October, 1971, I wanted not only our own people but also the outside world to know the cost in suffering, banishments, and deportations the diocese had faced for daring to expose the state. Behind me lay the wreckage wrought by the state in its attempts to silence us. First, it had made a determined attempt to split the diocese by forcing us to relinquish Ovamboland so that it could be pushed into a silent, forgotten backwater. When we refused to comply, the white authorities did everything in their power to wreck our work there—permits which were vital to allow much needed workers, nurses, doctors, teachers, and others to enter Ovamboland were simply withheld. This meant that an enormous strain was placed on the handful of missionaries left to run our schools and hospitals there. Nurses trying to run a hospital without a doctor collapsed from nervous and physical exhaustion. Students in our top standards tutored those in the lower forms. We were barely able to keep our institutions going as the state played out this vicious cat-and-mouse role with us. Of course, as always, it was the Africans who suffered the most.

I have no doubt that the state was trying to make it abundantly clear to us and to the other churches in Namibia that she could and would grind us into the ground. It is certainly a fact that by this time many of our own church leaders in South Africa were hostile to much of what we were doing and saying. I suppose, for their part, they would accuse us of recklessness in jeopardizing our work by "provoking the state." For our part, we felt that we had no choice: we were determined to stand by the Africans in their struggle and to live out the gospel no matter what the cost. We knew we were in the middle of a church/state confrontation; yet, though we were under considerable strain, there was also a degree of buoyancy among us. In fact, persecution made us even more determined to stand by the oppressed.

Why was our stand different from that of fellow churchmen in South Africa? First, whereas in South Africa, where there were strikes and political trials, Christian leaders could and often did allow others to take the initiative in standing by the oppressed, in Namibia there was no one else to do this and the church had to come out into the open, not merely with words but with effective action. Second, the very "style" of our ministry had its roots with the very poorest in our midst. They made up the overwhelming membership of our church and they turned most naturally to us for help. Third, in theological terms, we never separated political action from our understanding of the gospel, as often happens in South Africa. The overwhelming majority of strikers were Christians and many of their strike manifestos contained biblical passages and quotations. Fourth, the white churches in South Africa could not afford to alienate their rich white congregations on whose offerings they were so dependent; we, on the other hand, could not be intimidated by whites' withdrawing their money from the church since over 90 percent of our diocese was black and we drew our funds largely from overseas.

Our role in Namibian society was one which we discovered through our close involvement in the lives of its people. We had made a deliberate, conscious choice: we saw ourselves as part of a freedom struggle from which there could be no retreat, and we were determined to speak out and to defend those in our midst who were helpless. It was from the black people themselves that we drew strength and courage—if we were suffering in the face of oppression, blacks were suffering infinitely more. They inspired us neither to give up nor to sell out.

The 1971 synod was remarkable in many ways. In the past most Africans had been inhibited in their participation in debates, handicapped as they were by the difficulty of expressing themselves in a foreign language. We had now installed simultaneous translation equipment which allowed each person to express himself in his mother tongue, which was then immediately translated into different languages. During this synod, Africans hurled themselves at the microphone impelled by an eagerness to share with whites their deepest inner feelings. They were not afraid to speak their minds and spoke out courageously about the problems and sufferings endured by their people. The local press watched and reported our daily deliberations in full. Here were voices calling for a saner way to solving our country's problems which would lead to racial harmony. Here, in fact, was the church talking about real living issues and, though facing the distinct prospect of persecution, being neither daunted nor cowed in her task.

The work of this synod covered every aspect of our outreach as a church. A mere glance at the agenda paper clearly reveals that the church's main concern was with people—all people. We heard about the church's ministry to seafarers at Walvis Bay and about the problems facing the newest and poorest congregation in the western part of Ovamboland. We read the reports of a social worker in Katutura about the appalling conditions which pertained there in the old age home. We were reminded of those whom the state had forgotten in the dumping grounds of the Tses reserve. The church's motives were to reveal to society its obligations under God to the weakest and poorest in our midst.

This synod did more. Taking its courage in both hands, it totally rejected the policies of apartheid which the South African state was relentlessly pursuing with a callous fanaticism, and at the end of its deliberations it produced its own freedom charter, an outright condemnation of everything apartheid stood for.

The synod itself stood out in marked contrast to the South African government's method of operating in Namibia. Our delegates were all democratically elected and were representative of the entire people; the government's delegates were all paid stooges groomed to reiterate their masters' phrases and thoughts. Our debates were lively and often provocative—people disagreed with each other and said so. This contrasted with the state's policy, whereby any disagreements on major issues, especially on the part of blacks, were regarded as possible treason. Our debating chamber gave each person the freedom to express his opinion. The state locked up its opponents, branding any who disagreed with it as subversive.

As I listened to the debates in our synod, I felt a deep sense of pride in all the Anglican Church stood for in Namibia and in the courage of its people. The South African state could have learned something from us, but in fact, in the end, they had to destroy us, for we were becoming too great a threat to their security, challenging by the very freedom of speech we encouraged their whole monolithic system, which was aimed at gagging truth, suppressing all opposition, and outlawing any who resisted its policies.

Chapter Five

Windhoek: The Whites

Windhoek, the capital city of Namibia, has an estimated population of 80,000 people and lies 6000 feet above sea level in a dust-blown basin of bush and scrub encircled by high mountain ranges. For most of the year, the surrounding hills and peaks are baked a sandy brown, but during the rainy season they turn to a soft green. The corrugated red iron roofs of the old German shops have, over the years, faded into the color of peach, and the hand-cut stone of their facades makes a striking contrast to the concrete and glass of high-rise office blocks that now surround and dwarf them.

Windhoek is a city divided against itself. The racial policy of the government has forced the people to live in tightly segregated racial compartments. It is a boom town where fortunes are made at a frantic get-rich-quick pace—the only qualification is that you have to be white to make them. It is by no means unusual for the young immigrant mechanic from Western Germany to find himself a business owner after only one or two years in the capital. After four or five years, he can easily own a farm the size of an English county.

The crowds which jostle each other as they move along Windhoek's main street, Kaiserstrasse, make interesting character studies. Easily the most outstanding among them are the tall, imperious, graceful figures of the Herero women, whose long dresses of flaming multi-color sweep the pavement as they stroll majestically along.

The Afrikaner bureaucrat from South Africa is easily recognizable. He may be working for the Department of Water Affairs or the Bantu Administration or may be some minor government official in the Post Office or the Department of the Railways. He passes by in a South African tailored suit, a van Gogh beard, closely cropped hair, and a pinched, taut face. Politically speaking, he belongs to the master race and he knows it. His kind growls and shouts at the happy crowd of black messengers who spend endless hours waiting for letters and parcels at the main post office. He seldom proffers a thank-you as he receives money from the English-speaking community. He has all power, and at every opportunity he lets the rest of the world know it. His expression is dour and his manner brusque. One of the constant ironies of life in Namibia is that the oppressed can often find opportunities for laughter, the oppressor seldom can.

One also learns to recognize, quite easily, a member of the German community in Windhoek, some 30,000 of whom live in Namibia. He may be a mechanic walking along dressed in blue denim overalls with leather-peaked cap. He might be wearing a finely tailored European suit with expensive Italian shoes and earn his living as an exporter of karakul pelts or as an importer of building material, agricultural equipment, or mining machinery from Western Europe. Though his life style is far less Calvinistic than his Afrikaans counterpart and though he may wear his hair much longer, his racial attitudes are hardly more liberal than that of the Pretoria regime. Whereas the German community, who more than any should know the consequences of tyranny and the traumas it brings in its wake, should have been expected to have resisted the Nazi-style policies perpetrated by the Vorster regime, yet the sad fact is that they are lulled into docile acquiescence because in their daily lives they benefitted so much from the fruits of apartheid. The German in Namibia today feels he owes his very survival to the Afrikaner, and though he sees white colonial rule threatened and collapsing in other parts of Southern Africa, he has chosen to walk the tightrope of insecurity, giving his vote to Afrikaans-speaking white politicians rather than attempt to forge an effective opposition party which could act as a counterbalance to the Vorster regime.

As in South Africa itself, the English-speaking white is happy to make his fortune, enjoy his sport, drink his sundowner, and leave it to the Afrikaner to play politics. He lacks political fire, has abdicated, and therefore is irrelevant as an effective force in bringing a solution to the country's problems.

It is the black community that brings the bustle, life, and laughter to the city's streets. The Coloured girls from Rehoboth are easily recognizable with their pale and angular faces. They work as waitresses in the German beer gardens and sometimes become mistresses to the German farmers and businessmen. The Coloured women from the Cape, who live in a segregated township, pack the groceries and serve on the counter at the many new supermarkets. They are in a more elevated position than most African women in that they have been brought in to act as a buffer between white and black. Their menfolk are allowed such jobs as bricklaying and plastering, which are barred to the ordinary African. Their womenfolk perform the more menial jobs in society which previously had been done by poor whites.

As one watches the new office blocks rising on what had been waste ground in Kaiserstrasse, he notices immediately that most workers are African. These will be the contract laborers brought in from Ovamboland, who live in segregated, so-called "single" quarters in Windhoek's African township called Katutura. Their clothing on the building site is poor and ragged. Their lunchtime meal usually consists of half a loaf of bread which they share among themselves. These are Namibia's most exploited people. They are offered a mere pittance in return for their labor; yet it is their skills which are largely responsible for building Namibia's roads, schools, hospitals, administrative buildings, dams, bridges, and railways. Many of them are lucky if they take home $20 in their pay packet at the end of a month.

Seated or standing barefoot in the shade of an office block are the groups of black street urchins shouting out the names of the local newspapers, *Die Suidwester*, *Die Suidwes Afrikaner*, *Die Algemeine Zeitung*, and *The Windhoek Advertiser*. The first two are read by the Afrikaans-speaking community, the third is read by the Germans, and the last by English-speaking South Africans. My staff had such low esteem for the content and quality of the English newspaper that they irreverently referred to it as "The Two Minutes Silence." It was the only daily newspaper I have ever known which in the place of a daily editorial carried a four-sentence weather report.

Whites spend most of their leisure hours out-of-doors. Barbecues are very popular, so too is the drive-in cinema. At night white youths aimlessly drive up and down Kaiserstrasse in their highly polished motor cars, bored out of their minds. White women arrive at the hairdresser at 7:30 in the morning to have their hair made up in outlandish Madame Pompadour styles before going off to their jobs as typists and secretaries. Windhoek's shops are full of expensive clothes and shoes, imported from Germany, England, and Italy.

The German community has made some attempt at sustaining a cultural life and when we were in Windhoek had, among other things, a youth choir and an orchestra. From time to time they also imported artists to give concerts in a local hall. The English had a Shakespeare society and occasionally put on a play. Otherwise, Windhoek was intellectually and culturally dead. I rarely saw books in the homes of my white parishioners. Whatever thinking was done or whatever political opinion they had was based on the heavily slanted propaganda broadcasts from South African radio or on the outpourings of the local press. "Jesus Christ Superstar" was a bigger issue to the Calvinist ministers in Windhoek than the cruel floggings in public of black students and nurses in Ovamboland. If most whites in Windhoek lived in a "cloud cuckoo land," it was because they were cut off from contact with an outside world that politically, culturally, and educationally had passed them by. A certain German nostalgia still hung over the city. Next to the white Lutheran church was a statue of a trooper on horseback, a rather sad reminder to the Germans that they had once conquered and ruled this nation. Further up the hill, behind the statue, was a whitewashed Beau Geste type of fort—the Alte Feste—which had turreted walls. The proud Germans of Windhoek, who had seen their army fight the cruellest colonial war in Africa and had seen those same troops return victorious after that war of genocide against the Hereros, could now only boast that they were the best butchers, breadmakers, and confectioners in the city.

Though most of the German businessmen were staid and respectable in their day-to-day affairs, there were times when their hidden repressions broke through the surface. Once a year, at carnival time, these men would mount festooned trucks and parade up and down Kaiserstrasse dressed in party hats, dinner jackets, and white ties to the accompaniment of brass bands who played what I can only describe as oom-pa-pa music. They would blow on toy trumpets, throw a few sweets to watching children, and then return to the German sports ground for eight days of almost nonstop carousing. These occasions were noted for a certain amount of sexual promiscuity. Plane loads of people would descend on Windhoek from South Africa, and it was almost impossible to obtain a ticket on an aircraft flying from the Republic to Windhoek.

Visitors from Europe were often astonished to see three German schlosses dominating the hills of the city, an obvious hankering back to the romance of the Rhineland. Though the German community were nostalgic for their homeland, preserved many of its customs, and paid periodic visits to Germany, they often complained bitterly that Western Germany today was not the same place that they were proud of and had loved. They were shocked by what they regarded its permissiveness, dismissed its youth as long-haired hippie layabouts, spoke critically of its strikes and high cost of living, and felt that it had entered a period of irreversible decadence. My own feeling about them was that they themselves were victims of apartheid and had been mentally crippled by a regime which destroys both freedom and critical faculties.

There were other reminders of German life. Windhoek had a tiny but influential Jewish community. On occasion they would make nervous references to the warnings they had been given by the members of the Nazi Party in Windhoek during the last great war about what would happen to the Jews in Windhoek when the Allied Powers were finally defeated by Hitler. Whereas the new Germany has arisen and developed into an impressive, highly developed democracy, in Windhoek, it seemed to me, the old ideologies were longtime a'dying. I was often told that the Allies had backed the wrong side in the war and that if we had followed the policies of Hitler there would be no red menace today. They were quick to point out that Prime Minister Vorster, who had himself been pro-Nazi during the war, would no doubt agree with them.

The Pretoria regime had skillfully won the support of the German community by taking care to guard the German language and by allowing the West German government to pay for German-trained teachers to teach in the German schools in Namibia. Though the Germans largely despised the Afrikaners, yet they have embraced their policies in what can only be seen as a dance of death. An African worker told me that whereas his German boss regarded all Afrikaners as boorish and uncultured and referred to them as "those white kaffirs," yet he regularly voted for them in every election. Most Germans respected what they regarded as the strong government provided by the Vorster regime. If they secretly found the immorality laws irksome, if they believed that there could be concessions to the blacks in certain areas, they nonetheless put up with these irritants, quaffed their beer in their club, and remembered the size of their bank balance, allowing this to lull their conscience.

One or two exceptions in the German community stand out in my mind for their courage and outspokenness. I pay tribute to the young German pastors who desperately struggled to change the attitudes of their white congregations, but whose task was made almost impossible by the combined forces of the state which never hesitated arbitrarily to deport anyone who criticized its policies and the church bureaucracy which had lamely stood on the sidelines in silent acquiescence at the state's cruel racist policies and had sometimes openly supported them. So whether individual Germans wanted changes or not, no strong stand was taken by the white leaders of their church to encourage or guide them.

Pastorine Friederike Heller went out to Namibia to be a pastor to the German-speaking white community of Windhoek. In a letter to me, she describes the massive problems she and her fellow pastors found when they attempted to change the racial attitudes among members of their congregations. This is how she described her problems:

> We tried to convince our church members of the need to work together with black Lutherans.
>
> Our method was different from yours. We saw that your action, at the time of the banning of the Dean of Johannesburg, just shocked our people and made any discussions with them impossible. They called what you did provocation, and having given it that name, that was the end of it. So we tried another approach, the way of discussion. In private, they would agree that changes must come, but we underestimated the pressure of public opinion on them. As German passport holders, they felt that they were in a precarious position, because for them even to mention that change must come would be interpreted by the South African government as opposition to it. The pressure of the group was stronger than individual consciences. Many of our church members just could not cope with the problem. They could not stand out against what the group was doing and so collapsed.
>
> Though we are convinced personally that our church members' attitudes towards the blacks were wrong and unchristian, we felt that we couldn't blame them, for the church had never taught them to do otherwise. Because the church did not make a strong stand, the people could slip through.
>
> I think you also must take into account their history. Many of them tried to prevent a repetition in South West Africa of their experiences during the last world war, when their families lost everything. They are frightened and daunted by the idea that by giving in they can lose everything again. I know that all these last thoughts look like mere apologies for their wrong attitude towards the blacks and to any who sympathize with them. I cannot justify it, because it is evil in its consequences; I often say that though I understand it, I cannot sanctify it.

It was a constant source of amazement and grief to me that the white community of Windhoek was so insensitive to the obvious needs and sufferings of the poor who were all around them. The plain fact is that the overwhelming majority of whites in Windhoek cared neither for social justice nor the well-being of their black neighbors. One had merely to walk down Kaiser Street during any lunch hour to witness the deliberate rejection of the black people. In summer the white Windhoeker drove home in his car for a siesta period which lasted from one until three; the black worker would hang around, sitting on the pavement, or lie curled up on a piece of waste paper in the shade of some inconspicuous doorway. He was totally rejected from the cafés and restaurants of the city. The only toilet accommodation was provided at the magistrate's court, a place most black people dreaded and avoided at all costs.

The municipality had rejected a scheme for providing cheap food for blacks of the townships. They did nothing to assist African workers in the city who wished to study at night school. I felt strongly that the church should meet both these needs, and so I attempted a one-man soup kitchen and distributed food once a week in the Old Location. The whites in my cathedral held back, watched me do it, and contributed hardly at all. The English classes that I gave each Sunday afternoon in the cathedral hall were conducted under the gaze of a Special Branch officer who sat outside the cathedral in his car and watched my family and me teach each week. The needs were so enormous that I wanted to see the churches tackling them together. A caring center was needed in Windhoek where black workers could come for meals in their lunch hour, where they could conduct their own concerts, and hold exhibitions of their own art and crafts. We needed to provide legal aid for those blacks who were daily the victims of the vicious apartheid laws. Our Anglican diocese was poor and could not possibly raise the funds to do this, but help was to come from another direction.

My chance came when Dr. Carl Mau, secretary of the Lutheran World Federation, paid a visit in 1971 to the Lutheran churches in Namibia, of which there were three at this time. The German Evangelical Lutheran Church catered only to the blacks in the same area and had black and white pastors, the latter coming from Germany. The largest Lutheran church was in Ovamboland. This was the Ovambo-Kavango Church, staffed by black pastors and drawing its white missionaries from Finland. The head of this church is a courageous and outspoken African bishop named Leonard Auala.

I was invited to meet Dr. Mau at a simple evening reception given in the home of the presiding minister of the Rhenish Church. I went along not knowing quite what to expect, for ecumenical relations in Windhoek were tenuous, to say the least. The Dutch Reformed Church had a built-in fear and suspicion of the Church of Rome. The clergy of the Anglican Church were regarded as hotheads recklessly dabbling in politics who seemed to deserve the many restrictions that the state was placing on them. As churches we were divided by language, by the historic divisions of the Reformation, but most of all by our attitudes towards apartheid.

A dozen or more people crowded into a small room and were discussing various church problems with Dr. Mau as I entered. I sat back, quietly listening to a conversation conducted mostly in Afrikaans, with one or two German phrases thrown in by way of explanation. I recall that it was the whites who were doing most of the talking; the black pastors spoke little and quietly sat on the edge of their chairs.

The head of the white Lutheran church was explaining how difficult it was to make headway in race relations, given the attitude of the existing South African government. He spoke of missionaries being deported and permits for people to work in Ovamboland being refused at the whim of a junior official. The Africans present maintained a polite demeanor which never revealed their innermost feelings, but Dr. Mau began twisting and turning in his chair, grabbing at his knee, constantly changing his position, an indication of the increasing dismay he was feeling.

"Are you telling me that there is absolutely nothing that the church can do to improve race relations in South West Africa? Am I to go back to Geneva and tell my colleagues that we just don't have a solution?" He turned abruptly to me and said, in English, "I would like to ask Bishop Winter his opinion."

This meeting with Carl Mau was one of the most important moments in my ministry, but he caught me completely unawares as I was just contemplating how I could quietly leave that room without causing too much embarrassment to myself or my hosts. I had become increasingly frustrated as the meeting continued. I love the church and feel dismay when I see its ministers retreating from what seem to me the demands of the gospel. Here was a situation in which the state had tampered with the law, could imprison and torture at whim, practiced massive intimidation against any who opposed it, and needed to be faced by Christians who would exhibit the courage and boldness which the gospel demands.

I felt neither hatred nor anger towards these white pastors, for these men are clearly my brothers in Christ, but I was deeply ashamed. The Africans present seemed to be trapped by a system which had educated them, had provided them with their livelihood, and on which they were totally dependent for their future. Speaking up would have branded them ungrateful political agitators. It was clear that a frank reply was being asked of me. I had become sick of platitudes and felt that the church of Martin Luther and Dietrich Bonhoeffer had a glorious heritage to draw on in facing the tactics of tyrants.

I was strengthened, too, by the knowledge that several of the young German pastors were sadly disillusioned with their church's compliance with South Africa's racial policies. They felt strongly that their church had backed down too often and that now was the time for action.

My experience within my own church convinced me that the majority of white priests had little or no theological grasp of the crisis that Christianity was facing in Southern Africa. Instead of helping to evolve a theology to deal with this, they had decided not to become politically involved or had produced a sort of cheery religious piety which assumed that all things were bright and beautiful.

That evening, I told Dr. Mau that as churchmen we knew in our consciences that there were many things the church could have done, but that we had allowed ourselves to become paralyzed by fear. The same methods which had proved successful in silencing opposition in Germany during the 30's were proving equally effective here. To those among us who said that to oppose South Africa meant certain deportation, I had only one reply: it was not our job to defend the church or to protect our own careers in it. The need now was for the church to see Jesus in the starving, the naked, the hungry, and the exploited. I concluded by describing the two activities I had been engaged in, namely the feeding scheme and the night school classes. I then suggested that as an ecumenical activity the churches should cooperate on a center in the city which would provide amenities for all races.

Dr. Mau immediately took up the challenge, and my discussions with him continued into the early hours of the morning. When I left, he asked me to do everything in my power to involve the white pastors who had been present earlier that evening in the scheme for an ecumenical center. So I returned home tired, but filled with hope that after a ten-year struggle in South Africa my dream was soon to be realized.

After Dr. Mau returned to Geneva, we tried to follow through with the plans, but at the local level we came into head-on collision with pastors who were deeply worried by our whole attitude towards the state. I had stressed that if we were to obtain permission for building the new center we would have to represent it as in some sense a church. There was nothing in the present law which prevented refreshments being served in churches following church services. I saw the daily operation of our center as beginning with a short act of worship which would then be followed by the distribution of a hot meal. To ask explicitly for permission to build a social services center was to invite refusal.

The white Lutheran pastors, however, were troubled by this

oblique approach. They felt that if I was not actually breaking the law, I was badly bending it by not being completely honest with the authorities about the proposed project. I felt that we were standing on solid ground, for Prime Minister Vorster was repeatedly saying to the press that there was no church/state confrontation in South Africa. I felt strongly that there was a good chance of our getting away with this scheme if only because of the world publicity that would occur if a strongly backed ecumenical venture were finally to be closed by state action. What we were aiming to do was clearly demanded by the gospel. The final point I wanted to make was that the church could not afford not to do it if it was to have any future with blacks in Namibia. If it did not make a stand with them now, when would it?

The leaders of the Lutheran Church in Windhoek were not convinced by my arguments: in fact, I think they were terrified by them. Months of foot-dragging followed. When I sent communications to their headquarters, it took ages for them to answer. There were always excuses: "We've been busy with our church synods." Or "we've been too occupied with Easter." When I finally did meet with officials of their church, they were clearly disenchanted. At the end of a long discussion, an old German pastor summarized his strong misgivings with a well-worn text: "The powers that be are ordained of God." I came away from that meeting tired and frustrated. It seemed to me that there could be no progress.

But for other people the ecumenical center was a matter of urgent and vital importance. Great pressure was put on the local Lutheran church by the Lutheran World Federation in Geneva, where Carl Mau and his colleagues were doing everything in their power to get the plans underway. It was largely through their influence that the deadlock was resolved. They wrote and asked the leaders of the Rhenish Church to cooperate with us to the full and told us so in a letter.

This letter threw my tiny office into a frenzy of activity. We worked long hours into the night to produce a blueprint for a multiracial ecumenical center. It is a fine tribute to my small staff that when the Lutheran authorities received our illustrated brochure in Geneva, they said that it was the finest application for a grant that they had ever received. We were in fact making ecumenical history: it was the first time that an Anglican-conceived project was to be constructed from Lutheran funds. The cost was to be $165,000.

With the scheme duly processed, the financial costs estimated, and the architect's plans almost completed, my assistant, David de Beer, left with me for Geneva, where we presented our project to the staff of the Lutheran World Federation. We had left a country where we were hated and harassed and regarded by the overwhelming majority of the whites as traitors. Our own white church people would pass us in the streets glaring or muttering at us. At best, they would pretend not to see us. The love and courtesy shown us by the Lutheran Christians in their headquarters will remain always in our memories, in striking contrast to the daily hatred which surrounded us at home. We shall never forget their encouragement, their obvious friendship, and their generous hospitality.

Politicians and churchmen in South Africa frequently assert that the problems of their country can be solved only from within and are indignant at what they regard as outside interference. When I hear this, I immediately think of what Carl Mau achieved in Namibia. Without his coming, the Anglican Church would certainly have slipped further and further into a position of isolation. As an outsider, he was able to invigorate us at the very moment when we needed it most. He was neither aggressive nor discourteous, but he had every right to know what solutions we were trying to bring to the country's racial problems. As a detached, impartial observer, he could tell us frankly what he felt about our efforts. South Africa's Christians need to be challenged more and more by representatives from churches outside the country, and these representatives are failing in Christian love and concern if they did not speak out boldly on these issues.

Geneva wrote to inform us that our scheme had been approved and that the money had been totally subscribed. We were overjoyed and I felt that my dream was shortly to be realized. But there were grim forebodings at the local level. When asked to comment on the proposed ecumenical center, a Dutch Reformed minister in Windhoek said, "If Bishop Winter is ever allowed to build that center, he will become the most powerful man in South West Africa." For him, our scheme threatened to topple the whole fabric of the apartheid system and therefore needed to be resisted to the bitter end.

Chapter Six

Windhoek: Old Location

The poverty and suffering which were commonplace in Windhoek's Old Location have so burnt themselves into my mind that I can never forget the place. I remember the smell, the dirt, the tin cans, the garbage strewn about into heaps because Windhoek's municipality refused to collect it. I remember the drunks lurching about its stoney streets or lying senseless under a bush or tree, belly exposed to view. All the lost dogs in the world seemed to live there—snarling and snapping at each other and sometimes, hunting in a pack, attacking a cur more timid and emaciated than themselves. The children mostly ran barefoot and would occasionally stop to negotiate a part of the pathway where a dozen broken bottles could slash at the feet of the unwary.

Of course, there are more pleasant memories too. I recall the shouts and laughter of the children. I remember the Herero women strolling gracefully along, princesses in this ghetto slum. The Old Location was a place alive with activity, noise, humor, and inventiveness. The Africans accomplished amazing building feats. Using rusty old paraffin tins which they beat out and odd pieces of wood and sheets of corrugated iron, they would construct a home. Some of the shanties would lean crazily, held together by bits of sacking which had been tacked optimistically to a wooden frame.

Humor was often mixed with danger. I remember watching a swirling river race down the gullies in the streets after the summer rains. An excited crowd stood on the bank watching as a Damara man was swept over boulders and borne madly downstream. He was drunk and that fact may have saved his life: he seemed to relax as the torrents sped him past us. He could have had his brains smashed out on any one of the many rocks there, but he was dragged out at the end, soaking wet and dazed, by a happy crowd of spectators who surrounded him with their ribald laughter.

At the entrance to the Old Location stood a Red Cross clinic, in front of which was always a queue of patient African mothers, often holding in their arms the near-lifeless forms of babes who were the victims of gastro-enteritis and were often too weak to cry: they lay motionless, wracked by fever and dehydration.

The sight which most roused me was the endless procession of the crippled, on homemade crutches, dragging a twisted limb behind them, or literally dragging themselves along the ground by their hands. Windhoek's Old Location was a living reproach to the blind indifference of the white community, to the daily misery apartheid caused to the overwhelming number of blacks in their midst.

The Old Location was a health hazard, and one of the main reasons for this was that the public toilets provided for its occupants regularly overspilt their contents onto the unmade roads. Any wonder, then, that blacks living there were racked with fevers in summer and bronchitis and pneumonia in winter.

On the main road, a few hundred yards beyond the Red Cross clinic, was the burnt-out shell of what once had been the community beer hall. It is the practice of the South African government to equip each African township with a vast community hall where liquor is sold. In 1959 the white police force shot dead eleven inhabitants of the Old Location, and in retaliation the blacks ransacked and smashed up the building.

The unexpected was always happening there. Black workers would pool their weekly wages to purchase a worn-out truck or car from the white community. Dozens of wrecks stood on stones or rotted in the burning sun, monuments to the regular failures of optimistic blacks to make such vehicles roadworthy. I passed five men who were peering into the engine of a beat-up Ford truck. To their astonishment, the engine coughed, spluttered, then backfired, emitting a tremendous cloud of black smoke. The five jumped with delight and then proceeded to dance round the vehicle. They were quite satisfied, although, as far as I could see, they would never get it to move an inch under its own power. As I was leaving them, an old black patriarchal figure emerged from a tiny doorway. As I tooked towards him, I saw in amazement that he was wearing an old German military helmet with a spike on top of it, a relic, no doubt, of Bismarck's war against the Hereros.

Apartheid not only broke bodies, it also destroyed minds, and frequently the only escape was through liquor. A Damara woman staggers past me screeching abuse in the air. Stumbling over an unseen rock, she falls and cuts her face, and then, casually wiping away the blood from her mouth, she picks out a house at random, runs up to the front door, and beats at it insanely. From inside, the owners swear back at her, but don't trouble to come out. Seizing a broken bottle, she hurls it at a passing dog, who slinks away yelping. She calls down curses on all those who have robbed, cheated, and hurt her. One of her breasts dangles loosely from a gaping tear in her outer garment, which by this time is covered with filth; she looks as though she has just crawled out of Macbeth's heath.

If the Old Location spoke to me of poverty and misery, of racism and rejection, it was also a symbol of a people's determination to resist the white oppressor. If people continued to live there amidst all its squalor, it was because they were determined to show the whites in Windhoek that they rejected apartheid and everything it stood for. I found dignity there too. When it would have been so easy for Africans to have taken the easy way out, grabbed at a wine bottle, and ended it all, the overwhelming majority of the people in the Old Location maintained standards of decency and were determined to work for a better life for their children and for their nation. It goes without saying that they were very conscious politically; the grinding poverty around them was in stark contrast to the affluence and pampered lives enjoyed by the whites who dominated them. In such a cradle of exploitation and racial discrimination, the dream of a free Namibia was conceived and the plans for a revolution formulated.

I shall never forget the old people of the Old Location who week by week waited for me to visit them. They would sit in tiny groups shaded from the fierce heat of the sun under the thorn bushes or in the shadow of a nearby shack. An old Herero man with a khaki shirt worn outside his trousers sits quietly chatting to a diminutive, toothless Damara woman. The latter is blind and has been led there on the end of a stick.

The gathered skirts of the women are covered with beautifully laundered aprons. The old people clap and laugh as I approach them, and one by one they come forward to speak to me and shake my hand. I speak to one in Afrikaans, address another with a smattering of Kwanyama, and throw out to another a sentence of wildly ungrammatical German. It sounds madness now to say it, but there was a joy among these poor people that I have seldom found in Western Europe or America.

A thin, frail black hand stretches out from the crowd of people around me seeking contact with my hand. Her eyes are sightless and her face cruelly thin, but finally she finds my hand and holds it in her own, clasps it firmly, and then, reaching down, kisses it. She utters only two words, "Vielen dank," and then, throwing her head back, astonishes me by singing in German Luther's "Ein' Feste Burg." I watch the movements of those parched old lips, fascinated by what I am witnessing. The others just stand around smiling, one or two of them putting in extemporary harmonies as she continues, and then I open the urns which contain the hot soup that I have brought and distribute a quantity to each of them.

From the folds of their voluminous skirts, the women produce a variety of containers. Magdalena holds out to me a battered German field kitchen unit which had been salvaged from the war of 1904. Amelia hands me a pan which is so old and rusty that as soon as I pour soup into it, it pours out from a dozen different holes onto the ground. An old man calls her a silly old woman, and she stands there looking confused and helpless. Reaching back into the cab, I offer her a plastic container which she guards like a valuable treasure for the next two years. Afterwards, every time we met she would pat the container and then gently pat my hand—it was ever to be a sign of solidarity between us.

I am led away from the crowd to one of the shacks. I enter its darkened interior, look around, and am amazed at how neat and tidy everything inside is. It has only one room and one tiny window which has never been opened, firmly secured with rusty nails. A worn piece of linoleum covers the floor, and in the corner, lying on a heap of old blankets, covered with an old Army greatcoat, lies a very sick African woman. She is too weak to stand, tries to acknowledge my presence by lifting her hand in greeting, but even this effort is too much for her and she lets her arm slump back on the floor and closes her eyes again.

I pour some milk into a cup and kneel down by her side. The pain of her condition stabs at me too. As I gently cradle her head in my arms, I notice that her neck is like that of an ostrich—scrawny, skinny, and wrinkled. She does, however, manage to swallow a gulp of the soup. She closes her eyes again, shakes her head to indicate that she has had enough, and whispers a hoarse "Dankie." I hold her hand momentarily, say a prayer in silence, and leave the hut.

Sweat and soup are now trickling down my leg, flies begin to swarm over my knees, and the stench of the urinals is starting to turn my stomach. I want to run away, go home to my family, and forget this place altogether, but I can't. Two hundred more people have been squatting all morning in the hot sun waiting for me to bring a bowl of soup or a couple of pints of skimmed milk. So I climb into my truck again and slowly drive over the bumpy track with the words of a white South African Cabinet minister ringing in my ear: "We have no poor in South Africa."

As I climb out of the Chevrolet truck, I see twenty yards ahead of me a police car slowly patrolling the streets. One glance tells me that its white occupants are observing me menacingly from the top of the road. My instant reaction is fear, and though I try to put the thought out of my mind, because it happens every week, I still wonder if they will simply pass by or swing their vehicle down to where I am distributing the food and arrest me. I try to continue dishing out food as though I have not noticed them; fourteen years in South Africa taught me that this was the safest policy. Out of the corner of my eye, I see them hesitate, talk to each other, and then, with a screech of tires, roar past.

Dozens of excited black children have now gathered round the truck, and eager hands grab at the small packets of biscuits I am carrying. A two-year-old child jostled by the crowd has his biscuit knocked on the ground, and from nowhere a scrawny yellow dog darts in and devours it with snapping jaws. The child lets out a scream of protest and is comforted only when I reach out, lift him up, and sit him on my lap with a packet of biscuits.

All of a sudden, I am left alone, for the food has all been distributed, the last packet of biscuits hungrily consumed, and even the ladles in the milk urns licked clean by eager mouths. I watch the children scurry over the hill, leaping and shouting until they disappear from sight.

Death was a daily reality in the Old Location and could come in many forms—a flashing blade in a drunken brawl, the collapse of TB-infected lungs, the ravaging of pneumonia, unchecked by bodies weak from hunger. Africans can teach Westerners a great deal about facing the reality and consequences of death. Always the community rallies to the aid of those who mourn; the grieving are never allowed to become neurotic by having to face their grief in isolation from the rest of their people.

Typical of this solidarity was the funeral I attended of the father of Chief Clemens Kapuuo. The rocky streets of the Location were jammed with cars and trucks as hundreds of African people poured in from the reservations and the surrounding town to stand with their chief in his sorrow.

The dead man's house had been stripped of all its furniture, and in the front yard a group of thirty or forty women squatted on the ground. The men came and went, and some of them sat around on cheap wooden chairs talking quietly to each other. Periodically, there would be a movement among the group of women. Their bodies, which had been motionless, would suddenly begin to sway, and a high-pitched moan would come from the lips of an older woman, which would then be taken up by the whole group. It was rather similar to the noise that bees make when they swarm and seemed to have a valuable purging effect on all those present.

The black community was always left to mourn alone. Though Clemens Kapuuo was a chief, such was the indifference of the white administration that there was not a single government representative present. Apartheid was to be carried even into the grave.

I had been asked to take part in the committal service, which was to be held in the barren wastes of the African cemetery. As I followed the vast crowd of Africans in the procession to the grave, we filed past the simple monuments to the African dead. Pathetic little crosses had white letters painted in clumsy writing on them. One noticed how many graves contained the bodies of mere babies. They showed me to my place on a mound made by the rock and rubble that had been dug out of the grave itself. There was a danger that if the heap collapsed we would be plunged into the grave, and as I moved my feet from time to time a stone would clatter down and land on the coffin.

An African brass band played some Lutheran hymns, and the people sang them slowly with great feeling. There were three or four ministers present, and as an act of courtesy I was also asked to speak. All that I had seen around me cried out for comment, and so I began, "In Namibia as elsewhere, death is the great leveller. It is good to remind ourselves that we will all stand one day before our God, and as there is no apartheid in heaven, so a person's color, wealth, class, or education is no guarantee of a place in eternity."

With the thought of those tiny crosses that I had seen over the graves of the infants still gripping my mind, I continued, "When a nation forgets to share, when it holds down the overwhelming majority of its people, when it has replaced mercy with a hundred racist laws that cause misery and hopelessness, then that nation stands under the judgment of God. Namibians yearn to be free people; yet for over a hundred years they have had to suffer the consequences of white domination and white greed. We stand at the graveside of an Herero brother who was a member of a nation almost exterminated by a bloody colonial war. Yet that people, along with the Namibian nation, have resisted and still wait for their deliverance. It is up to each and every one of us to ask God to give us strength to continue to resist until that day of liberation arrives."

When people accuse me of mixing politics with religion, I reply quite unashamedly that I see no dichotomy between the two. A new political system which brings with it justice for the oppressed, a more equitable distribution of the wealth of the nation, equal opportunities for all, and more just and sensible laws must surely replace the manifold inequalities and injustices that apartheid has erected. It was such contacts as I had with the African people that day in the cemetery and the shattering effect of seeing the graves of so many young children who were the helpless victims of a political system which wrecklessly pursued its policies irrespective of the cost in human suffering that made me determined to resist by every means available a regime which I had now come to see as anti-Christ.

After a heavy day's work, my staff and I would often stroll in the cool of an evening along the well-lit pavements of Kaiserstrasse, window-shopping and chatting as we went. Quite the most outstanding of all the shops were those of the German jewellers, who were master craftsmen in their art. Their windows were ablaze with the semi-precious stones from Namibia presented in modern settings. Amethysts, agates, tigers' eyes, hewn from the rocks of the Namib and Kalahari Deserts or discovered in thick seams on some obscure farm, were by the skill of these German goldsmiths transformed into modern artistic creations often of astonishing beauty.

The neon lights of Windhoek's main streets brilliantly lit up the white section of town, but as soon as one entered the buffer zone, which by law must separate white and black, one entered darkness. The African ghetto called Katutura was an ill-lit place. Africans had been forcibly moved from their homes to Katutura when bulldozers smashed down the Old Location in 1968. Whites cared little about conditions in Katutura and hardly ever visited it, since this required a permit. For most whites, therefore, Katutura was a mere name, a faceless place filled with faceless people.

Dominating the township itself and menacing all who passed by its walls was the vast fortress of Windhoek's prison. The blacks of Katutura had to pass it every time they entered their township. It was built there with the clear intention of warning all blacks that the price of political agitation or resistance of any kind was inevitably arrest and detention.

Prisons are never pretty places, and whenever I drove past Windhoek's gaol, I was tense and afraid. Its designers had included narrow, open slits in its walls which could be used as machine gun turrets. Every morning, khaki trucks full of black convict laborers would roar out of the huge, studded gates. These laborers were rented out to white farmers and householders at ten cents a day per man.

A vast wire fence had been thrown round the Old Location itself, and it was obvious at a glance that within minutes the whole place could be screened off, surrounded by armored cars, and isolated from the white community should the blacks ever decide to rise up against their oppressors. Between the gaol and the entrance to the Location itself stood a seven million dollar hospital which had been completed for the African inhabitants. It is an impressive building, but it is one of the enigmas of apartheid that, having built such a fine modern hospital, the administration could not find enough blacks to staff it. After fifty years of South African control of Namibia, there were only three black doctors in the whole territory. Further, the whites in Windhoek were incensed that this hospital had ever been built at all and felt that the administration was pampering the blacks. Though their own hospital was relatively new, they demanded that a new one be built for them, fearing that they might be upstaged by the one for the blacks.

At the entrance to the Location stood the police station and the pass office. As in South Africa, the black man in Namibia can hardly move without first obtaining a permit. If a friend wished to come and visit him from a nearby reserve, a pass was needed for him to stay in his house. If his wife was sick in the homeland, he needed a pass from the magistrate to visit her. If he wanted to look for work in a nearby town, a pass was needed for that too. No adult male above eighteen could reside in the township unless he had a pass, and it was an offense punishable by fine or imprisonment for any black to be in a white area for longer than forty-eight hours unless he had a permit. So the police vans, which daily patrolled the streets of the Location, were there to harass and intimidate the black people. Many hours are spent by the blacks queueing up to obtain permission from white officialdom to seek work, to visit friends, or to reside in white areas. Failure to produce a pass when demanded unleashes the violence of a hostile state. Pass raids are sickening sights to watch. So the black men and women stand for endless hours, begging permission from a half-educated bureaucrat to live and breathe for the next few months. And if they laughed and joked among themselves as the queue inched up to the counter, it was simply to release the pent-up frustration and fury that ate into their hearts.

By contrast, the lives of white people are leisurely and fairly carefree, a combination of sundowners, barbecues, and sport. Just occasionally, they too would be caught in the web of state bureaucracy, as when they had to spend a few minutes queueing to pay the municipal tax for their black servant. Employers are supposed to provide a shower, a bed, and a toilet for an African servant, and a "poor white" employee of the municipality would be dispatched to see that this was so. I never heard of anyone being turned down for not having properly equipped quarters for his servant. Some whites did provide excellent accommodations for their African employees, but by and large the conditions for the contracted black laborer would never have been tolerated for a moment in a free society. Blacks living in white homes in servants' quarters were relatively secure from police violence and harassment, but this was not so for the ordinary inhabitant of Katutura.

As in Nazi Germany, police raids were always launched in the early hours of the morning, with the sole objective of producing maximum terror among the Location's black inhabitants, thus reducing their will to resist. For their part, the authorities gave as their excuse that they were looking for work-shy Africans and for illicit liquor. The first indication the inhabitants would have of a raid came when the metal doors of their tiny homes were hammered on with heavy truncheons. Not waiting for the terrified occupant to open the doors, the police would kick them in and burst into the house, shouting and swearing. The people would be indiscriminately beaten as the police demanded to see their passes. The men would rarely be given a chance to find them. Instead, they were beaten and kicked and shoved into waiting police trucks, to be driven to gaol. Often, they were naked.

Next day, when a terrified wife presented the proper papers at the police station, she would be forced to pay an admission of guilt fee before her husband would be released. He would then be allowed to go home, often still half-clothed.

For nearly 5000 African contract laborers, living quarters were the compound, which stood opposite the police station at the entrance to the Location. It was a cheaply constructed, white-washed building to which entrance was gained through a high wire gate. The dormitory accommodation it provided consisted of a concrete slab which was used for a bed, underneath which was a tin locker. Men were herded together into overcrowded rooms which were crawling with lice and vermin. Their food was served to them on shovels; sanitation was of the most primitive kind.

There was only one tarred road in the township; the others were tracks strewn with mica rocks and sharp stones, so that a constant pall of dust hung over the Location itself, penetrating the houses and the lungs of the children. Respiratory problems were a daily hazard in the place.

The houses provided the Africans were of the most rudimentary kind, with doors limited to the front and back entrances—it was unthinkable that African married couples would want a door on their bedroom. Each of the houses had large numbers painted in white on the doors, with a capital letter prefixing them. This letter denoted what ethnic group the occupant belonged to. Not content with dividing the blacks from the white community, the inhabitants of Katutura had to be further subdivided from each other into smaller groupings so that there was a Nama section, a Damara section, an Ovambo section, and so on. Apartheid's iron hand pursued them even into their tiny shacks. If the blacks found a unity among themselves during the few hours they spent in their homes, this could be a threat to the white man's dominance.

One of the cruelest aspects of life in Katutura was the appalling condition under which old black people had to live. Blacks are described as "work units" in South African political jargon. When a black is no longer able to work, he is immediately endorsed out of the white area and removed to the reserves. Some old blacks managed to cling on in Katutura until the authorities decided where they should be sent. Since they were nobody's immediate responsibility, they were shuffled off from one department of government to another. Some of them were blind, many were weak, and at least one of them was mentally deranged. But desperate as their condition was, no one in authority took responsibility for them. They lived in a collection of single rooms in the most appalling squalor. I came across them quite by accident when I found one old lady scratching around in a rubbish heap looking for old bottles and bones which she would later sell to buy food. I then visited the "home" once a week to take in bread, tea, tobacco, and fresh milk.

This is the description of the home which was presented at our diocesan synod in October 1971:

> The building consists of twenty adjoining rooms, all strung out in a line. Most of the windows are broken and the holes covered with old pieces of tin and cardboard. Curtains of mealie-meal and flour sacks are hung at some windows. The cement and brick walls—once painted white—are filthy, blackened with soot, bugs, spiders, even excreta. They are covered by old paper, dirty blankets, ragged clothes. There are no wash-basins in the rooms; the inhabitants literally bathe in the toilet since the shower is directly above a cement hole in the ground.
>
> In summer, the rooms—under the corrugated iron roof—are

> unbearable, hot and stuffy and constantly filled with dust. However, in winter, the lack of insulation and heat is equally unbearable. Often, inhabitants build fires in the centre of the rooms, right on the floor, leading to carbon monoxide poisoning, not to mention the danger of burning down the whole building. Despite the cold, one blanket is the most that anyone is allowed. No furniture is supplied. What exists has been collected by the inhabitants: three chairs in the whole place, pieces of wood or tin, old bathtubs. There are no beds. Most rooms have more than one occupant; a few people have rooms of their own (5 x 7 paces). The most active inhabitants are rats, cockroaches, lice and fleas, wasps, and moths; they have the run of the place. Obviously, this increases the danger of disease.
>
> The average age [of the occupants] is between 60 and 70. Most are crippled with arthritis; two are blind; some, mentally unstable. One of the blind men is now in hospital: he was burned trying to cook on a primus. An old woman, suffering from malnutrition, tries to care for her mentally retarded child; both are clad in rags. One old man—an outpatient at the local mental hospital—must climb through the jagged edge of a broken window to his room, for the door is locked and the key long gone. He has not so much as a blanket in his private room. The people cannot care for themselves, yet are expected to keep their rooms clean. One more active man helps the others to get around and stay tidy; he is receiving treatment for TB. . . .
>
> No cutlery is provided. If inhabitants lack an old tin or container, their food is given to others.

This report was compiled by Sister Shabalala, Sister Durkie, and Gillian Nicholson. They inquired and were told at the Windhoek Municipal Offices in Katutura that there was no one in charge of the "home." The Bantu Administration stated that it is not policy to have an old age home in Katutura, as the people must be returned to their "homelands." They, therefore, refuse to put anyone in charge of the premises. They are not certain what is to be done with people who have no "homeland" to which they can be returned—for example, a Liberian. The inhabitants themselves are unwilling to be sent away, since they know that the last time this was done, all the people died.

The most crushing condemnation I ever heard of the South African regime came from the lips of an old Nigerian over eighty years old who lived in the home. A Kruman, he had come to Cape Town with the English navy and had been unable to save enough money to return home to Nigeria. With immense dignity he said to me, "Old as I am, it is still my hope to get out of this country one day. I hate it here and I don't even want to leave them my bones. I want to go back home and die a free man in a free country." He never achieved his wish.

In August 1973 one of the women who compiled the report wrote:

"Last year the 'home' was cleaned up and painted. . . . This was organised by Sister Shabalala, who is in charge of the clinic. Several of the people have been removed to their homelands." All of these died soon after their removal.

If one man could epitomize, in his own physical presence, the people's hopes and dreams, that man was Hosea Kutako. During the lifetime of the Old Chief, a myth, an aura of grandeur had grown up around him. Anyone following such a man was bound to have problems, and Clemens Kapuuo's task was formidable when he took over the reins of power.

The South African authorities chose the moment of his accession to move in against the Old Location. First, they rushed through legislation in the municipality saying that the Old Location had become a health hazard. They themselves had frequently cut off its water. They had refused to remove its garbage until this became piled high and stank. They continued to remove its night soil only because any epidemic which struck down the blacks in their township would be equally merciless among the whites so close in the adjacent town.

Having gotten the law passed, they moved against white employers. Realizing that any attempt to move out the blacks by force had been resisted by the whites, they aimed to starve the whites out. Any white employer who kept in his employ a black residing in the Old Location would be fined $75 a day. The white employers were forced by government demand to move their employees or fire them.

In such a situation, the white government in Pretoria could sit back and claim total innocence if such a scheme backfired. It was purely a domestic matter between the white administrators of the city of Windhoek and its black township which had now become a health hazard. Healthier quarters, piped water, earth closets awaited the blacks in their new township. Only national stubbornness and backwardness, they said, made them cling to the old ways.

The municipality acted first against its black employees. Hundreds of cleaners, road workers, office boys, nurses, teachers, laborers were told: "Leave the Old Location by the end of July or you starve. If you are without a job, you may not stay in Windhoek. You will be shipped back to the reserves."

Propaganda was churned out to persuade the Coloured community to leave the Old Location. They were wooed by promises that they were to have special privileges in the new township which placed them a cut above the Africans. Their Afrikaans culture was to be preserved. They could go to slightly better-constructed houses in a place called

Khomasdal. Because they had white blood in them, they were not to be considered on the lowest rung of the ethnic ladder, as were the "primitive" Bantus.

The press moved in and played its part. The thin trickle of people at the beginning of the process became a flood at the end. The Hereros resisted as best they could, but they were obviously isolated, left in solitary confinement to defend a heap of rotting, rusty shanties. About three hundred of them sat in solitary occupation as the massive yellow bulldozers, hired from a local businessman, ripped into the shanties around them. Time was running out.

Three or four telegrams were sent to the United Nations. The Africans waited in vain for an answer as that body stood remote, helpless, mute.

The bully-boy methods that had been used to break the people's resistance in the Old Location appalled me. Day after day, as I drove in there, I passed vehicles of the South African police force. I felt sickened and ashamed as I passed their armored cars.

No white voice was raised in protest in the city. The contest was now merely a question of time before it was declared over and the land could be parcelled out and sold to white developers and entrepreneurs as some of the best building land in Windhoek.

Heartsick and depressed, I entered the Location again. For some months, I had been sending food out to the reserves through the help of an old Herero. But it seemed that someone should defy the ban on employing an African in the Old Location. So as a small token of solidarity with the blacks, I asked Aaron, an Herero, if he would work for me. I offered him $30 a week to distribute Bibles among his people. He agreed and set out from my house with a small quantity. As I watched him depart, I wondered how long I would be living in Windhoek.

The matter never came to the test, for the next day he came back looking uncomfortable. Speaking to me in broken English, he pointed out that he was the only one in the Old Location who now was earning any money at all.

"I cannot do it. . . . I must be the same as my brothers." So he resigned.

On the last occasion that I drove into the Old Location, the final group of Hereros were leaving. I watched them sadly as they climbed into the waiting trucks which were piled high with household possessions. Ten families or more could be accommodated in one truck. They had with them a few possessions—the odd chair, a table, a primus stove, a worn mattress. I felt ashamed as I watched the women in their long stately dresses file past me.

The white administration, wishing in victory to be seen as a benefactor, had sent along a couple of underlings who were to offer the people mealie meal or flour for their journey. Some of the reservations to which they were travelling were hundreds of miles away; poverty and overcrowding awaited them there. The local press had made much of the fact that the removals were conducted with as much humanity as possible on the part of the white administration.

The two white men stood beside full sacks of mealie meal and flour. I watched the Herero women pass them. Their faces were expressionless; with heads held erect, they glided past the officials who tried to hand to each one a small sack of flour. Not a single woman so much as looked at them or recognized their presence; they were completely ignored.

One little Herero boy held out his hand and accepted a parcel. His mother responded immediately by dragging the child to the side and beating the contents from his hands onto the ground. She then handed her son safely into the arms of her friends who were already seated on the truck.

Chief Kapuuo walked from truck to truck, staying with his people to the end. They greeted him quietly, and he chatted awhile, encouraging each party and asking after their well-being. There they sat, surrounded by the twisted tin and broken spars of what for them had once been home.

Chapter Seven

Windhoek: Coloured Community

There was a small community of Coloured people in Windhoek, numbering less than a thousand, who lived in a segregated area of town called Khomasdal. Their tiny township was on the same side of the city as the Katutura location, and like the Africans, they too lived in a twilight world of rejection. Many of them had come from the Cape or from some of the more obscure parts of Southern Africa, attracted by the high wages and the many jobs which were made available to them. Not that the white community ever accepted them as people or had any social contact with them; they were tolerated because they had skills which the whites needed and did the type of manual work which most white people found unattractive or physically too demanding. The men were the skilled bricklayers, carpenters, painters, and stone masons employed by the booming building industry. The women worked as shop assistants, packed clothing in the dry cleaners, worked in the storerooms of the supermarkets, or pressed and ironed clothes in the local laundry.

No less a person than the Administrator warned them that they could never regard themselves as permanent settlers in Namibia, and soon after he made this statement, vans of railway police began closely examining the documents of all the Coloured people arriving by train from South Africa. Any who did not possess written permission to be there would be immediately sent back to the Republic. Despite this constant police scrutiny, many did in fact manage to slip through. For those who evaded the police cordon, their future existence, though not as thwarted with dangers as that of the Africans, was precarious since they could be forcibly ejected from their jobs and removed within twenty-four hours from the territory.

The effect of all this was crushing on the personality of the people. Their cramped and overcrowded township lacked any real amenities, and they were barred from the cinemas, restaurants, and sporting facilities provided for the white community. In consequence, alcoholism was rampant among the men, and their children, though charming, were usually timid and unsure of themselves. They seemed to lack drive and social cohesion and were constantly arguing and fighting among each other. It was almost as if a death wish had come over them, the culmination of years of rejection by the whites.

By providing them with houses separate from the people of Katutura, the white authorities were trying to drive a wedge between them and their African neighbors. The Coloured people had a few privileges which were totally denied to the blacks. They did not need to carry a pass, and the luckier ones were able to have their wives and families live with them. Their homes were rather better constructed, more money was spent on their education, and they had a greater choice of jobs and employment. They were not viciously hounded by police, and though no amenities were provided for them at beaches or game parks, they could at least travel the country quite freely. Because of all this, they were the most isolated of all social groups in Windhoek.

Most of them came from farming areas where their forebears had been employed in conditions of cruel poverty and neglect. Consequently, TB was rife among the Khomasdal community. Though there were facilities for treating this in the local "non-white" hospital, many of the men absented themselves from treatment after a few weeks. White officials reacted with insensitivity and hostility and accused their patients of reckless stupidity for their lack of cooperation, but the plain fact was that if a Coloured man was to spend six months in a TB hospital, his family literally faced starvation. A sense of social justice among the white community would have gone a long way to eradicate this problem.

Though the Coloured community squabbled among themselves, and could not be bound together for united social action, yet I shall always remember their generosity and their outstanding gifts as music makers. This they derived from their ancestors in the Cape, who had a special love for dancing and for music.

One of my staff, Cathy Roark, a young American volunteer from Tucson, Arizona, had a special responsibility for working among the young people of Khomasdal. Though she had no training as a youth worker, had learned only a few words of Afrikaans, and came from a middle-class American home, she communicated with these young people better than any other member of my staff. She was an accomplished guitar player and taught the young people Negro spirituals and freedom songs. This music was the key which would unlock their hearts.

We had a small, white-washed church in the township, and one winter's evening I stood there waiting for Cathy to bring a party of young people who were going to discuss their plans and activities with me. As I stood on the concrete strip next to the church, I watched the lights of the township flickering in the African night. Trucks carrying construction workers home to the Location drove past me, forcing me to turn my head and bury my nose and mouth in my handkerchief as clouds of thick mica dust rolled over me. There were only two tarred roads in the township and both of them were on its perimeter, so that the inhabitants here suffered from the same respiratory sicknesses as afflicted their counterparts in Katutura.

Dogs barked in the distance, and the silhouettes of workers were outlined against the sky as they drifted past me, hot and tired, after their day's work. It was Friday, pay night, and so the inevitable cries and curses assaulted the darkness. Somewhere by a clump of trees a woman or a girl screamed and continued screaming, yet no one paid much attention. She could have been drunk or quarreling or being raped. Violence erupted in Khomasdal every Friday night. One felt helpless to deal with it.

As I stood there in the dark, I thought about the people I knew in this township. There was Mrs. September, who was now living with her seven children in the garage of a friend's home. Her husband, a carpenter, had been forced to leave Namibia and return to Cape Town because when he changed his employer he had not notified the Department of Coloured Affairs. It went without saying that he would sneak back into the territory eventually. Since he was a reliable worker, his boss would reemploy him, and he would continue to live in this same garage, moving around by stealth until he was again deported. It meant that he could never live in a municipal house and that his family would be brought up under conditions of acute discomfort.

Some of the Coloured people could pass as white, and though they lived under the great strain of possible detection, it was financially and socially well worth the risk. I thought of Frank Jansen, who though married to a Coloured woman and though Coloured himself, had a near-white skin. This, together with a gift for repairing machinery, got him the post of manager in a local factory. He rarely mixed with his Coloured neighbors, but chose instead friends from the German community. The strain of this dual existence took its toll, and such was his fear of detection that in the end he left his wife and children and slept on the floor of his factory.

My eyes settled on the outline of a school for Coloured children. Its principal, Johannes Kluter, was a willing accomplice of the white government, dispensing their racial theories among his own students. He rode around Windhoek in a large American car and would often call on white businesses to get extras for his school. Since whites had helped to create the Coloured race and had feelings of guilt for their existence, Kluter did well both for himself and for his school. He owed his entire position to the white racist regime, and he was eager to show his masters that he had fully assimilated all its doctrines and was imparting them faithfully to his staff and pupils.

One of the teachers on the staff described what it felt like to work for Kluter:

> Here was a sell-out on a big scale. As his teachers, we were also his victims. He would even send us into the African location to see if there were any children there who looked like Coloureds. We were then to tell them that they didn't belong there, but had to come to the Coloured school. I had to manufacture a name so that I would be admitted. My mother was an Herero, but the Coloured school had better facilities, so naturally, my parents wanted me to have a better chance of a decent education. The situation became unbearable for me. I lived in the Old Location at that time but I didn't feel Coloured. I just wanted to be me. When I later came and taught at his school, I was hounded by paid informers and men from the Secret Police. The kids used to tell me: "Pasop, juvrou; dardie mense is naby" ("Watch out, Miss; those people are near").

She told me how the white government had imported Coloured teachers from South Africa and paid them inflated wages so they could brainwash their own people into accepting the racial classifications of the whites. Kluter was a happy and industrious collaborator in this. The system produced in her feelings of guilt that she was black, and she recalled vividly the fantasies of her childhood:

> Of course, as a little girl in that school, I used to have these dreams. It wouldn't have mattered if I had been turned into the oldest white woman alive, I would have even preferred to be that than to be black! Why, even the dog of a white person has a better life than we blacks. I used to have uncles who had worked all their lives for South African Railways and the day they retired, wore the same overalls and boots that they'd been issued with when they started.

Though an African, she returned to teach at the Coloured school because there were obvious financial advantages. Her father had taught African children and after thirty years was earning a mere $60 a year. By posing as a Coloured teacher, she could earn that in a month.

She then described to me what conditions were like for the little Coloured children in that school in Khomasdal:

> They used to sleep in hostels, but they did not have proper blankets. They used to sleep in hessian sugar sacks. The worst I remember was that there were no flush toilets, and one of the jobs the children had to do for Kluter was to empty the teachers' toilets by hand. They were given tins to do this. I used to see tape worms in those cans. It was terrible.

She lasted little more than a year in the school before the whole system broke her. She felt that she was betraying her African past and her own people:

> The first words I spoke were Herero, so why should I masquerade as a Coloured? I just wanted to be me. You see, I couldn't possibly sing the Afrikaner National Anthem, and so I was dogged by the Secret Police and taken for questioning by them time and time again. I was living in a world of terror. There were so many old people and poor folk and so many children that were hungry that there was nothing left out of my wages at the end of the month because there were so many hungry mouths to feed. I wasn't even able to buy myself a dress, so I decided to get out.

Together with a few companions she hired a truck and was driven through the Kalahari Desert to within several miles of the border fence. Their driver did not dare approach too close to the border for fear of being picked up by South African Police patrols; so the girls were dropped off and then had to walk for three days through the desert without food and with just a little water. They nearly died. Exhausted and hopelessly lost, they were beginning to lose hope of ever reaching the Botswana border. In the distance they saw a flock of goats, and summoning up what strength was left, they caught one of the animals and milked it.

My informant today lives in Holland with her husband and little boy and has a degree from a Dutch university. She waits for the day when she can return to a free Namibia.

Kluter was not so fortunate. Driven by an insatiable ambition, he was launched by the government as the mouthpiece of a Coloured political party. Inevitably, however, the crash came, for after selling out his people, he was imprisoned for embezzling his party's funds. Yet today this is the man Prime Minister Vorster has made one of the chief representatives on the Advisory Council which purports to speak for the people of Namibia.

And so I stood that evening at Khomasdal, waiting in the darkness, and watched the lights of approaching vehicles and smelled the smoke from a hundred wood fires. The lights of a truck dazzled me as it swung into the churchyard. It was packed with two dozen youngsters singing their hearts out.

> Going up the mountain, children,
> I never come here to stay:
> If I nevermore see you again,
> I'll meet you on the judgement day.

The truck lurched over a pile of rubble that had been pushed to the side of the road by a road grader and came to a halt in a swirling cloud of dust. Several of the children ran to collect wood with which to build a fire, while the rest gathered excitedly around Cathy as she strummed her guitar and prepared to teach them a new song. Within moments, they were harmonizing as she played, "We Shall Overcome."

> We are not afraid,
> We are not afraid,
> We are not afraid today.
> Deep in my heart, I do believe,
> We shall overcome some day.

I looked from each shining face to the next, saw the reflected light of the fire shining in their eyes, and suddenly Khomasdal, with all its smells, its lusts, its knifings and betrayals, receded and was purged by the spark of freedom that had been kindled in the hearts of these youngsters.

Quietly leaving the group, I walked into our little church. From outside, the light from the fire cast shadows on the walls of the sanctuary. The crowd of youngsters had now swollen to well over one hundred who were sitting around Cathy, clapping in time to the music or dancing unselfconsciously at the fringe of the group. Their song reverberated over the housetops as they sang out in defiance:

> One man's hands can't tear a prison down,
> Two men's hands can't tear a prison down:
> But if two and two and fifty make a million,
> We'll see those walls come down.
> We'll see those walls come down.

Chapter Eight

Community of Simon the Zealot

The activities of the Secret Police were not confined to keeping a constant vigilance and harassing the staff at my diocesan headquarters in Windhoek. The police launched a deadly campaign to paralyze and, if possible, destroy the effectiveness of the Anglican Church throughout the entire territory. In retrospect, it is still incredible to me that our tiny church—poorly financed, badly organized and ill-equipped—could have posed such a threat to the white regime, but it obviously did, and the state used every device imaginable to work havoc among our members. They had agents who were ready to fan the flames of discontent not only among our laity but also among the clergy. In one instance, they were supremely successful.

Prior to my being elected bishop, some brief talk had arisen about the possibility of dividing our diocese, which was a vast, sprawling, and unmanageable area of 318,000 square miles. It would certainly have been easier for two bishops to have managed, but there were two important considerations. First, such a move could be made only after approval by the Synod of the Church of the Province of South Africa. The Province would have had to be convinced that two smaller units could be economically viable given time and that each would have a sufficiently trained administrative staff with which to function. Given our situation, they might have been persuaded that this could eventually have been achieved. The second consideration was a much more serious one: The overwhelming majority of our church members lived in Ovamboland and were black. These people were proud that they belonged to a church which, in theory at least, was open to all men and women of whatever race. To have divided the diocese at this time would have played right into the hands of the government's Bantustan policy, which aimed at carving up Namibia and separating people into their various ethnic groups. Had Namibia been a free society without these hated racial categories and classifications and had the decisions come from the people themselves, I would have accepted the division of the diocese as necessary for its better administration. As it was, none of the African clergy wanted this; in fact, they felt that if the diocese were divided, they, their families, and their people would suffer by not being allowed to move out of the confined and restricting sandy stretches of Ovamboland. Therefore, I was opposed to its division.

One single clergyman, a black, newly ordained deacon named Petrus Kalungula, felt otherwise. Whether initially he was prompted by motives of personal ambition or had been bribed by the Secret Police, one cannot be sure, but the police used him to spearhead a campaign of violence against my clergy and against the policies that I was attempting to introduce.

Our church had been slow to share with the African clergy and people positions in the power-making body of the diocese. Africans naturally felt a deep sense of grievance that for almost fifty years they had been shut out of the effective decision-making bodies of the Church. In consultation with the Rev. George Pierce, a young priest who had come to us from the American Indian community of Pine Ridge, South Dakota, I set out a Board of Inquiry to look into the structures of our mission. Certain white missionaries felt threatened by this and two of them resigned shortly thereafter. Petrus Kalungula immediately moved in, and the mission was wracked with student disorders and protest as a result.

When some of our old priests attempted to say Mass in outlying churches, Kalungula would prevent them by blocking their entrance and in one or two cases by physically assaulting them.

Finally, after all reason and persuasion had failed with him, we appealed to the local magistrate to restrain him from impeding our clergy from peacefully executing their religious duties. To our utter astonishment, the action of the local magistrate in Ondangua was swept aside on the authority of the Secret Police, and Kalungula was able to harry and menace our clergy at will.

By this time the unholy alliance was out in the open, for he was now travelling throughout Ovamboland in vehicles provided by the South African police. He moved with impunity wherever he wished, boasting that he would soon have the Bishop deported and that he himself would take over the Anglican Church in Ovamboland.

He visited every single congregation in an attempt to persuade the people to join his newly founded schismatic church, and he boasted of having government support at the highest level. Furthermore, he threatened people by announcing that those who remained faithful to a church which was outspoken in its criticism of the government would be dealt with. He was a powerful and persuasive speaker and at the beginning drew great crowds by the strength of his personality and by the brilliance of his oratory.

At the beginning of this struggle, two Africans were chosen by a representative body of clergy and people to be our church leaders in Ovamboland. They were Archdeacons Lazarus Haukongo and Philip Shilongo. Because of their position, they were singled out for special attention by Kalungula. It is a tribute to their remarkable gifts of leadership and courage that not a single black priest defected from our church during these troubles.

For all the state's determination to crack us and for all the strain and tension it created, there was often a gaiety among my fellow workers. At times diocesan helpers were being skittled like nine pins, and yet young people constantly arrived out of the blue to replace them.

When I became bishop in 1969, my entire staff at diocesan headquarters in Windhoek consisted of one part-time secretary who came in for four hours each morning; May Harte, a wonderful woman who did the books; and Frank Haythornthwaite, who as well as being canon of the cathedral also acted as diocesan secretary and treasurer. We were desperate for funds, and so I decided not to move into the bishop's house but rather to rent it and use the money to help pay clergy stipends. The first job I did as bishop was to paint out the garage of the house I lived in, remove all the junk, and turn it into a much-needed diocesan office.

Dave de Beer had lasted one week as hospital secretary in Odibo before the government deported him from Ovamboland because of the outstanding part he had played in student politics in South Africa. I immediately made him the administrator of the diocese, responsible for all financial matters. At twenty-one, he was probably the youngest diocesan administrator in the Anglican communion. As bishop I was determined not to become a bureaucrat, and I relied totally on David's expertise in commerce and accountancy to free me for the task of being chief pastor to my clergy and people. I had total confidence in him not only in financial matters but also in political insights.

When an African walked into Windhoek from a distant mine and wanted to greet his bishop, it was vital that he should be received with courtesy and love. Thus, no meeting was too important to prevent me from greeting him. Many of these African workers were volunteer, unpaid evangelists who not only were teaching their comrades to read and write, but were also preparing them for baptism and confirmation. From the start my priorities were that people mattered more than things. I owe it to David that his business competence was so great that it gave me the freedom to do this.

African and Coloured people began to flock to our small diocesan office, and it became a meeting point for Africans from the mines, Coloured office workers, as well as black students. Because of our contact with blacks of all levels, we were able to gain deeper insights into their problems and were able to gear the church's ministry to their needs as they themselves saw them. A grass-roots ministry was being hammered out in response to the heart cries from the contract laborers themselves.

A building boom was going on in Windhoek at this time as mining companies moved in to prospect for minerals or to take over mines which had already been started. From South Africa, men were recruited to staff various jobs in the white administration. Insurance companies and other commercial enterprises in South Africa sent up their representatives to cash in on the expanding economy. White civil servants were given beautifully constructed and well laid out modern houses at a subsidized rent of around twelve dollars a month. The picture for blacks was wholly different: they got little comfort and a few crumbs. Rusty corrugated iron shanties for construction workers and their families leaped up overnight outside the city's boundaries on the Okahandja road. This squatters' camp was about seven miles outside Windhoek, out of view of the general public, but similar to thousands of such camps throughout Southern Africa.

David was asked to visit the camp and went out Sunday after Sunday just to spend a few hours visiting with the people who lived there. Heavy drinking took place on weekends, which was often followed by quarrelling and fights. So suspicious were the white authorities of us at this time that David took the precaution of wearing an old black cassock of mine in the hope that the management of the construction firm would take a more tolerant attitude towards his visits if they thought he was a church worker.

The black workers were delighted with his visits and so responsive to his presence that they got together and built their own church. Like their houses, it was constructed of rusty tin sheeting and twisted scraps of metal, but it was a real labor of love and acted as the only meeting place for the whole community. An abiding picture I have of David is of him entering the battered, weather-beaten door of the shanty church holding the hand of a chubby little African child and being followed by a crowd of African children.

All my staff were able to make lasting friendships with the black community, and it was this fact, as much as any, which evoked the animosity of the state and caused it to regard us as a threat. Paid informers were employed to watch our every movement, to report our conversations, and to ask us loaded questions which might lead to our arrest or deportation. One such victim of this process was Larry Weeks.

Larry Weeks was a young Harvard graduate whose father was an Anglican priest in Tucson, Arizona. I had met him when I had been a guest in his father's parish and he seemed just the right sort of person I needed to help me with an important project. I wanted a detached, impartial study done on the effects of apartheid upon urban blacks in Windhoek. It seemed to me that as a church we were floundering in our attempts to serve the black community by continuing the same style of ministry which we had inherited from medieval times in Europe. In fact we were offering the Africans a style of Christian ministry much of which was being discarded in present-day Europe. At best, our priests were struggling manfully on, but often seemed not to understand the massive problems, tensions, and pressures that life created for an urban black in our city. At worst, we were guilty of the same inexcusable fault as the South African government: we were telling the blacks what they needed without first asking them what they wanted.

Christianity was breaking down under the daily strains of living in Katutura. So often, we used the Sunday morning sermon as a means of lashing our people instead of applying healing balm to their wounds and scars. Furthermore, the churches were used for just a few hours on Sunday and apart from being poorly attended at weekday services were largely left empty for the rest of the time. I felt a study might reveal that there was a need for them to be used as crèches where the young African children could be cared for during the week while their mothers were away working in factories or the homes of the whites. I felt too that the study might reveal a need for them to be open as centers which could offer literacy classes and provide training in handicrafts and other skills for men, while offering classes in domestic studies, child care, and other subjects for women. But basically I wanted to know from the people themselves how they saw their own problems and where they felt the church could help.

Larry Weeks had agreed to make his way to Windhoek as a sightseer who would be housed as a guest in one of our houses in Windhoek. Students often came to this house from universities in South Africa, and we felt that he would be less noticeable if he joined them rather than staying with me. I stressed the need for absolute secrecy to him, explaining that the survey he was going to conduct, although it would be used to improve our pastoral relations with our people, would be regarded as subversive by the white authorities, especially when conducted by an American.

Unfortunately, I was in Ovamboland when Larry arrived in Windhoek, so I could not brief him more fully about the local situation than I had been able to do when I had last seen him six months or so before in Tucson. He was well prepared for the first visitor, a white man claiming to be an insurance salesman, who dropped in to see him the very next day after his arrival. The young Harvard student was noncommittal to the many searching questions that were asked him, gave nothing away, and knew from the start who his visitor was and why he had come. What he didn't know was that there are black paid informers too. That same night, he fell victim to one of them.

The Coloured parishioners of our church in Khomasdal gave a barbecue that evening to raise funds for their church, and Larry was delighted to be invited. When he arrived, a small group of musicians were playing out in the open, and the Coloured people received him with warmth and enthusiasm. The whole atmosphere was relaxed and happy; this might have put him temporarily off his guard. He found himself listening to the criticisms and comments about the effects of the apartheid regime. He nodded in sympathy and was outraged at some of the examples they gave him of their people's suffering. Later in the evening he had a deep discussion with a Coloured woman who was a social worker and asked her about the problems she faced in her work with the Coloured community. During this discussion, she was able to pry out of him enough information to damn him in the eyes of the Secret Police.

Though nothing he told her would have convicted him in a court of law, though nothing he was about to embark on could have led to violence or threatened the position of the state, yet within a week he was deported from Namibia by order of the Minister of the Interior.

During the time that Larry was in Windhoek, a party of white students from the Afrikaans University of Stellenbosch were staying with us. They had made a thousand-mile journey from Cape Town to come and work with the Coloured people in Khomasdal. For many of these young whites, this was the first occasion in their lives that they had been free to make friendships with people of different races. It was also the first time that they had been able to see people of a different race as people. They rejoiced in their new-found friends and in their new-found freedom. Larry's deportation came as a shattering blow to them all. Several of them wept openly at the shame of it, and at a farewell party given to him in the back garden of my house, they made a sad and sorry sight. Yet, even his going, traumatic as it was for him and for us all, was not without its witness. Several of the students from Stellenbosch later came back to act as volunteer workers in the diocese itself, made more resolute in their determination to work with and for the black people of Namibia by having experienced themselves one sordid aspect of the apartheid system.

David had many contacts with student groups and organizations in South Africa and a constant stream of visitors came to see us from the Republic. Before very long it was clear that accommodation was needed to house them, so that they could live together in a commune which would have a loosely structured life style but which could be a meeting place for all races. I provided them with a small house in Klein Windhoek, and it was here that the Community of Simon the Zealot took shape.

This community had a rapid turnover of personnel, faced and overcame several tensions, and made a unique and vital contribution to the life of the diocese. At one period, it managed to bring together people from South Africa, Namibia, America, Britain under one roof. A steady stream of Africans and Coloured visited there and a spirit of comradeship and gaiety always prevailed among its members. The society produced a magazine, ran a newspaper for the Hereros, taught blacks English, and coached them for internal examinations. Its members travelled to outlying farms and mines to participate in services with Africans; they offered hospitality to visitors from all parts of the world; they were a link with newsmen, television crews, politicians, and diplomats. They wore their Christianity naturally and without fuss, often sharing in the daily Eucharist of the cathedral and making Christianity come alive through agape meals and experimental acts of worship with people of different nationalities. Above all, they offered courageous resistance to apartheid. The majority of them worked for no money and were supported by those with secular employment.

Marge Schmidt, who rented out her home in Denver, Colorado, to come and work full time as my secretary, is remembered for her Groucho Marx sense of humor and for a mind which cut like a laser beam through hypocrisy and half-truths. In America she had worked in television and had also been a highly efficient secretary. Best of all, she was an all-purpose tranquilizer. I see her now calmly walking into my office, sitting herself down, secretary's pad and pencil at the ready, calmly preparing me for a mind-blowing crisis with words such as, "We will remember to keep our cool and not go charging around like an Irish bull in a china shop, but will keep repeating to ourselves that as a bishop, we have a certain degree of dignity to maintain. . . ." Marge Schmidt, with her two daughters, Tina and Lisa, stepped out of a loving and supportive parish into a community seething with gossip and frightened out of its wits through the intimidation of the dark forces used in a police state. It was a situation which could have crushed a lesser being, yet she held her own right to the end, saw my staff and me deported, and returned to America only when someone else replaced her. She was not swayed by the shoddy behavior of fellow white Anglicans who were ready to blame me and the Community of Simon the Zealot for the majority of the racial problems that existed in Namibia. She steadied me with her loyalty and with her unswerving dedication to the things she believed in. No bishop could compromise on racial issues with Marge Schmidt as his secretary.

John Witherow came to us direct from a public school in Britain, which according to Britain's own unique form of logic is a private school. Though John came from an upper middle-class background, he arrived in Windhoek wearing blue jeans and sporting a Scandinavian peaked cap with a pom-pom and streaming long hair, all of which was enough to have him immediately dubbed as rabid Communist by some of our white Anglican Church goers. The task he settled into was to teach in our program for urban blacks. The need for such a program was urgent in the light of current events. The black student body in Namibia was rapidly becoming the mouthpiece which articulated growing black unrest and dissatisfaction. The white administration had the choice of entering into dialogue with the blacks in order to understand and then to resolve their problems, or crushing them by making an example of their leaders and treating them as trouble makers. It chose the latter course. Students were carefully watched in Namibia, paid informers abounded in their midst, and the state moved in with speed to smash any opposition before it got a grip on the black community at large. It was not unknown for an entire school to be closed and the greater part of the black students expelled for what was termed "political agitation." At one period, it was estimated, at least 1000 black students had been forcibly removed from school with all chances of furthering their education blocked to them. Sometimes the state would agree to have them back on the condition that they submitted to a flogging. So our diocesan office became a center which offered educational facilities for blacks to study by correspondence. John acted as tutor, counselor, and friend.

Daily he could be seen in our tiny office sitting beside grown men coaching them in English, mathematics, and science, impervious to the clatter of typewriters and the general bustle of office routine all around him. Through his initiative, a London-based publisher presented us with reference books to the tune of £2000. A new world was opening up for African students; it was a world which did not regard them as so many faceless "labor units" offering them a restricted form of education; under John's tutelage they were entering a world in which their minds could develop and in which they were treated with genuine dignity.

Not all the members of the community were intellectuals or following scholarly pursuits. Others were attracted to it who came from a totally different background. Such were Rob, Dick, and Patrick, three miners from Cumberland, England. Rob, their leader, had also been a farmer, a paratrooper in the English army, and a deckhand in the merchant navy. He had travelled down the Amazon River by canoe and had hitchhiked across America—in short, he loved the life of a wanderer.

I had found the three stranded in Windhoek and penniless. On a blazing hot Sunday afternoon, I caught sight of an assorted crowd of blacks and whites who were examining a battered and very dusty vehicle parked outside Barclay's Bank. Windhoekers were used to seeing all types of trucks and safari vehicles in their city and were rather blasé towards them, but this was something different. It was a twenty-five-year-old ex-hospital ambulance which the group had acquired for sixty pounds at the end of its sedate life of carrying village people to the hospital in an English county town. Now it was festooned with badges from different countries in Europe and Africa and it had their names listed in black paint all over one side. A combination of sheer guts and mechanical ingenuity had brought that vehicle through the Sahara Desert right down the East Coast of Africa until it had come to a clanging halt on Windhoek's main street. The little group had been able to overcome every natural hazard posed by rivers in flood, treacherous unmade roads, and boulder-strewn tracks, and had met with hospitality and helpfulness at every stage of their journey. That hospitality stopped dead on their arrival in Windhoek. They had not eaten for three days and had only the dregs of a bottle of Portuguese wine to sustain them. They hadn't a clue what would happen to them when that finished. Every attempt they had made to get a job had been frustrated. Haulage drivers were urgently needed in Windhoek, and so they went along to apply. A hefty German foreman agreed to employ them on one condition, "Get your hair cut, come back, and then I'll give you the job."

"Go to hell," Rob West replied, and the three walked out of the shed, preferring hunger to compromise.

I edged my way through the crowd of gawking onlookers and poked my nose through the open window of the ambulance. Though its occupants were somewhat startled to see a man with a clerical collar peer into their vehicle, they responded with warmth to my invitation to them to join my family for a meal.

Their ambulance just about made the hill which led up to the cathedral, and they parked their vehicle on its grounds. Worshippers arriving for Sunday services were somewhat startled when they had to pass through two clothes lines on which the men had hung their washing, but after a while got used to them and invited them into their homes.

Bored with hanging around Windhoek for five days, the trio asked me if I could give them some work so that they could get their muscles toned up again. They painted the cathedral, the church hall, and my house. In the evenings, after work, they completely stripped down the engine of the ambulance, repainted the outside, and thoroughly cleaned out the living section.

Their industry was a source of amazement to passers-by, who would slow down their cars and even stop to take in this remarkable sight, which was unique in Namibia—white men stripped to the waist working with picks and shovels. They became members of the Community of Simon the Zealot and shared their earnings with the rest of the group. One of them returned to help organize and run our diocesan construction company, which was a multiracial cooperative.

What did this group bring to the community? Well, first of all, they introduced a certain earthiness. With them involved, the community could never be overreligious, pietistic, or snobbish. Next, they brought to it, in a very special sense, the generosity and naturalness of mine workers. Everything they had, they shared; this came naturally to them. They had an easygoing manner, cared little for authority as such, and regarded apartheid as total nonsense. They could not understand it and they were not cowed into submission by those who tried to impose it. All workers were fellow human beings to them with whom they would share their last cigarette, their last dollar, their last piece of bread. Rob West, who was the foreman of our construction company, would be stripped to the waist, sweating, shovelling, hammering blow for blow with his brother African workers. For the first time in their lives, these blacks found a comradeship with whites in their daily work. This was unique in Namibia.

Their humor never deserted them. Dick Blair was an avid darts player who enjoyed nothing more than to take part in the weekly dart matches arranged in one of the local bars. One of the local Afrikaners developed a friendship with Dick, attracted no doubt by his unconventional manner and lack of snobbishness. He wanted to learn more about Britain and had a problem: he couldn't understand how a modern industrial country could get by without cheap black labor, and he wanted to know who did the dirty and menial jobs in English society. He put his question like this: "Who are the 'boys' in England?" Through a haze of tobacco smoke, Dick Blair retorted, "I'm th' bloody boy in England." The conversation, the game of darts, and the friendship came to an abrupt end there and then.

People had different motives for joining the Community. Steve Singleton was a machinist, and he belonged to a pop group which played in the north of England. His parish raised the money to send him out to us when he expressed the desire to do youth work with African and Coloured young people. He loved music and his motivation was a simple one: he just wanted to communicate this love to the blacks living in our ghetto.

Toni Halberstadt had tried teaching the pampered children of rich, white South Africans in an exclusive school for white girls in Natal. For the most part, she found these young white ladies unteachable. Lacking in motivation, committed to a life of leisure, they had no interest in education. The experience had been shattering for Toni, and she came to the Community in Windhoek just to have a look at us and to try and evaluate her own life. As a student at the University of Witwatersrand, she had known David, and she had an idea at the back of her mind that she might possibly have something to offer in black education.

I met her for the first time as I was emerging from our tiny cathedral one weekday evening after conducting evening prayer. Walking up the hill towards me came a shortish girl with a pony tail bouncing rhythmically as she approached. She wore a kaftan and open sandals, and was smoking a cigarette.

"Hi, Colin, I'm Toni, how are things?" was how she greeted me. Her approach was direct and her whole manner informal and friendly. She brought these same gifts to Ovamboland, where we sent her to teach blacks in our high school. She had a very precious gift of being able to draw out the shiest and most inhibited of her students. At this time, Ovamboland was alive with political activity which the police were doing everything to suppress with the usual severity. Dogs, baton charges, tear gas raids, floggings, and arrests were all used as means of silencing and intimidating those students who dared to take part in demonstrations or to protest the indignities suffered by the people under the apartheid laws. No white was free from criticism, and many missionaries were not only ill-equipped to cope with the new situation but resented the new militancy which the blacks had adopted. Because of her political insights and her contacts with black and white students in South Africa, Toni was neither threatened nor intimidated by the new situation. She encouraged her students to express the grievances they felt, whether against the state, the church, the missionaries, or herself. She set aside one classroom in the school and lined its walls, from ceiling to floor, with newsprint, so that the African students could go there at any time to write down their complaints. By thus being able to express their outrage, they were able to rid themselves of tension and find an outlet for their pent-up feelings.

The first lesson she conducted each day dealt with the complaints on these sheets. They were fully discussed by the students, who then outlined a course of action to make whatever improvements could be made. The students' attitude towards authority changed overnight, and instead of seeing a teacher as part of a rival, antagonistic force, they saw in her both ally and friend. She was later to be deported from Namibia after the government had expelled her from being principal of our high school in Odibo.

Namibia is five times the size of New England, roughly the size of Italy and France together, and my diocese includes all of it. I often stood before a huge wall map which showed in colored pins where the scattered community of Anglicans were situated. Mariental, Keetmanshoop, Ariamsvlei, Welwitschia, Abanab—all these were reached only by hours of driving along lonely roads through desert tracks. My ministry was perhaps the most costly in the world, for I could travel five hundred miles to bring communion to ten people. I can still picture the heat shimmering from the road ahead; the steering wheel becomes too hot to hold with the full hand. I steer using just the tips of my fingers, the car surging at eighty or ninety miles an hour, the sun dipping below the horizon behind vast foothills of wind-eroded mountains, surrounded by the ludicrous, bulbous shapes of the primitive baobab tree. I see, too, the tiny clusters of farmhouses with a filling station and bar. Perhaps twenty whites would live here. And then a couple of hundred yards down the road, one passed the inevitable conglomeration of shanties of the forgotten, unwanted African and Coloured people. At the approach to several of these townships stood the tents of corrugated iron shacks for the contract workers from Ovamboland. If the whites in these areas were cut off from the outside world, the plight of these Africans, dumped by the side of the road, away from their wives and children, was unbearable.

As bishop, my problem was how to meet the needs of both these groups. I tried as I journeyed through the territory to drop in on any of the people who lived in these outback regions, but the plight of the Africans on the reserves, especially the old, was grim. They obviously needed more regular visits and a priest who could love and provide for them in their extreme poverty and isolation.

The Tses reserve was a wasteland of a place into which the African aged, now no longer able to work, had been dumped. There was often not enough fuel for them even to boil a pot; removed from living in the white urban areas because they were no longer "labor units," they were given a small, two-roomed shack and a subsistence allowance of food which barely staved off starvation. I had seen a stick of wood, not more than six inches long, smouldering all day slowly warming mealie porridge. Fuel was so scarce that it could not be wasted and so the old folk waited several hours just to cook a handful of meal. What we needed was a priest of unusual stamina, able to cope with long hours of travel, willing to forego the comfort of a settled home and the stability offered by normal parish routine, and able to work on a pittance.

In this context, the coming of Richard Wood was a blessing. He arrived on my doorstep one day, clothed in veld shoes and a safari suit, and carrying a haversack.

"My name is Richard Wood. . . . I hitchhiked here from South Africa. I read about the new community and want to give it a try."

He had a good working command of Afrikaans, was natural and loving with people, and a man for whom no job was too trivial or undignified. His whole aim in life, now that his wife had died and his children were through university, was to dedicate himself to the ministry of the poor, and he wanted to live as close to their life style as possible.

He hitchhiked 1300 miles through the South, stopping at Ovambo work camps, being fed by his hosts wherever he happened to land. In attempting to thumb a ride through the Namib Desert, he suffered from exposure and was ill for two weeks with a pneumonia-type infection. It was only after I heard this that I succeeded in my demands that we be allowed to buy a Volkswagen microbus for him.

Richard yearned for the church to be effective in healing the wounds of an apartheid society and felt that one way of achieving this would be through an Africanized form of monastic life as lived out under the rule of St. Francis. To this end, he made a trip to visit as many religious communities as he could in South Africa, and journeyed to England to see for himself what was to be gleaned from the Franciscan headquarters at Cerne Abbas. We had high hopes that he would settle in the wooded part of Ovamboland called Oshandi, begin a center for village crafts, and gather a community of men and women around him, the beginnings of the monastic life for the diocese which would have an African character about it from the start. That was the plan.

God had other ideas. Richard offered to chaperone Cathy Roark as far as London on her way home to Tucson; they fell in love, married, and returned to Damaraland, where he was consecrated assistant bishop after my deportation.

It was at a meeting in Durban attended by Alan Paton, the South African novelist, that I met Ed and Laureen Morrow. Ed was a company director deeply disturbed by the starvation wages being paid to blacks in his firm in Durban. A draftsman, builder, craftsman, and executive, he had resigned from one firm in protest at its shocking treatment of black laborers who were being paid twenty cents (U.S. twenty-three cents approximately) a day. He came quietly over to me after I had spoken to Alan Paton and asked if there were anything he could do for my diocese. NOKI Construction Company (South African officials refused us permission to register our company as Ikon Construction Company, so on Arthur Dibble's suggestion we merely reversed the lettering) was made possible by that meeting.

Ed's coming to us meant that the Church could now not merely denounce the exploitation of black workers, but could launch a workers' cooperative which could clearly demonstrate that fair sharing and imaginative partnership in industry were possible in Namibia. We had no money to launch the company, no tools, no equipment, no personnel, just the quiet determination of Ed Morrow: this was more than enough.

In the chapel of the seminary at Odibo, I met with the twenty African members of what was called the Bishop's Advisory Board. This group met three or four times a year to guide me in policies affecting Ovamboland. All its proceedings were in Kwanyama, and its members were drawn from a diverse background, reflecting the outreach of the mission. Older and younger, black and white, all argued with, coaxed, scolded, challenged, laughed at, and encouraged me. We had been given the mite box offering from the Episcopal Church in the United States, and it was during a discussion on how best this money was to be used for the benefit of the African people that the

NOKI venture was first presented. The blacks immediately grasped its significance and were its ardent supporters from the start, as the majority of them knew the poverty of the contract laborer. This was an opportunity now for the church to blaze the trail towards justice through partnership in industry. They voted immediately to loan the $6000 sent from the States to NOKI.

When the news about NOKI got around, Africans poured in to work. The men were split up into small teams and were sent out to various kinds of work. One team began repairing and rebuilding a garage and an old German house that was falling apart. Another group started on a subcontracting job building a wall. A house was needed in the African location for our African priest there. We decided that it should be the best we could build, so NOKI was called in to do it. Business grew, and Ed Morrow was able to compete with other firms and obtain contracts at lower prices. Whatever profits were made were shared with the men and used to pay off the loan from Ovamboland. If there was money left over, it could be used to help with the work of the diocese.

There was a lighter side, of course. After negotiating for a contract which was costed at several thousand dollars, the men embarked on the task with great pride. The job involved the repair, renovation, and redecoration of an old German hotel in the town. In their eagerness to create a good impression, some of our men got carried away. One of the Africans swung lustily with a pick into the concrete floor, which was split wide under the blow. In the process, the chief water main was severed and, within minutes, the hotel was covered in a deluge of water.

NOKI's small Volkswagen van was loaded with ladders, wheel barrows, and shovels. Unlike the other vehicles that left Katutura in the early hours of the morning with sullen cargoes of Africans, our van carried African workers in comfort, happily chatting to each other in perfect amity. Once a week, Ed and Laureen invited the men round for a meal. Discussions were held then, progress reports were given, suggestions were received, or news of impending jobs was shared. One look at those meetings gave even the most casual observer pause for thought: this could be the shape of future industrial planning in a free Namibia. Men were learning skills hitherto denied them. They were earning wages which on the open market greedy businessmen denied them. Chiefly, they were communicating with each other and sharing as fellow human beings.

Steve Hayes, a young white South African priest, joined my staff as a worker priest in 1969. He was a quiet revolutionary who loved children, cats, and London buses. Because we were too poor as a diocese to pay him, he also worked for the *Windhoek Advertiser* as a proofreader. He had the God-given gift of saying the right thing at the wrong moment—something which the Church neither thanked him for nor enjoyed. There was a touch of the mystic about him, and this no doubt was gleaned from his study of and love for the Orthodox Church.

He had read theology in Durham, had driven a London bus, worked with sailors in the Mission to Seamen Institute in Durban, but felt dissatisfied with this ministry. He had a deep love of theology and yearned for an area of work where he could apply it to the problems of South African daily life. For holding a multiracial service in a Durban church where he had told the congregation they could dance in the aisles if they felt so inclined, he was removed as a paid minister of the church in Natal and was jobless. I was appalled that the Church could act so callously, and on Dave's recommendation wrote him a letter of sympathy and offered him a place in the diocese as a worker priest.

At first he would often sit on the floor at our weekly staff meetings, quiet and withdrawn. But as he made contact with the blacks, his whole personality came alive. He produced an Herero newspaper called *Omahungi Vehi* (*The News of the World*); organized closer contacts with black leaders and students; penetrated the African reserves where the old and infirm were dumped in cruel poverty; drove his truck to take services for isolated Ovambo miners, and hunted out the tiny shanty towns of the lonely construction workers. Through Steve Hayes, our whole ministry took on new dimensions.

He was a challenge to all that could be called "established Christianity." What Cathy Roark was doing for the people of Khomasdal he was doing for the black contract workers. Nothing and no one daunted him.

One of his most striking contributions to the diocese was the organization of a conference with the Chiefs in the Kaokoveld. This area, which covers the northwestern part of Namibia, is a place few whites have penetrated. Cut off from the rest of the territory, it teems with herds of elephant and rhinoceros. The Ovahimba people who inhabit it have suffered cruelly from South Africa's policies and yet, due to the remoteness of their area, few people knew about their sufferings and poverty. They are cattle ranchers but have been forbidden by the South African government to sell their stock, which is their only source of income. The suffering and the enforced poverty of these people still stands out in my memory. The greed of the white farmers to the south of them had determined the government's policy of not allowing blacks to sell their cattle. At first, they were told that their animals were sickly and a threat to health. They were told that if they inoculated them, all would be well. They were fobbed off with excuses and driven to the point of rejecting totally all that the white South African government stood for. The following extract, from Steve's notes, describes the meeting of the Chiefs with members of our diocese in Windhoek on August 31st, 1971:

> Bishop Winter welcomed the headmen and said that the Church was interested in their problems and would try to help them in any way possible.
>
> Munjomaherero: Thanked the Bishop for his words, and said that what the Bishop said was great words. Hereros and Himbas have many problems, and they do not know what will take these away.
>
> Ndjai: There are many problems. Life is difficult. We have cattle but cannot sell them because the government does not arrange sales.
>
> Bishop: What do you want for the Kaokoveld?
>
> Muatjeuri: Ongutukiro! (Freedom)
>
> Bishop: Do you want to be ruled by South Africa?
>
> Ruiter: Your question makes us cry. You have heard about passes. We are not allowed into certain areas in Kaokoveld. I cannot go to a funeral if a relative or my Chief dies in the police zone. I must make an application.
>
> Questioner: What is your attitude to the government proposal for an independent homeland in the Kaokoveld?
>
> Ruiter: South West Africa is one country, from one end to the other.
>
> Questioner: Has the government asked you whether you want to be an independent homeland?
>
> Ruiter: This question makes us cry. The government tries to separate the Kaokoveld from the rest of the country, and says that this land (ehi ndi) is yours, and is different from the rest of the country (ehi ndo). We tell them that the graves of our ancestors of people in the police zone are in the Kaokoveld. The government is trying to separate a child from the breast of its mother. If a white man's father or relative dies, he can travel to Pretoria for the funeral without restriction, but a black must make an application for permission to travel to attend the funeral of his relatives.
>
> Bishop: The South African Government tells the world that the Ovambos and Hereros would fight if the South African Government were not here to keep them apart.
>
> Ruiter: It is not us who create hostility, but the South African Government. Long ago, we used to travel freely between Kaokoveld and Ovamboland, and we would trade with the Ovambo and they would trade with us. There was no hostility before this government came.

One Saturday afternoon, Steve took a party of the Windhoek diocesan staff to a nearby mine to hold a service. As he gathered a crowd of men around his truck, handing out Bibles and small tracts, a white Afrikaner foreman drove up in his car and ordered Steve off the premises. Dave and he explained that they had come to hold divine service with the men, were doing nothing unlawful, but had a pastoral concern for the Africans. The Afrikaner seized one of the Bibles on display, flung it open, and shouted at the astonished Africans: "You can't read these books. I forbid it. They are Communist Bibles." He then ordered Dave and Steve off the property and said he would call the police if they refused to leave.

Underneath the humor, the rebellion, the mysticism, the pranks and eccentricity beats the heart of a Christian priest burning at the injustice, and offering himself in love to the thousands of broken hearts and bodies that apartheid has strewn the length and breadth of Namibia.

When I look back to the time we all worked together as a remnant, St. Paul's words about the early Christians come to mind. God had indeed chosen the weak things. We were daily conscious of that weakness, but somehow there was a feeling of strength. To say we felt our cause was right sounds smug to a degree; but we certainly felt that here was something worth living for and, if the time should come, worth dying for.

Others who worked alongside me have tried to assess their feelings of our time together. I don't think that any of us could put the whole thing better in perspective than the following account written in a magazine called *Pink Press*, by which the Community of Simon the Zealot kept in touch with people throughout the world. This was their last issue before they were banned into silence by Vorster's laws. The writer: Steve Hayes.

> Looking back on nearly three years in South West Africa, it is the good things which stand out. Perhaps, now that I have to leave, I forget that there was much that happened that was depressing, and which made me time and again want to leave of my own accord. Looking ahead to the future of South West Africa, there is still loneliness and despair and the feeling of non-achievement.
>
> I came here because there was nowhere else to go, there was no alternative. I did not know why I had come, nor what I had come to do. It is only now, looking back at the past, that I can see a pattern and a purpose.
>
> SYMBOLIC EVENT
>
> One event stands out, and seems to symbolise the whole of three years. I was standing at the edge of a newly-dug grave. The

veld around was dry and drought-stricken. The sun was hot and flies were buzzing around. At the bottom of the grave was a cheap wooden coffin, and rocks and earth were thudding down on to it, while the Herero congregation was singing a Russian Easter hymn:

> Kristus ua penduka mondiro,
> Mondiro je ua nata pohi ondiro,
> Ajandja omuinjo ku imba mbe ri meendo.
> Kristus ua penduka mondiro.
>
> Christ is risen from the dead,
> Trampling down death by death,
> And on those in the tombs bestowing life.

Then I knew that God had brought me to South West Africa to bury Aletta Tooromba.

She lived in the Ovitoto Reserve, at a place called Oruua. It is not marked on any map. It is about 90 miles from Windhoek, 40 miles from Okahandja, and the last 13 miles is along one of the worst roads in the country.

The funeral was on 12 February 1972. It started with a Requiem Mass. Because of the large number of people present, it was held outside, with the altar at the door of the house. On one side of the doorway was the red flag of the Herero nation, and on the other, an ikon of Christ pantokrator.

Two months before, I had come here and Aletta Tooromba had received her communion. She had been a faithful Anglican all her life. In the time I knew her, she was old and crippled. She could not walk, and had to be carried out of the house. She lived in an isolated place, cut off from the sacraments of the church. The government tried to make it as difficult as possible for her to receive communion by not giving permits for priests to enter the reserve. Nevertheless, she was faithful and loved her Lord. Now she had gone to be with him, and yet our Lord had promised that he would be truly present with us in every eucharist. And so she was truly present with him and with us, in this eucharist. Not in that fragile decaying body lying in the coffin, but in the communion of saints of the Lord.

After the Mass was over, we went to the cemetery, bumping along a narrow rocky track (the name of the place, Oruua, means 'rocks'). Ahead went a battered old Ford bakkie (truck) with the coffin, and the red flag flying from the canopy. The others followed in three other cars, all fully loaded. As we went, we sang 'Matu tja ndangi, Mukuru' (We thank you, Lord.) At the graveside, there were speeches by members of the family, and by ministers of various denominations—St. Phillips Faith, the Apostolic Spiritual Healing Church, the Oruuana Church. All spoke about the resurrection of Christ and none of the words were gloomy. It recalled one of the prayers sometimes said at compline—"Lord Jesus Christ, who at the sad hour of compline did rest in the sepulchre, and did thereby sanctify the grave to be a bed of hope for your people. . . .''

God had brought me to South West Africa to bring Aletta Tooromba her communion before she died—and it was worth coming just for that. George Pierce, the last priest who had visited Ovitoto, three years before, said once that if it were not for faithful little old ladies, the church could not survive. Aletta Tooromba was one of these who remained faithful in spite of difficulties. And now, at last, she is with her Lord, where neither death nor life, nor principalities nor powers, nor magistrates nor policemen nor the Department of Bantu Affairs can separate her from communion with her Lord. To her belongs the inheritance of the Kingdom of Heaven, where God will wipe away every tear from their eyes, and death shall be no more, neither shall there be mourning or crying or pain any more, for the former things have passed away.

ONDATUMISIRO

There were many other things too during these three years that stand out in memory. There was Thomas Ruhozo, a Himba man from the remote Kaokoveld, who came to Windhoek at the time of the last Diocesan Synod, and went back as a catechist to preach the gospel of the freedom of the sons of God to his people. There were the headmen from the same place, who came to Windhoek to see their Chief, Clemens Kapuuo—men of amazing patience. They say that they are eager to have the gospel preached in their land. When asked what problems they faced, an old man, Kapika Munjomaherero, dressed in the leather apron of the Himbas, replied "Ondatumisiro! Ondatumisiro! Ondatumisiro! (Oppression! Oppression! Oppression!)''

There were other funerals too, of the old Herero chief, Hosea Kutako, of the aunt of Abraham Hangula, of the father of Clemens Kapuuo. And all were triumphant occasions.

There is the change in attitude I have seen since I first arrived. When I came, blacks were fearful, not daring to say what they really thought. Some were cringing and subservient. Others were aloof and reserved. Others still were bewildered. In the last nine months, these attitudes have virtually disappeared. The advisory opinion of the World Court, the open letter to the South African Prime Minister from the black Lutheran churches, the Ovambo workers' strike, all in the second half of 1971, brought about a drastic change. Blacks are becoming conscious of their humanity, and they are walking tall in the streets. They greet me with a smile, and the word 'baas' has disappeared from their vocabulary.

Also not to be forgotten are the faithful white Christians. Those who have many doubts about the teaching of the church on race, on political and social injustice. They have to face ridicule from their friends and those they work with, often for things they do not fully understand or support. Yet, they remain faithful. One of the most surprising things of all was to be stopped in Kaiserstrasse by one of the indigenous white inhabitants of Windhoek, at the height of the Nationalist campaign against the Anglican church. He shook my hand, and said, "You people are doing a great job. Don't be discouraged, a lot of us are for you. Keep it up."

Yes, on looking back, it is the good things that stand out. The bad things—the smear letter sent to parishioners by a brother priest, the packing of a vestry meeting with nominal Anglicans who hardly ever came to church, the loneliness, the betrayals—these are fading memories.

AFTER DEATH . . .

The death and resurrection is seen in the church too—at the final farewell service, where four church workers were leaving, the Bishop ordained four new priests, to continue to preach the good news to the poor, recovery of sight to the blind, liberation to the oppressed, release to the captives. They are Peter Beard, Abraham Hangula, Edmund Dawson, and Polycarp Haihambo. Pray for them as they take up the task that God has given them.

I will leave with happy memories of the people of South West Africa, Kalanami, Namibia, call it what you will. And the sorrows and sufferings and hopes and aspirations are symbolised by Aletta Tooromba. She suffered with her people, suffered poverty and contempt and oppression. She suffered from bodily weakness and disease. She suffered loneliness and isolation.

But she was faithful unto death; unto her belongs a crown of life.

Chapter Nine

The Bite of the Snake

When South Africa assumed responsibility from the League of Nations for Namibia, she solemnly swore to allow freedom of movement to those undertaking missionary work on behalf of the black people. Time and again she has violated this aspect of the trust by hampering clergy and missionaries from following their lawful callings. Realizing that many of them were dedicated to the welfare of the African people, the white authorities quickly appreciated that they could intimidate those missionaries who were critical of their regime by delaying permits or by refusing to issue them altogether for such essential workers as doctors, nurses, and teachers.

Missionaries quickly learned the lesson that any utterance on their part which was even mildly critical of South Africa's racial policies in the territory would not only land them in trouble, but could jeopardize the future of an entire hospital or school. Often this faced them with agonies of conscience: they would witness a black pupil beaten up by the police officers who would call in the missionary to help in the process. Knowing how desperately the Africans depended on the Christian churches in the vital areas of medicine and education, the individual missionary frequently had to weigh the consequences of outspoken protest against the possibility of the closing down of a school or a hospital. It is only fair to these men and women for the world to understand this, for too often they have been pilloried for acquiescing with the regime and remaining silent in the face of its horrible excesses.

For a white person to enter an African township or a reserve, an official permit was needed. This had to be produced at the office of the local magistrate, or in the case of entry into Ovamboland, to the police on duty at the border fence. The strictest scrutiny was undertaken before individual missionaries were "cleared" and issued a permit to enter their respective working areas. Papers had to be completed and then dispatched to Pretoria for written approval, and this process could often take months.

When I first arrived in Namibia, the whole process of entering Ovamboland was fairly relaxed and casual, but within months of my becoming bishop, every delaying tactic and excuse that the Department of Bantu Affairs could make to harass and intimidate us was used. Whereas in the past I had been given an annual permit which would allow me entrance and exit into Ovamboland as often as I needed to go and was renewed without fuss by a junior clerk who simply extended the date and signed the document, that policy was drastically changed. Now I was regarded with suspicion and increasing hostility. The government officials were beginning to lean on me to demonstrate the power of the state and to warn me that by the stroke of a pen they could summarily close off my access to the overwhelming majority of Anglicans living in the North. They gave me no rebukes, they entered into no discussions, but one could see merely by looking into the faces of their junior bureaucrats that the Anglican Church was in for a rough ride.

I was due to go to Ovamboland on a six-week safari in order to conduct confirmations in the remotest parts of my diocese. It was only the day before I was to leave that one of my colleagues noticed that my Ovamboland permit needed extending, a mere formality in the past. One of my staff drove down to the office of Bantu Affairs to deal with this and returned an hour or so later with the news that he had met with a blunt refusal. They were not prepared to issue me with a permit to visit Ovamboland, and I must now submit new forms which would have to be sent both to Pretoria and Ondangua for their approval. This would take at least three weeks.

Quite by chance, the evening before I had made a pastoral visit to the home of a young South African water engineer living in Windhoek whose firm was engaged in the construction of dams and reservoirs in Ovamboland. He told me that he had been given a year's permit to travel to and fro in Ovamboland and that there had never been any trouble about its being granted. In fact, such were the cordial relations between him and Bantu Affairs that he could obtain other permits for his staff merely by phoning the office.

I mentioned this to my staff member when he returned with the news of the refusal and sent him back again to the department to speak with a top official this time and to be emphatic that I was going to Ovamboland the very next day to do confirmations and that great inconvenience would be caused to the African clergy and people who had been looking forward to my trip for months and who had made careful preparation for it.

Within half an hour, he phoned back to tell me that the clerk had confessed that he had it on top authority not to reissue my permit. I asked that the senior official, a Mr. de Wet, be brought to the phone. When he spoke to me, he alleged that he had never been told of any application on my behalf, but when I asked him whether he was going to issue the permit, he stalled and made excuses saying that he would have to think about it. I exploded into the phone and said, "Either I have that permit in my hand by five o'clock this afternoon or I'll see that the whole matter is raised at the United Nations."

I got my permit and subsequently left for Ovamboland. I also got the full fury of his revenge, for thereafter permit after permit for teachers, doctors, nurses, clergy, mechanics and housekeepers was refused with sickening monotony.

My troubles as bishop with the authorities were trivial by comparison to what the Africans had to undergo. At the end of a period on contract, most Africans would carefully parcel together their few belongings, bought with their hard-earned money in the Police Zone, and transport them by bus back to their kraals in Ovamboland. Before the military road which joins Cape Town to Luanda in Angola and passes through Ovamboland itself had been completed, the old muddy track ran through the vast game reserve called the Etosha Pan. It was here that the Germans had built a Beau Geste-style fort at a place they called Namutoni. It is famous in South Africa as a rather exotic tourist center, a headquarters from which whites ride out in Land Rovers and other vehicles to observe the herds of elephants, giraffes, kudus, and wildebeests which abound in the Pans. The place had a romantic appeal, and most whites revelled at the prospect of spending a night in a genuine old-fashioned fort. Blacks hated the place and for very good reasons.

Namutoni was a checking-in point for all black contract laborers as they returned from their twelve- or eighteen-month stint in the mines, factories, or farms of the South. They were made to dismount from the dusty, battered railway buses that had brought them from the mining town of Tsumeb, and young white policemen, on pretext that they were searching for stolen goods or arms, would force them to empty their cases on the ground and would rip open their carefully packed parcels. Sometimes the police would claim that they were searching for diamonds, but the subsequent actions of the young policemen laid bare their real intention. As they inspected the collection of goods on the ground—bicycles, blankets, radios, mattresses, beds, and trinkets—they would demand to see the receipts whereby the blacks could claim ownership of the goods. Rarely, if ever, were receipts given to Africans, and when these could not be produced, the police would confiscate the property, shouting to the protesting owner that the goods had been stolen. This was a cruel act because the goods which were confiscated often represented the greater part of an African's earnings for an entire year. Later, the Africans alleged, the police would privately dispose of the confiscated property and pocket the money themselves. Resentment about this smouldered in Ovamboland, and in the early 50's it had come to the notice of an Anglican priest named Father Theophilus Hamuntubangela.

Father Theophilus was a mountain of a man, six foot four inches tall, with massive shoulders, powerful frame, and huge hands. He was a poet and had remarkable gifts for translating hymns from English into Kwanyama, the language of his people.

He decided to take action on behalf of his people. One Sunday morning during Mass he declared in a sermon that he was "fed up" with the large number of people who were coming to him at regular intervals to complain that the police had stolen their legitimately acquired property. His great church of Christ the King, which has well over 5000 members, was packed to capacity when he invited members of the congregation to remain behind if they had grievances against the police.

An eyewitness informed me that three hundred men stood up on that Sunday afternoon in April 1954 and laid out their complaints in detail to their parish priest. My informant, an African priest, recorded for me the impression of that meeting. This is what he told me:

> Eliaser Tuadeleni, an African worker in Ovamboland, had written letters to the native commissioner at Oshikango and also to Windhoek. He complained to them about the ill treatment of the African contract workers who were being robbed by the police. These were written in January, 1954. It was in April of that same year that Father Theophilus met the assembled people, who were openly angry with him. The people told him, "You pastors always keep quiet while your people suffer from robbers."
>
> Father Theophilus then took down the names of those that were robbed and noted what had been taken from them. Men were jumping up all the time and saying, "I was robbed of a blanket . . . they took a coat from me. . . ." He then sent off a letter of protest to the United Nations. Nobody knew about this organization then, only him. The way he explained it to us was as follows, "Our country belongs to this organisation."

The priest's sister-in-law had married a white Portuguese trader who owned a shop close to the Ovambo border in Southern Angola, and when he had finished writing his letter, it was quietly given to her to be posted in Angola. If it had been dispatched from Ovamboland itself, the white authorities would have intercepted it and it would never have reached its destination. The amazing thing is that simply addressed as it was to "The United Nations, New York, U.S.A.," it did reach its destination. What is more, the United Nations sent a reply to the priest which he received in August that same year. The gist of the reply was that the U.N. wished to hear more from the priest about actual conditions for the Africans in Ovamboland, and they thanked him for the concern he had shown for the well-being of his people. They were not the only ones who wished to hear more—by this time the Secret Police were on to him, and in September, two plainclothes detectives came to the Mission of Christ the King, having driven up from Windhoek. They were accompanied by an African policeman who acted as their interpreter.

When they arrived at the mission, the priest was seated with a group of his catechists and students on the veranda by the church office. The newcomers began the interview by addressing Father Theophilus in Afrikaans, a language which is detested by many blacks and which brought an immediate reaction from him. With a voice full of scorn, he said, "You are not from the government, you are from the bush. Please speak to me in English."

My informant continues the story:

> First of all, they cautioned him and asked, "Are you Father Theophilus? Are you the one who wrote to the United Nations about the situation in Namutoni?" To which he replied, "Yes."
>
> They then continued, "As you say that your people have had some trouble, why did you not try to speak to the government, or take your problem to the magistrate or even to the administrator in Windhoek? How often did you try to do this and fail to get an answer?"
>
> Father Theophilus thought for a moment and then he replied, "I have never heard that someone who has been bitten by a snake would go to another snake to get the poison taken out. I wrote to the United Nations to defend poor people. I don't believe the police in Namutoni can do anything without getting their orders first from Windhoek."
>
> The detective continued the interview. "You say you got a reply."
>
> "Yes," the priest answered, "I did get a reply, and they have asked me to send more information."
>
> "Did you do that?"
>
> "Yes, I did," the priest replied.

"May I see the letter they sent you?" the senior detective then asked. Father Theophilus then stood up and showed by his manner that he was becoming more and more impatient with the interview. He demanded, "Show me your identification papers first."

This apparently threw the captain into a certain amount of confusion and he asked him, "Why do you want to see them?"

"Because I intend to send them to the United Nations headquarters along with my next letter."

The policemen then all left the mission.

Such outspokenness was not to be tolerated, and the authorities began plotting means to bring about Father Theophilus' downfall. Things were quiet for him until the end of 1955. At that time the Native Commissioner of Ovamboland ordered him to appear before a tribal court at Ohanguena to stand trial. This court was to be a real trial of strength between the white authority and the Anglican priest. More than a thousand Africans gathered there to demonstrate their support for and their allegiance to their priest who had now become their champion. He was first accused of violating tribal law by doing things without first obtaining the necessary permission of the local African headmen. The "judge" in his case was to be a certain Mr. Ireland, a native commissioner who had been specially imported for the occasion from Windhoek. Ireland called out, "Is Father Theophilus here?", whereupon the priest stood up in the center of the vast arena.

"A priest should stick to the priesthood and not meddle in politics," the commissioner began. But he got no further. Violence almost broke out as the Africans supporting Father Theophilus surrounded their priest, lifting him bodily from the ground.

There were shouts of "This is our hero . . . this is our fighter. . . . We don't want him to answer any more of your stupid questions." As they lifted him onto their shoulders, the rest of the assembled crowd thundered applause in support of his actions. That day Commissioner Ireland was thwarted and retired discreetly from the gathering for fear that physical harm should be done to him.

The commissioner returned to Windhoek, where he had a long interview with the then-Anglican bishop of the diocese. Rumor had it that the authorities were contemplating the deportation of the priest to the dreaded swamps of the Okavango, a place teeming with malaria. He was to be placed in a detention camp there, removed from his parishioners and his family. This was the place where the African chief, Epumbu of the Okwambi, had been sent to his death in 1932. One wonders if the bishop knew that he was being asked to be part of a scheme which sought to destroy a courageous African patriot and spokesman.

The bishop ordered Father Theophilus to leave Ovamboland at once and to come and live in Windhoek. His wife and children were to remain in their kraal in Ovamboland, and he himself was to live for two years in the tiny dusty vestry of St. Barnabas Anglican Church in the Old Location.

While he was in Windhoek, the priest's resistance to the regime continued. He held regular political meetings with such men as Mr. Sam Nujoma, the leader of the South West Africa People's Organisation (SWAPO). His spirit was not broken, and because he was so outspoken in his views, the authorities were forced to send him back to Ovamboland. He returned there in 1958, but because of the strain he had undergone, he had become a sick man.

The authorities still had not finished with him, and now launched a carefully prepared campaign of slander, something which is fairly common in Ovamboland. It was alleged that he had slept with the wife of a certain headman named Nehemiah. Though it was known that this man was afraid of the priest and hated him, and though the wife herself strenuously denied that the event had ever occurred, Father Theophilus was dragged again before the Headman's Council at Ohanguena, where his enemies were both prosecutor and judge. The African priest who related the story to me observed:

> If you are hated by the white government, then it means you will be hated by the African headmen, who are just their puppets to do what they are bidden. These, then, move around to persuade people to do things against you. As I see it, it was the senior headmen who persuaded the junior headmen to fight against people like Father Theophilus. Before a man can be convicted of adultery in Ovamboland, he has to be caught in the very act, but this could never have been so in the case of Father Theophilus.

Again, the priest was deported to Windhoek; when I arrived in the territory in 1964, I found him working as a laborer bending bars in a factory. Today, he is still a sick man, scarred by the suffering he has borne on behalf of his people, a people who regard him as one of their martyrs in their struggle for justice and independence.

Chapter Ten

The Contract Labor System

From the time when the German flag was raised in Lüderitz in 1884 and throughout the entire period of South Africa's occupation of Namibia, the black man there has been regarded solely as a "labor unit." As in South Africa, he would be allowed into the so-called "white" areas only under terms which were acceptable to and profitable for whites. The contract labor system was therefore devised as the most efficient and effective way of controlling the black man's movements and exploiting him for his master's convenience. The "native" existed for only one thing: to work for the white overlord for the minimum cost with the aim of producing the maximum profit.

This was clearly spelled out in no-nonsense terms by one of the early German conquerors of Namibia:

> This land, of course, must be transferred from the hands of the natives to those of the whites. So the natives must either give way and become servants of the whites or withdraw to the reserves allotted to them.

Time and again, in Namibia's history, black subservience to white demands has been rammed home by the master race. In 1922 a small group of blacks called Bondelswarts resisted tax demands made on them by the white administration. A massacre followed in which one hundred blacks were killed and 458 wounded, among them many women and children. Laws were passed in Namibia to ensure that any black over the age of eighteen who was unemployed could be removed from the white area and deported to the reserves. He could also be imprisoned if thought to be work-shy. In the reserves themselves, every adult male was forced to pay an annual tax. Since there are no industries in the majority of the reserves, the white government ensured that there would be a plentiful and cheap labor supply for the mines, farms, shops, and homes belonging to the white community.

The black man was thus forced out of his homeland through the burden of taxation, through hunger, and through the desire to obtain a better life for his children. But he was completely at the mercy of the white employer. He was not allowed to join a trade union, which is illegal for blacks in Namibia, and if he dared to strike or refused to carry out an order he could be lashed by order of any local magistrate.

In the main cities, huge barrack-like buildings were constructed in which the contract laborer was forced to live. Denied the right to have his wife and children live with him, he led a life of loneliness in surroundings which were not only barren and devoid of even the most primitive comfort, but which were psychologically and morally devastating. Violence was often the outcome of this segregation. The Windhoek police openly admitted that they dared not enter the compound in Windhoek after five in the afternoon.

The task of recruiting labor for the mines and other industries was given by government concession to the South West African Native Labour Association (SWANLA). Men would come to the recruiting center at Ondangua and would be placed into one of the five categories. The strongest men would be creamed off for the copper mines at Tsumeb or the diamond mines at Oranjemund. Others would be recruited for jobs on the railways or for private firms involved in construction, dam building, or commercial enterprises. The government officially tried to discourage recruiting domestic servants, and occasionally clamped down on this supply. The lowest category was that of shepherd, for which the pay was a few dollars a month and for which the conditions of labor were poor. These men often dressed in rags and would be heavily fined if one of the sheep in their charge died. Even children could be recruited under the category of "Piccanin." The worker was not able to choose his employer, nor was he able to negotiate the wage for which he would work. The government allowed SWANLA to fix rates of employment which were much lower than anything paid in the Republic of South Africa, and yet the cost of living is generally much higher than in any city in South Africa.

The ordinances decreed that the laborer be provided with an overall and a pair of boots. He was also given a copper ring which was clasped on his wrist showing his contract number. (It is interesting to note that in Kwanyama, the same word is used for contract as for human excreta.) At Ondangua, he had his medical inspection. This was particularly obnoxious to the Africans as they were stripped naked and part of the procedure was the examination of their anus and sexual organs. From the center at Ondangua, they boarded railway buses and were transported to Grootfontein and from there were dispatched to wherever they were going to work. Once in the compound, they would be herded together into dormitories sleeping as many as thirty men each.

For over forty years, the churches in Namibia had condemned the contract labor system for its dehumanizing effects both on the African and on the whites, but their pleas went unheeded. Yet the missionaries were in the best position to judge what the system was doing to the people, and unlike the chiefs, they were not in the pay of the government. They were, however, intimidated: any missionary who became too vociferous would soon find his permit of residence withdrawn and he would be forced to leave the country.

A Finnish missionary, Miss Rauha Voipio, who was a lecturer at a Lutheran Seminary at Otjimbingwe, published a report on the contract labor system which was released by the South African Institute of Race Relations. Miss Voipio had been a missionary in Ovamboland for many years, spoke fluent Kwanyama, and wanted to discover from the Africans themselves what they thought of the contract labor system. She chose Ovamboland because this area provided by far the greatest labor pool for contract laborers in Namibia. When her report, released in December 1972, was received by the South African press, many newspapers there registered shock and amazement at the conditions which existed for the blacks in Namibia. By contrast, whites in Namibia itself were largely indifferent to the matter. Told that a white butcher had raised his workers' wages from $1.40 to $14.00 a week, a white housewife remarked to Miss Voipio, "But the Ovambos don't have social obligations like us; they don't have to arrange parties and entertain guests."

Miss Voipio pointed out the moral consequences of the system: black workers in the South became lonely and formed adulterous relationships with local women. Venereal disease rose seriously among the workers, while in Ovamboland itself, divorce and illegitimacy became a new phenomenon, for three-quarters of the worker's married life could be spent away from his wife and children.

Black workers would say to her, "When I came home, the children fled from me"; or, "To my own children, I have become a stranger."

The black worker had nothing but contempt for the Ovamboland government, a group of white-appointed chiefs and headmen who not only refused to condemn the system, but seemed to be making a profit out of the suffering of their own people. One worker said, "The contract is a very bad thing, but it has been forced upon us by our headmen." Another added, "Our headmen in Owambo trouble us in their collaboration with whites, because they have good jobs and are paid enough. They no longer look after their people . . . but have turned their backs on us and give us a snake when we ask for fish."

Before Miss Voipio's report had been circulated, whites in Namibia could hide behind the excuse that they did not know the facts of the contract labor system and its effects on the blacks. After its release, there could be no excuses left; yet the system remains, with one or two minor changes. For daring to produce her booklet, Miss Voipio's permit to visit Ovamboland was withdrawn.

I was one of the few whites ever to have gained entrance to the African compound in Katutura. Often after saying Mass at St. Michael's Anglican Church, I would drive into the barrack-like building to meet some of the men who lived there. Africans would emerge from their doorways just to see who this white visitor was. Washing hung from a dozen clothes lines stretched across courtyards; men naked to the waist washed themselves in huge concrete tanks while others did their washing. The authorities had made no attempt to make the place liveable, so the men could only sit on a concrete step in the shade or lean against a wall which provided little shelter from the heat. Many of the huts had doors which had broken off on their hinges, and I could see the slabs of concrete beds inside, row after row of them in monotonous succession.

Many of the Ovambo workers enjoyed trading and spread out brightly colored blankets on the ground, on which they placed small articles for sale. I saw batteries, tins of fish, corned beef, tiny packets of sweets, razor blades, and small packets of tea, all neatly laid in rows on these blankets. There were also articles of clothing for sale, as well as sunglasses and children's clothing.

On one occasion as I drove from the compound along the road which led to the white side of Windhoek, I saw black and white policemen conducting a pass raid. Africans returning from work or out for a morning stroll were made to stop and show their passes. The whole exercise was an act of uncontrolled violence. The black and white police were hitting out indiscriminately and kicking at the legs of the African men as they walked along the pavement. One man was being struck in the face for no apparent reason; all hell was being let loose on that pavement as police screamed at them in Afrikaans, "Waar is jou pas?" ("Where is your pass?")

Behind this particular raid was the complaint of some of the white city fathers that blacks from the compound were obtaining an extra dollar for doing Sunday work in the gardens of Windhoek's white residents. The city fathers felt that this seriously threatened the whole basis of the contract labor system: by receiving these inflated wages, the blacks might ask for more money in their monthly wage packet or else become "soft" in the process. The municipality clamped down on Sunday morning work, but since the majority of the blacks could not read, they had not seen the ordinance placed in the columns of the local newspaper. The whites who had driven up in their cars to pick up a laborer for a day's work soon got the message, turned their vehicles around, and quietly returned to the city.

If the conditions in the compounds of the cities were appalling, the conditions for contract laborers on most farms in Namibia were worse. The pay was the lowest in the territory, and housing conditions were of the most rudimentary kind. African laborers were forced to live in small, corrugated iron shanties which were like ovens during the day and were freezing cold at night. They complained that the blankets issued to them were filthy and threadbare, that their food was of the poorest quality, and that their employers would beat them or lash them for trivial reasons.

A man we shall call Jeremiah Hivateli was recruited as a contract laborer in Ovamboland and was sent to work on a farm owned by a German in the Otjiwarongo district in the South. His one ambition in life was to earn enough money to become a teacher. But when he saw the deplorable conditions under which his fellow laborers were working, he decided to escape. While he realized that he ran the risk of imprisonment, he knew that he could get a better job with higher wages in the fish factory at Walvis Bay.

Together with a young companion, he slipped away from the farm in the early hours of the morning. With only a handful of bread between them, and with no money, they survived by eating leaves from bushes and drinking from cattle troughs as they furtively made their way under cover of darkness a distance of two hundred miles to reach their destination.

After working for a few months in the fish factory, Jeremiah was caught in a pass raid and sentenced to three months in prison for being in a white area without permission. On completion of his sentence, he was given a travel document and repatriated to Ovamboland. Since there was no one to escort him there and because he wanted to continue working to earn enough money to obtain his education, he happily sold his bus ticket to an African contract laborer. With the money he bought a pass from another African and continued to work in the area for about six months.

All went well until a paid informer reported him to the police for having a pass that was not his own. He was sent to prison for a further three months. In all, this happened three times! The whole process was farcical, yet white-made laws had made a man a criminal whose driving motivation would have been altogether commendable in normal society.

David de Beer, my young diocesan treasurer, had travelled many miles taking services in the mines around Windhoek and had an intimate knowledge of conditions under which the Africans lived and worked for a radius of up to five hundred miles from the capital.

On March 22, 1971, he had been invited to give a lecture to the students at the University of Witwatersrand. While staying with some Anglican monks in Johannesburg, he had picked up a copy of *Christianity and the Class War*, by Nicholas Berdyaev, and the following paragraph was imprinted in his mind as he came to give his lecture:

> When a man is deprived of elementary economic rights and has no control over the means of production, he is forced to sell his labour as a commodity; that is co-ercion, and a regime which allows that state of things is based on despotism. If the workman is ill-used, if he has to put up with bad conditions on pain of losing his job and consequently his livelihood, though his work may be called free because he can leave it at will, nevertheless, there is frightful pressure put on him and his liberty is an illusion.

In his speech to the students, David condemned the contract labor system in Namibia as a form of slavery. Next day, *The Rand Daily Mail* gave the story banner headlines. The newspaper article read as follows:

> The Leader of the South African legal team at The Hague, Dr. David de Villiers, did not know what he was defending when he defended conditions in South West Africa, Mr. David de Beer, diocesan secretary to the Anglican Bishop in Windhoek, said yesterday.
>
> In a lecture on conditions in the territory to students of the University of the Witwatersrand, Mr. de Beer referred to the contract labour system in South West Africa as a form of "slave labour" and said that the government had turned Ovamboland into a "labour pool" where the inhabitants could not get jobs.
>
> "In Windhoek you have an Ovambo compound of 5,000 contract labourers. The police are afraid to enter the compound because of the violence and frustration of the people who live there."
>
> One of the authorities he had spoken to about the problem had only been able to suggest legalised brothels to solve the problems of the compound.

David then described the type of persecution church workers experienced when they tried to establish pastoral contact with African workers living in lonely or scattered communities. Whites not only were unable to understand that Christians would want a loving relationship with blacks but reacted violently to the mere presence of church workers going about their normal pastoral duties. David described the occasion when he and some friends had been ordered off a mine by a white Afrikaner who was the foreman there. The newspaper reported him as follows:

> Mr. de Beer described a visit by a group of Anglican church workers to a mine where they had begun distributing religious literature to Ovambo workers. A White foreman had snatched one of the Bibles they were distributing and called it a "communist Bible." The foreman said he would tell his "boys" not to buy books from the group and added that he would sack any worker who attended the religious service that the group were planning to hold.

Later, David explained to me that he had not meant the speech to be political at all. Rather, he had taken four characters at random from Namibia to indicate the tragedy that apartheid was causing not only to blacks but also to whites. As a Christian, he was deeply concerned with the dehumanizing effects the system had on all races living there.

Newspapers in Namibia are frequently used by the Secret Police to prepare the public for action they wish to take against elements in our society they dub "subversive." The pro-government newspaper *Die Suidwester* launched a vicious attack on David shortly after the appearance of the article in *The Rand Daily Mail.* White Anglicans felt threatened that a spokesman of the Anglican Church had dared to make such an attack on the contract labor system, and they sent scores of letters to the editor of the newspaper in which they were quick to disassociate themselves from him, denounced him for mixing religion with politics, and demanded that as his bishop I "unfrock" him. Since David was not an ordained minister of the church, this request posed a certain difficulty.

What was vital was that as his friend and bishop I should not only be seen to stand by him in support, but also make it clear to the world at large where I stood on the subject of contract labor and what I thought about the whole system. On March 25th, 1971, I released a statement addressed to the editor of *Die Suidwester.* It read as follows:

> I have read with a feeling of great concern your editorial comments on the talk given by Mr. David de Beer, the Treasurer of the Diocese of Damaraland, to the students at the University of the Witwatersrand. As his Bishop, I fully support his state-

> ments and stand solidly behind him. I believe that what he said is based on fact and on truth. Even were I to disagree with him on any of his views, I must point out that this would not give me the right as Bishop to discipline or to silence him. Every shade of political opinion is reflected in the Anglican Church. As a Church, we are proud of our tolerance of those who hold views which may be in conflict with our own. As a Church, we would never attempt to coerce our members to express one shade of political opinion, nor would we attempt to suppress people when they are attempting to define truth as they see it.
>
> Your article amazes me for the following reasons: An English newspaper in this town rightly drew the public's attention to the appalling state of affairs in the compound of the Windhoek location. I think it did our city a service in emphasising the shocking situation which is festering in our midst. Surely this is the function of a newspaper, to reveal to the citizens of a community situations which if left undealt with will become explosive. Your newspaper made no comment on the right of the newspaper to do this. Why deny the same right to a Churchman when he speaks out from conscience? The Dutch Reformed Church has expressed its gravest concern at what it calls the "cancer" in our society and the effects of migratory labour upon African family life. Again, I think you would be wrong to deny them the right to speak out clearly and forcibly against evil as they see it in our midst.

After a series of bitter attacks by Anglicans and other people in the daily press, worse was to come. Up to this point, we were used to our mail being opened and our telephones tapped. Now it was obvious that the Security Branch would step up its efforts to frighten and harass us. We started to receive abusive phone calls. We would lift up the receiver of the phone to hear heavy breathing on the other side or the tinkling of bells or maniacal laughter.

The Security Branch even tried to hang a charge of fraud on David. One of our priests in Ovamboland wished to invite a visitor to the mission from South Africa. Since there was a massive delay in the postal service between Odibo and Windhoek, he had asked David to submit a letter on his behalf to make a formal application for the visitor to be given a permit to enter Ovamboland. So eager were the police to get at David under any pretext that they took this trivial instance and tried to make capital out of it.

The first I knew of their intentions was when one afternoon a knock came on my office door and I looked to find Arthur Dibble standing on the threshold. Calmly he said, "There are three gentlemen here to see you, Bishop. They are from the Secret Police."

The police remained in my office for several hours that afternoon and said that they had come to confiscate all the typewriters. I reacted by immediately calling in a young South African advocate, Chris Nicholson, who was our legal advisor. It was obvious to us all what was happening: for espousing the cause of the blacks my staff and I were regarded as enemies of the state and would be hunted and hounded by every device that the state had at its disposal.

From here on, none of us had any illusions; imprisonment or deportation would be our ultimate fate.

Chapter Eleven

A Time to Listen

There is no doubt in my mind that the year 1966 marks a turning point in the history of Namibia, for it was at this time that the leaders of the South West Africa People's Organisation decided to launch the armed struggle against the South African regime illegally occupying their country. Their decision came to our notice in a dramatic raid on the white commissioner's house at Oshikango, only a mile or so from our mission headquarters at Odibo. The roof of the house was set ablaze and gunfire was exchanged, after which the freedom fighters silently retired into the bush.

Whereas in the urban areas Africans were constantly hunted and harried by white police applying the laws of apartheid, the situation in Ovamboland was more relaxed for the simple reason that so few whites lived there and the Africans were relatively free to follow their traditional patterns of living. Paid informers and police raids were not unknown, but generally speaking one felt more at ease in this part of the country away from the violent conflict of the major cities.

Priests like Canon Lazarus Haihambo moved among their people as gentle pastors, listening to their problems, visiting them in their kraals, and lovingly tending their sick and aged. Like the peasant priests of Greece, they would tend their gardens, plant their corn, and in the evening sit in one of the kraals of their neighbors listening to them recount anecdotes of bygone days as the flames of a log fire lit up the night. Then as the final cup of millet beer had been passed round and consumed, the priest would quietly gather his neighbors together and they would all kneel under the stars to recite the evening prayers. He would then tramp through the dusty tracks that led to the round mud hut where he would spend the night. Canon Haihambo was an old priest, gentle in his ways and loved by all his people. He radiated by his bearing and way of life those principles of peace, good will, sharing, and compassion that he had derived both from the Christian gospel and from the traditional values of his own people. Unlike Father Theophilus, he could never be regarded as "a political agitator," for he saw his role supremely as that of a pastor. Yet he was one of the first victims in the massive reprisals that took place after the raid at Oshikango. As he lay sleeping peacefully in his hut, a police truck drove up to the kraal. White and black policemen, with shouts and curses, threw him out of his bed onto the ground and beat and kicked him into a state of semi-consciousness. His old wife managed to protect him by throwing her own body across his as he lay dazed on the ground. A rain of blows fell on her as the police screamed at the old man, "You are a Communist." Canon Haihambo managed to crawl out of his hut and to hide in the bush until the police went away. He was in such a state of shock and fear that he remained in hiding for two or three days before daring to return to his kraal.

Why would such a gentle, old man elicit such violence from the regime? The policy had systematically searched his kraal looking for weapons and ammunition and had found none. It was apparent that they had singled him out because the Anglican Mission headquarters was close to the house of the commissioner that had been fired on. Canon Haihambo was an Anglican, and therefore, by deduction, he was obviously connected with the raid. It mattered little that his kraal was fifteen miles in the opposite direction. It was enough for the authorities that he belonged to a hated church.

The raid also produced far tighter control at the border fence at Oshivelo, which became a check point for people entering and leaving Ovamboland. A huge tubular steel gate was built and no one was allowed in or out without careful police scrutiny. It was manned day and night and came to be regarded by the blacks with the same loathing as the Berlin Wall.

The fence lies about an hour's drive north of the American mining town of Tsumeb and is approached by a single tarred road which passes through fairly dense bush. Often wild animals would dash across the road, so one had to drive with a great deal of caution. I used, particularly, to watch out for rogue elephants which would stray across the highway or for giraffes or kudus which could dart across one's path and then disappear, plunging wildly into the thick bush. Unsettling as the prospect was of meeting these beautiful animals, it never matched the grim foreboding and tightening of the stomach that always gripped me as I approached the Oshivelo gate. If Africans were travelling in my car, conversation would come to a dead halt as they too became tense and nervous.

For most whites the procedure was relatively uncomplicated. Their position as government officials, drivers of huge trucks, engineers journeying to inspect irrigation schemes, tourists visiting Angola made them privileged visitors in the eyes of the border guards. I certainly was not, but was regarded with deep suspicion and was usually treated with hostility and contempt. It was clear that they regarded me as an agitator, and the fact that I was a bishop was no protection. I would be delayed for upwards of an hour, during which time the captain of the outpost would often be summoned, the contents of my car or truck meticulously inspected, and my passengers made to get out of the vehicle so that they and their parcels could be scrutinized as well. All this was done in a bullying, condescending manner. These border guards regarded me as having become black by association. They took a delight in harassing and delaying me, and I got the distinct impression that this bit of bishop-baiting gave a touch of relish to an otherwise hot and boring day.

The border police never allowed a black's vehicle to pass through the fence without a thorough search of its passengers and its contents. Under a burning hot sun, the Africans were shouted at to dismount, while their suitcases, bundles of clothing, and parcels were thrown out of the truck with no thought given for the safety of their contents. All the time, their owners were being pushed, bawled at, and cursed.

On one occasion I had given a lift to a Lutheran pastor, who was journeying with his two grandchildren in my truck from Windhoek to Ovamboland. He had carefully put together a few household possessions, meticulously sewn up in sacking for use in his kraal, and was delighted when we were able to squeeze them in the back of an already heavily loaded truck containing sacks of cement, desks, water closet basins, books for our high school, a paraffin refrigerator, and dozens of other articles. Our truck was also crammed full of people. Three Africans sat with me in the front, with another three sitting squashed and uncomfortable on sacks in the back. So we came to Oshivelo.

At the border gate, we were all ordered out as usual, and the Africans were conducted by the police to a small canopy arrangement at the side of the road where their passes would be examined. I was directed to an old wooden railway carriage, which was being used as an office by a young, white South African policeman. I could tell at a glance that his mood was ugly. Sure enough, he immediately became belligerent and rejected all my efforts to engage him in a conversation, snapping back monosyllables and clicking his fingers at me as he demanded to see my documents. Always the cheerful optimist, I offered him an apple in an attempt to relax him, but he pushed away my hand with a gesture of contempt and I felt for one awful moment that he might even be contemplating booking me for attempting to corrupt a police officer in the lawful execution of his duty. I took a deliberate bite of the apple myself just to reassure him that it wasn't poison. By then he had spotted my African companions. Pushing past me, he hurried over to where they were standing and began demanding to see their passes. Though these had all been examined, they nevertheless had to be produced again for him to scrutinize. A feeling of impending doom spread over our entire group as it was quite obvious from his manner that he was not going to let us go without victimizing one of our number.

Today his victim was to be a slightly built, undernourished African woman who was now trembling with fear as she handed a crumpled travel document for him to examine. The change that had come over her was quite shattering to me, for in the truck she had laughed and chatted away as she shared with us a small packet of sandwiches. At that moment, I was very conscious of witnessing a process of dehumanization as she lost more and more of her confidence. Her replies to the white policeman's questions became barely audible monosyllables mumbled through lips paralyzed with fright.

By this time, even he realized that he could not get coherent answers from her, so he called out to a black policeman to come over and interrogate "this thing." Up until now, the black, a sergeant dressed in khaki uniform, had been chatting light-heartedly with the Lutheran pastor and my other friends, but under the glare of his superior he had to assume another air. He grimly approached the woman and asked her in Kwanyama, "Edina loje, Meme?" ("What is your name, my mother?") To which she replied, "Ame Christofina." ("My name is Christofina.") This produced the next shock, because when I had asked her her name in Tsumeb, she had told me in a rather shy, sing-song voice that she was called Rebecca. I knew at once why she was afraid. She was using someone else's pass. The others knew this too, and we stood by helpless watching her intently as she struggled and lied to preserve her freedom.

The white officer held the scrap of paper in his hand and flicked it with the index finger of his other hand as he spoke to the black sergeant in menacing tones. "Look at the date on this pass. It expired more than a month ago. Ask her where she got it, why she went down to Tsumeb, whom she stayed with there, and why she's coming back so late. Tell her she's broken the law and I can send her to prison for this."

He then placed his hands on his head, stood with his feet astride and looked as though he was really enjoying his moment of glory.

The black sergeant had been caught somewhat off guard, because by this time he was busy shaking hands with me and asking after the health of my wife and children and how the "brothers" in Windhoek were getting on and whether we'd had much rain there lately. He was getting tired of the white man's game and was somewhat embarrassed to be seen associating with him in front of his pastor. So he turned towards her and said in a soothing voice, "He asked me to ask you why you come so late, my mother."

Even this could not allay the fears and suspicions of the African woman, who blabbered repeatedly, "Ame Christofina . . . ame Christofina." She then said nothing but kept on looking at her feet waiting for the inevitable blow to fall.

With the competence of a veteran actor and with an eloquence that was as inventive as it was stunning, the black sergeant turned to the white policeman with a sort of pirouette and tiny bow and said "Ag, baasie (Master). She says her old grannie dropped dead in Walvis Bay and she had to stay behind to make all the necessary arrangements for the funeral. You know how these things are, baas, all the guests coming and so on, but she says she's very sorry for the inconvenience and she won't do it again, baas." By this time, the white policeman was thoroughly confused. He turned abruptly, threw down the woman's pass onto the tarmac, and walked towards the railway shack saying over his shoulder, "They can all blerrie well die for me and the sooner the better."

We remounted our truck and continued on our journey.

As early as 1917, a South African expeditionary force launched itself against a startled King Mandume, chief ruler in Ovamboland. In a joint operation with the Portuguese army, which moved against the king from the north, the South African forces descended on him and found him unarmed inspecting the corn in a field of millet. Without a word to him, they hastily mounted a machine gun on the top of a truck and mowed him down where he stood; then a white sergeant strolled across to where the corpse lay and nonchalantly hacked off its head with a machete. For some undisclosed reason, the head was carried to Windhoek, where it was buried in a small garden on the road that leads to the railway station. No one knows for sure what purpose lay behind this horrid act, but the violence done to their king was keenly felt by the entire people, the more so because the authorities refused them permission to honor him with the traditional ceremonies as befitted his rank. The Africans, however, have had the last word. Today when a Kwanyama steals from a white man, he regards it as an act of reparation. As he pockets the goods, he will smile to a comrade saying, "I am mourning Mandume."

With the elimination of their chief, the Ovambos were given a white-controlled form of government. Chiefs and headmen who were mere puppets of the white regime were set over them, but the real power lay in the hands of the white officials who gave the orders for the headmen to carry out. Behind the so-called black leaders is the coercive violence of the white state.

The majority of headmen in Ovamboland were illiterate peasants, many of whom had never left their native villages. The youth speedily outstripped them in education, in political sagacity, and in understanding the outside world. These young people embued with a spirit of idealism and yearning to see their country develop were bitterly frustrated by the antics of their so-called black "leaders," who because they received fat pay checks stood mute and unprotesting at the daily outrages which were inflicted on their people. The three hundred dollars that a headman could be paid each month often represented a year's salary for the average black contract laborer. It goes without saying, therefore, that the youth and overwhelming majority of workers turn to SWAPO as the one organization which is prepared to expose the vicious conditions under which blacks live in Namibia and to stand up to the white exponents of apartheid.

What has been enacted in Ovamboland is part of a huge farce aimed at selling apartheid to the outside world; it is window-dressing meant to lull uninformed observers into believing that South Africa is producing a form of democracy there. At several points in Ovamboland, vast tribal offices were erected to function as debating halls and administrative offices for the puppet chiefs. These buildings, constructed in brick, steel, and concrete, with huge roofs spanning hundreds of feet, stand out in stark contrast to the general poverty surrounding them. Few blacks are taken in by the erection of these buildings and speak with amusement about them. Many understand clearly the game South Africa is playing, for no matter how much hot air is released in these debating chambers, the hand that holds the gun dictates the policy and controls the state.

Despite the huge sums that have been spent on the trimmings in these Bantustans, South Africa is backing a loser, for the people despise both the system and those blacks, as well as whites, who administer it. They know that far from surrendering power to the Africans themselves, the South African authorities are using the Bantustans as an effective way of maintaining their control over the black people, by limiting the effective powers of the black leaders who are attempting to make them work.

The young see this most clearly. The students of our high school in Odibo were summoned to listen to a talk by a white official sent to explain to them what the Bantustans were and how they would be applied to Ovamboland. He stressed that the Pretoria government wished at all costs to preserve the traditional cultural patterns of the African people. He referred to the "extinction" of the Indians in America and asserted that that would never be allowed to happen in South Africa. He stressed that the authority and rule of the chiefs and headmen were to be maintained at all costs and that the Ovambos would be ruled by their own people. His oration over, he ended his speech with the following words, "And so, you see, my government has ensured that democracy has come, at last, to Ovamboland." He then sat down and asked for their questions.

An African girl rose to her feet to ask the first question. "I just want to ask the speaker," she said, "who signs the laws that our headmen and council pass, because they can neither read nor write?"

"That's a stupid question," the speaker replied angrily, "I haven't come here to answer silly questions like that."

The chiefs and headmen in Ovamboland have had opportunity after opportunity to speak out clearly about the wrongs done to their people, but with sad regularity they have missed these chances. Either out of fear or ignorance they have maintained a shocking silence, so much so that after Oshana Shimmi, a former "paramount chief" of Ovamboland, died in a car crash when the Land Rover he was travelling in skidded out of control, the contract laborers in the compound of Katutura danced, sang, and clapped among the mica rocks.

Three things have combined to sound the death knell of the Bantustan system in Ovamboland: the first is that education has developed the critical faculties of the youth. They will no longer tolerate propaganda which they know to be lies and a system which enslaves their people. The second is that the government-appointed chiefs, by refusing to criticize the evils of the white apartheid regime, have lost their credibility and are regarded by the Africans as mere government stooges. The third is the astonishing growth and influence of SWAPO, the freedom movement which has succeeded in binding the people together in unity and producing among them leaders of great courage who are not afraid to stand up and be counted. The result of all this is that Namibia is in the midst of a revolution which the white government is desperately trying to quell with everything at its disposal. They go to absurd lengths to suppress student activity. On the one hand, the government has built a magnificently designed high school for blacks in Ovamboland at a place called Onguediva. By any standards, it is a splendid piece of architecture, and it is a point of call for visiting VIPs, who are often shown around it. What visitors don't see is that it stands as a monument to white racist ideology. Inside the school are separate kitchens and common rooms for the white and black teaching staff. A white member of staff brought a small pistol into his class laying it on his desk with a knowing look that said he wanted the blacks to realize who was master.

Yet the students have refused to be intimidated. When German missionaries were deported from Windhoek, it was black students who came out to the airport and sang freedom songs and held banners and placards to demonstrate their solidarity with their white friends. SWAPO youth leaders have been imprisoned and tortured by the Secret Police, but others have replaced them as the struggle for independence continues. History will judge these young students as having played a crucial and courageous role in the awakening of the African people and in leading them in their determined struggle for freedom.

For forty years, individual church leaders had condemned the enormities of the contract labor system, but their protests had been ignored. In the early 1920's, Bishop Fogarty, the pioneer Anglican bishop of Namibia, refused point-blank when asked by the government to do everything he could to encourage Africans to leave their wives and families and go to work as cheap labor in the mines. The Administrator replied to his letter of protest by saying that he hoped the Bishop would do all in his power to encourage the natives not to be "idle."

Two other events have forced the churches to make a stand on behalf of the oppressed. These were the decision of the World Council of Churches to make grants available to various freedom movements in Southern Africa and the International Court's decision of June 1971, which by an overwhelming majority of thirteen votes to two—Britain and France dissenting—declared South Africa's presence in Namibia illegal. This decision at The Hague caused a sensation in Namibia. There was dancing in the African location. But the whites responded with a sullen silence and then later declared that they were indifferent to what they felt was "a political decision."

By this single act, years of indecision, of tortuous arguments and compromise, had finally been swept away. The World Body had been extremely patient with over fifty years of South Africa's wheeler-dealering policies. When South Africa had refused to place Namibia under the trusteeship of the United Nations, the World Court was of the opinion in 1950 and 1955 that although South Africa was the then-effective administrator of Namibia, she could not legally annex it. Bitter outrage prevailed at the United Nations, especially among those delegates from African countries who knew the daily indignities and sufferings that fellow blacks in Namibia were undergoing. So in 1960 Ethiopia and Liberia—the only two black African states to have belonged to the original League of Nations—were allowed to petition the World Court again. The world waited until 1966 for a decision. When it came, it was shattering, because on the vote of a white Australian judge, Sir Percy Spender, the World Court declared that it was not competent to make a decision. The group of judges was severely depleted and so the opinion given was no real opinion at all and left the basic issues hanging in the air.

The new decision of 1971 altered all that. Now the highest court of appeal that the world knows was, in effect, saying to South Africa, "You have no legal right to be in Namibia at all." It was also saying to the Africans of Namibia that they and they alone did have that legal right.

In order to deal with the new situation, the South African Security Police moved in with speed. Three Anglican clergymen in South Africa were deported for saying that they did not regard the grants of the World Council of Churches as an attempt by that body to provide arms to guerillas. They saw it as the World Body making a moral stand on behalf of the oppressed and those who were struggling for freedom. Further, they felt that by its action the WCC was condemning the compromise and double talk that existed in all churches in South Africa and their failure to make a clear stand on issues that were condemned throughout the world.

Church leaders were approached by the Special Branch and asked to give their views on what the WCC had done. Within South Africa itself, the overwhelming majority of white churchmen condemned the World Council's action, no doubt greatly influenced by the act of intimidation against the three Anglican monks.

One of those approached by the Security Police was Bishop Leonard Auala, the head of the Lutheran Church in Ovamboland. The Bishop received the men courteously and remained calm and composed. When asked his opinion of the World Court's decision, he replied that the opinion of one individual was not worth much. Would it not, he asked, be far better for the outside world to know what the members of the Lutheran Church in Ovamboland, which numbered some 300,000, thought of the whole business? A questionnaire was produced and distributed among all the congregations of the Lutheran Church in Ovamboland, and the results were eagerly awaited.

At this same time, the South African government was proposing to hold a referendum in Namibia which would decide by a majority vote whether or not the people there wanted South Africa to rule them. The assumption was that the overwhelming majority of the whites, who number about 90,000, would vote in favor of South Africa. And whereas the numerically smaller Herero group would undoubtedly oppose South Africa's rule, this vote would, it was hoped, be cancelled out by the "gentle, simple, smiling Ovambos," who would vote for the white men. The result of Bishop Auala's referendum shattered that illusion forever, and South Africa has never since offered a plebiscite to decide on the continuance of South African rule. When asked, in their own language, by people they trusted, for their opinion on the world ruling, the people of Ovamboland returned an overwhelming vote: they totally rejected the continuance of white rule from South Africa. Bishop Auala had pulled off a brilliant diplomatic coup, because not only had the Pretoria regime asked him for his personal opinion and agreed to a referendum among his church members, they had also given him an opportunity to let the world know the feelings of the overwhelming majority of the Namibian people. Bishop Auala and Pastor Gowaseb, the joint signers of the Open Letter to Prime Minister Vorster which contained the results of the referendum, had put together an historic document which will rank as Namibia's Declaration of Independence. The South Africans had given the Bishop his chance, he took it and rocked the Pretoria regime back on its heels.

OPEN LETTER TO HIS HONOUR THE PRIME MINISTER OF SOUTH AFRICA

The Church Boards:
Evangelical Lutheran Ovambokavongo Church,
P.B. 2015,
Ondangwa/Ovamboland,
and
Evangelical Lutheran Church in SWA,
(Rhenish Mission Church)
P.O. Box 5069, Windhoek.

His Honour,
The Prime Minister,
Mr. B.J. Vorster,
PRETORIA.

His Honour,

After the decision of the World Court at The Hague was made known on 21st June, 1971, several leaders and officials of our Lutheran Churches were individually approached by representatives of the authorities with a view of making known their views. This indicates to us that the public institutions are interested in hearing the opinions of the Churches in this connection. Therefore we would like to make use of the opportunity of informing your Honour of the opinion of the Church Boards of the Evangelical Lutheran Church in SWA and the Evangelical Lutheran Ovambokavongo Church which represents the indigenous population of South West Africa. We believe that South Africa in its attempts to develop South West Africa has failed to take cognizance of Human Rights as declared by U.N.O. in the year 1948 with respect to the non-white population. Allow us to put forward the following examples in this connection:

1. The government maintains that by the race policy it implements in our country, it promotes and preserves the life and freedom of the population. But in fact the non-white population is continuously being slighted and intimidated in their daily lives. Our people are not free and by the way they are treated, they do not feel safe. In this regard, we wish to refer to Section 3 of Human Rights.
2. We cannot do otherwise than regard South West Africa, with all its racial groups, as a unit. By the Group Areas Legislation, the people are denied the right of free movement and accommodation within the borders of the country. This cannot be reconciled with Section 113 of Human Rights.
3. People are not free to express or publish their thoughts or opinions openly. Many experience humiliating espionage and intimidation which has as its goal that a public and accepted opinion must be expressed, but not one held at heart and of which they are convinced. How can sections 18 and 19 of the Human Rights be realised under such circumstances?
4. The implementation of the policy of the government makes it impossible for the political parties of the indigenous people to work together in a really responsible and democratic manner to build the future of the whole of South West Africa. We believe that it is important in this connection that the use of voting rights should also be allowed to the non-white population. (Sections 20 and 21 of the Human Rights.)
5. Through the application of Job Reservation[1] the right to a free choice of profession is hindered and this causes low remuneration and high unemployment. There can be no doubt that the contract system breaks up a healthy life—because the prohibition of a person from living where he works, hinders the cohabitation of families. This conflicts with sections 23 and 25 of the Human Rights.

The Church Boards' urgent wish is that in terms of the declaration of the World Court and in co-operation with U.N.O.

---

[1] A South African law by which the most skilled and best jobs are reserved for whites only.

of which South Africa is a member, your government will seek a peaceful solution to the problems of our land and will see to it that Human Rights be put into operation and that South West Africa may become a self sufficient and independent state.

With high esteem,

Bishop Dr. L. Auala,
Chairman of the Church Board of
the Ev. Luth. Ovambokavango Church
and
Moderator Pastor P. Gowaseb,
Chairman of the Church Board of
the Ev. Luth. Church in SWA
(Rhenish Mission Church)

Windhoek, 30th June 1971.

There were mutterings from senior white officials in Namibia that Auala would not be allowed to get away with what he had done and that reprisals were being contemplated against him. The press swung into the attack, quoting these officials as saying that the Bishop was really a rather naive man who could not be expected to know or appreciate the full political implications of his statements, which they felt had rather got out of hand.

Fearing for the Bishop's safety, I felt that the other churches in Namibia should immediately rally to his support. In the past, individual Christians have been persecuted simply because the church has not rallied solidly behind them. It seemed to me that two things were needed: first, that as bishop of the Anglican Church I should give Bishop Auala my moral support, and second, that by doing so, I should try to somehow prod the other churches in Namibia into declaring what their position was. Accordingly, I wrote the following letter of support, which was distributed to the worldwide press on July 25th, 1971:

A TIME TO LISTEN

Bishop Leonard Auala and Moderator Paulus Gowaseb have produced an important document. It behooves all people of this territory, and especially those who govern us from Pretoria, to read it, but best of all to listen to what these men are saying. From just living in this land, one knows from experience that it has taken a great deal of courage for two black leaders to dare to say the things these men have said. South Africa does not take kindly to criticism of her policies. Time and again, such people are dubbed "agitators," "communists," "anti-South Africa," "fanatics." Abuse and rejection and sometimes violence are the lot of those who dare to express opinions contrary to those of the government. When will the white rulers of South

Africa, and the vast majority of whites, listen to the sincerely-held opinions of the blacks of this land? Surely if ever there was a need for a round table conference with black leaders, that time is now. To continue to reject what they are telling us is to return to a never-never land of make believe. These two Christian leaders are calling us back from a path that all of us in our heart of hearts know can only lead to bloodshed. We cannot ignore or suppress black opinion forever. My question is, Will they be listened to by our rulers and by the majority of whites in this country?

May I, as a Christian Bishop, be allowed to comment on the effects this document has had on me personally?

First, it confirms what all of us who have contact with the blacks know to be true, that the overwhelming majority of blacks in this land totally reject apartheid. The Bishop and the Moderator make five points why this is so. They are 1) that blacks are not free people in this land; 2) that free movement is denied them; 3) that blacks are afraid to express their opinions for fear of reprisals; 4) that voting rights are denied black peoples; 5) that job reservation hinders the development of black peoples and destroys their family life.

Apartheid has been foisted onto the black people against their will. It is in essence the white man's way of rejecting his black brother, no matter how much successive South African governments toy with words or battle to define ideologies. What Bishop Auala and Moderator Gowaseb's document is saying clearly to me is that we whites have deluded ourselves into thinking that we have found any solution to this country's problems in the apartheid regime. They expose apartheid as a violation of the Declaration of Human Rights upon which every free nation of the world bases its laws. New schools, new hospitals, new roads, new Bantustans all beg the real issue. The black man is still suffering in this land, is still exploited, is still denied those basic human rights without which life in the modern world becomes intolerable. These two Christian leaders are telling me loud and clear that they and their people are not free, that they yearn for freedom and that they can never be free in a state which bases its legislation on racial discrimination.

Because these men are Christian leaders of respected Christian churches, because they are black leaders in touch with the mood of their peoples and therefore better able than most of us to speak for the black man, they have the right to be heard throughout the free world. Will we listen to them in South Africa? Experience teaches me to doubt it. We whites for the most part have not only become deaf, but have silenced our consciences as well.

Christian leaders such as Bishop Auala and Moderator Gowaseb must not be allowed to stand alone. For this reason, and because I know them to be men of integrity, I wish to say that I agree with their assessment of the situation as it exists in South West Africa today, and that I stand by them in their views. It is vital that all Christian leaders in this territory make their views known also. Men such as these must not be allowed to carry the brunt of the consequences of what they have said. The Christian Church as the conscience of this nation must now speak out with clarity and without fear. Apartheid must be denounced as unacceptable before God. Who else but the leaders of the Churches can do this?

Chapter Twelve

Strike

In December 1971, the black workers of Namibia stunned the white South African authorities and finally awakened the world to their plight by going on strike. Over 13,000 men, mostly contract laborers from Ovamboland, downed their tools in mines, factories, and farms and walked out of offices, white homes, and railway yards in a single united protest. From its very inception, the organization of the strike had been a shared responsibility of the African workers themselves, and hard as South Africa tried to find the one heroic figure behind it so that they might arrest him and crush the strike, they failed. The strength of this movement of workers was that the strike was totally democratic both at its planning stage and later in all its developments.

The strike began in Windhoek in what was the beginning of the Christmas holidays for whites. Incensed by the allegations of David de Beer that the contract labor system was a form of slavery, Mr. Jannie de Wet, the Chief Native Commissioner of Ovamboland, was quoted in *The Windhoek Advertiser* as saying, "The Ovambos are quite happy with the contract labour system." This statement was the spark that ignited the whole powder keg and gave the contract laborers the challenge that led to the strike.

A series of letters went back and forth between the contract laborers in the compounds of Walvis Bay and Katutura in Windhoek. In the past the workers had tried to acquaint the tribal authorities in Ovamboland and the native labor recruiting agency with their deep grievances, but to no avail. De Wet's statement was a clear indication to them that no improvements would come unless the workers acted themselves. The following letter, written in Ondanguan, was sent from the compound at Walvis Bay to the workers in the compound at Windhoek:

> We are having problems with the white man, J. de Wet. You are having similar problems. We said we ourselves want to be on contract, because we come to work. But we must talk about ending system. We in Walvis Bay discussed this. We wrote a letter to government of Owambo and SWANLA. We will not come back. We will leave Walvis Bay and the contract and will stay at home as the Boer J. de Wet said.

The next letter called for caution and unity. Its author was later brought to trial as one of the twelve accused of inciting the strike:

> Honoured friends: greetings. We meet 3 p.m. today to listen to what is read. Do not be afraid. We have friends. They come to tell us their thoughts. We have decided to break the contract. On Monday, we must not go to work or eat in the kitchen. Those who disagree with this must leave or they will get hurt. Those who work at night must not return to the compound or you will die.

A further letter expressed the workers' indignity against the system itself—their yearning to be seen as human beings and to move freely in their own country:

> Love your neighbour as yourself. We don't want contract—it does not allow us to be seen as men. De Wet said at Oshikati—15 November, 1971—the Ovambos themselves want contract. We don't want contract as Mr. de Wet said. If contract not ended, we must have enough reasons. We want the right of free movement in Namibia to work where we want to.

Since the overwhelming majority of the strikers were practicing Christians, Biblical sentences were often used in their statements. A fairly brief letter said just this:

> 17th December, 1971—some are cowards. I was in Ongwediva. Do you want to go to the Kingdom of God? Don't be afraid. There are many hands.

A further letter expressed the yearning among the blacks to be regarded as people:

> M.C. Botha said on 15 November, 1971, that we want contract. We don't want it anymore. We want to be seen as people. If my employer doesn't want me, he sends me back. But, if I don't want him, I cannot leave.

The last letter rejected the contract labor system on Christian grounds. It said simply:

> The Bible says that Christ died to free all men, but I am not free under contract. Give us chapter and verse [to justify the contract].

Thus de Wet, the great white father figure and the Afrikaners' apostle to the blacks, had succeeded in a single sentence in bringing about a black and white confrontation which, as it developed, he found increasingly difficult to interpret, let alone control. A banned leader of SWAPO confined to the black location of Walvis Bay voiced the contempt that the overwhelming majority of Ovambos felt towards de Wet when he said, "If I were Mr. Vorster, I would sack Jannie de Wet."

On the 10th December 1971 de Wet grudgingly admitted to an astonished and totally unprepared white electorate that rumors about an impending strike were correct. *The Windhoek Advertiser* broke the news in the following manner: "Mr. de Wet confirmed that a strike would take place on 14th December should the plans to put it into effect materialise. On that day, hundreds of contract labourers intend handing in their contracts."

At this stage, de Wet was handing out reassurances and exuding confidence, asserting that "the situation at Walvis Bay was being carefully watched. Attention had already been given to the matter and there were ample recruits in Owambo to proceed to Walvis Bay should the situation require it."

By December 15th the compound in Katutura was hemmed in with a cordon of police armed with guns and batons and with riot vehicles standing at the alert and ready to go into action. For their part, the Ovambo contract laborers were seeing to it that no one got out to report for work. Panic spread through the white community as not only mines and businesses were being threatened. Goods were piling up in the railways, litter and garbage went uncollected, there were no deliveries of milk, and other essential services were threatened. White schoolboys, largely teenagers, were hired to haul the garbage at wages of over R100 (U.S. $140) a month—ten times what black adult workers received for the same work. The whites saw nothing incongruous in this.

Savage action was aimed by the police at the strikers. From time to time individual policemen burst into the rooms of the contract laborers and smashed up their radios and other possessions, clearly wishing to intimidate the strikers into going back to work. Yet, thousands of blacks remained inside the compound itself demonstrating incredible solidarity. There was little food to be had, as they had boycotted the notorious kitchen. For the most part, white opinion clung tenaciously to the belief that once the black workers became hungry, they would "come to their senses" and come crawling back to their employers seeking their old jobs back. De Wet echoed this opinion when he said, "Many Ovambos will escape to their employers tomorrow once they have been set free of that virtual prison." But the workers stood together and remained inside the compound.

The strike was now spreading the length and breadth of the territory, and what had begun in the compounds of Walvis Bay and Windhoek had now extended to the mines, the factories, the farms, and all places where black workers were employed as contract laborers.

The American-owned mine at Tsumeb predicted that no trouble would occur there, but was, in fact, among the worst hit as the overwhelming majority of its black labor force downed tools. This action forced the white staff to man the huge copper smelter, whose closure would have cost the company thousands of dollars.

Individual blacks working on farms heard the news over the radio that their comrades had come out on strike, and they too quietly handed in their aprons and work clothes, leaving the farms to join them.

The strikers then demanded that they be repatriated to Ovamboland; they wanted the outside world to know their total disenchantment with South African rule by dissociating themselves from it, and they expressed their vote of no confidence by a massive withdrawal to their own part of the country. Special trains were provided which carried them back by the thousands to Tsumeb from where they were transferred by bus back to Ovamboland. A manifesto was released on January the 12th which outlined the grievances and the demands of the strikers. It was issued under the names of two men, Johannes Nangutuuala, a magistrate's clerk from Ondangua, and an unknown person who simply signed himself, Antindi. The following is a summarized translation of what the strikers were demanding, as recorded in *The Windhoek Advertiser* of 12 January 1972:

> We do not want the contract system to be improved or that it be given another name. We want the barricade [the twelve-foot fence at Oshivelo which prevents freedom of movement from Ovamboland] to be removed, and in its place there should be a legal agreement. All sorts of ways aimed at selling people meet with our disagreement.
>
> We want employment agreements including the following: liberty for those to do the work they want to do and of which they have experience and knowledge; the freedom to change

> one's place of employment without the fear of landing in gaol first.
>
> We also want the freedom to take our families with us and to have the right to visit people when we want to. Let a man get payment for the work he is doing and not according to his colour. Let all be given the same treatment.
>
> There should be employment bureaux in all tribal regions and towns. When an employee looks for employment, he should know what wages are paid for the work. There should be mutual respect between employer and employee.
>
> Employees should be paid sufficiently to buy their own food and to provide their own transport needs.
>
> In the place of the existing passbook, we want an identification card, which should contain the following: name, tribal area (with the insertion of South West African Citizen behind the name of the region), sex, identity number, photograph of the holder.

These demands were moderate, but sounded like bloody revolution to the whites.

On the 12th of January 1972, after reading the published demands of the strikers, de Wet commented to the press: "The intimidation in Owambo is at an end. In my opinion, there will be no further incidents." In addressing the plenary session of the Ovambo Council on the 14th of January, he went on to claim that the Ovambo contract labor system, as it had been known for four decades, was on the eve of drastic changes and revision, and that, in fact, an entirely new system was about to be launched. This referred to the setting up of labor bureaus.

Once the contract laborers had returned to Ovamboland, a state of emergency was declared there.

In South Africa the government gazetted a series of regulations aimed at suppressing the strike which were especially vicious. All gatherings of more than five people were forbidden; freedom of speech was removed with the words that it was an offense to make "subversive or intimidating statements." Chiefs and headmen could impose fines of R100 (U.S. $140) at random and magistrates were empowered to dish out fines of U.S. $840. The most frightening aspect of the whole procedure was that it swept away all rights of the Africans to appeal to the courts against wrongful arrest, malicious accusations, or torture. "No persons arrested or detained under the regulations may, without the consent of the minister or person authorised by him, be allowed to consult with a legal advisor."

Prime Minister Vorster said in Cape Town that the South African government would deal with the situation in Ovamboland: "Any further incidents would be settled as speedily as possible."

They were, indeed. Africans were gunned down and six were killed after a church service. Students from Onguediva and other schools were arrested for taking part in demonstrations, and their schools closed down. The strike leaders were imprisoned and people were held without trial in temporary gaols. A reign of terror was let loose of such savagery that certain missionaries at my church's headquarters in Odibo telephoned to tell me that they could not bear to pass near the police post at Oshikango because of the screams coming from it. Hundreds of blacks, including an Anglican priest, were placed in corrugated iron "cages." These men suffered greatly from thirst in an area where temperatures can often reach 100°F. in the summer.

The situation in Ovamboland was deteriorating rapidly as government officials resolutely refused to meet with the accredited leaders of the strikers to discuss with them their grievances. Instead, great wagon loads of troops patrolled the border road between Angola and Namibia, descended on any group of workers who were gathered to discuss the strike, beat and manhandled them, and in some cases shot them.

In a statement issued from Oshikati on the 13th of January 1972, Mr. de Wet assured the Ovambo people that the paramilitary forces, armed with automatic rifles, who by now were swarming in droves all over Ovamboland, had come at the request of the Owambo Legislative Council, the very black puppet leaders scorned as quislings by the strikers. He said, "I wish to assure you that they are not here to force anything on the Ovambo people, but only to prevent disturbances. They will act only in the event of Ovambo intimidators trying to prevent other Ovambos from working in Owambo or elsewhere by threatening or injuring them."

He asked all the people in Ovamboland to remain calm, because this was the best way to meet any crisis, and added, "I wish also to give you the assurance that this whole matter will be solved to the satisfaction of all by the South African Government as trustee of the Ovambos and the Owambo government." (Four years later, the state of emergency still exists.)

De Wet's perennial optimism was shattered time and time again. On the 17th of January, reports were released that three policemen were injured at Etomba. This came close on the heels of reports in the same newspaper that all was peaceful and calm in Ovamboland. Furthermore, no Ovambos had yet come forward to be recruited for the mines, which were now virtually paralyzed. Again, de Wet the optimist: "It appears as if all are waiting for the Grootfontein conference to be held on the 19th and 20th of January."

Just before that meeting took place, indications that things were far from peaceful in Ovamboland came in a statement to the press that the headmen there had asked police to break up "illegal meetings" and to prosecute the organizers of such gatherings. Once again, the black government stooges were being used to cover up police aggression.

Two events blew up in the face of the public on the very day before the meeting in Grootfontein. The border fence between Ovamboland and Angola was cut in several places and confrontations with police and strikers took place in the process of this. Secondly, a booklet by Miss Ruaha Voipio was released which showed the misery and suffering caused to the Ovambos by the contract labor system. De Wet dismissed the booklet in just a few words, saying it contained "replies to questionnaires sent to Owambo."

Mr. de Wet refused to comment on the fact that from Bonn eleven Social Democrat Members of Parliament sent an open letter to the churches and to trade unions calling for support for the strikers and their families in Namibia. Clearly, the significance of the strike was moving beyond the confines of Namibia. The letter said that "The Ovambos risk life and limb in a struggle for basic human rights which we take for granted here."

When the Grootfontein meeting finally took place in the Agricultural Hall, it was attended by M.C. Botha, South Africa's Minister of Bantu Administration, and two directors of SWANLA, J.H. Louw and A. Rothkegel. A cryptic note revealed that the contract labor force would be represented by the Executive Committee of the Owambo Legislative Council, the very body which had called in the police to arrest the strike leaders and to smash all meetings of workers in Ovamboland. In all, the conference was attended by forty-two people. On January 19 the first meeting was held between the Department of Bantu Affairs, the Executive Council of Ovamboland, and white employers.

Details of the first day's meeting were released to a waiting and anxious public by the press secretary. Neither Minister Botha nor Commissioner de Wet spoke. Mr. J.C.B. Eynsen admitted that the Ovambo spokesman at the conference had asked for the removal of all whites from Ovamboland. He went on to answer questions about the killing of three policemen near Oshikati. According to the press account,

> Mr. Eynsen said that one of the policemen was stabbed twice, a second was dealt a hammer blow, and the third was shot with a

> bow and arrow. He also said that a meeting held near Oshikango had been addressed by strike leaders who demanded that stock inspectors from South Africa be removed and that the border fence between Ovamboland and Angola be done away, the latter being a protest of the division of the Kwanyama tribe into two parts by the white-erected fence.

The conference between the ministers began in siege-like conditions. Twelve Owambo and Kavongo deputies arrived in shiny black limousines from the north, surrounded by plainclothes detectives and security men. Minister Botha and his deputy minister, Piet Koornhoof, shook hands with the Ovamboland delegation. The press were allowed to photograph the delegation from the north but were ordered to leave the grounds when the minister arrived. When the conference proper began, uniformed police put up a road block to the entrance road.

The Owambo delegation consisted of seven members of the Executive Committee, the most important being Silas Iimpumbu, singled out by the South African government as "Minister of Labour and Works." Not a soul had known about him or about his position before the conference!

Minister Botha carried in his pocket a draft of prepared statements—sixteen in all—which it was reputed had been discussed at the conference the previous day. He made no statement to the press, but said that they could be present for the historic occasion when the statement would be signed setting up the new deal for African labor.

Here was an exercise in window dressing for the benefit of the whole world. South Africa's reply was woefully characteristic: she wished to shuffle off her responsibilities by asserting that Ovamboland was now almost an independent territory being assisted to nationhood by the guiding hand of South Africa and therefore responsible for her own problems. At the conference, South Africa spoke about the Ovambo and Kavongo "nations," using words such as "Minister of Labour" and "Executive Council," and holding top executive meetings with men who represented nobody and then preparing for world consumption sixteen points pulled out of a minister's back pocket.

"The Owambo government will provide labour employment offices in the different regions where work-seekers can be registered and employed." The worker would know beforehand what his wage would be and any fringe benefits. All details would be furnished in a "Bantu language." His rights and those of his employer would be pointed out to him. It would no longer be difficult to change from one job to another. SWANLA would disappear. These conditions would later become applicable to other "homelands," namely Damaraland, Hereroland, Namaland, and Bushmanland.

South African authorities presented Chief Philomen Elifas with a golden pen; flashbulbs from the South African press lit up the room; Jannie de Wet stood guard over the whole proceedings; Headman Silas Iimpumbu stood in the background just to add weight. The full text of the agreement was to be released in Cape Town next day.

The press in Namibia greeted the deal as a landmark in the history of South West Africa. If the contents of the released statement had been prepared beforehand and were not the result of the working of the South African delegation, well, that just went to prove that South Africa was going to change the contract labor system anyway. Then speculation arose as to the meaning of the words used in the text. Just exactly what did Minister Botha mean when he said that the Ovambo should be allowed "to maintain contact with his family"?

One paper made the following prediction: "From this, there is one easy inference to be made—the worker will be permitted to bring his family—if the accommodation is available. This conclusion appears to be correct, and in view of the workers' demands, and the great distances involved, one fails to arrive at any other definition of the meaning of 'maintaining one's family ties.' " The paper was wrong, as was the rest of the world, in assuming that improvements to the contract labor system were just around the corner. The Ovambos were being tricked in an attempt to get them back to work with vague promises that drastic changes would come.

By the 24th of January it was reported that workers were trickling back to Ondangua expecting the new deal to come into operation. Commissioner de Wet, by the 26th of the month, had the onerous task of telling the white farmers that the golden days of exploitation were over and that they would have to increase the wages of their black employees, and then of trying to calm their fears. News leaked out in Windhoek that the mines and fishing industry accepted the new deal, but that the farmers (who employ over 20,000 Ovambos as contract workers) were not at all happy with what they had heard. The Nationalist Party in Namibia depends almost entirely on the support of the farmers, who would resist any government attempt at forcing them to pay higher wages to their black workers.

Ovamboland was now seething with unrest and discontent. Still the South African Government refused to meet with the workers or to discuss their problems. By the 31st of January, a peaceful, nonviolent strike by 13,500 Ovambo workers who had been shipped back to Ovamboland had escalated into a state of open warfare between the black workers and white troops. The government expressed its account of the situation in the following terms:

> The government has taken note of the fact that under pressure by a limited number of intimidators, disturbances of the public peace and good order, a threat to the security of the individual, as well as damage to property and particularly the destruction of international boundaries, had occurred in parts of Ovamboland, that attempts were made to disrupt the normal course of public life by hindering officials in the execution of their duty. Cattle kraals and fences were destroyed; trouble makers have prevented workers from returning to work in and outside the country.

General Gideon Joubert of the South African forces assured the public that they had nothing to fear, but admitted that in the previous forty-eight hours his soldiers had shot and killed six Ovambo men. The wife of a headman was in the hospital after being attacked with a panga, several policemen were injured, and a headman was in the hospital. In Angola 1600 Portuguese soldiers had been sent south to patrol the border.

The strikers' frustration was now turned against the government-appointed black leaders in Ovamboland. The headman Philipus Kaluvi had been given special responsibility for dealing with the contract laborers. In a press interview on the 18th of January, de Wet admitted that Kaluvi's kraal and general dealer's shop had been burned down by "arsonists." At this time, Kaluvi was one of the highest-paid black officials in Ovamboland; yet he was a man who had only rudimentary education and was totally out of sympathy with the sufferings of his fellow Africans.

Johannes Nangutuuala, a spokesman for the striking Africans, was promised that all the demands made by the workers would be met and a completely new system would be brought into operation. Convinced of the reasonableness of the workers' demands and thinking that the government had at last come to its senses, he went on Radio Ovamboland to say that he was happy with the government's new proposals and that the strikers could now go back to work. Two thousand contract workers returned to the recruiting center demanding that the new deal be delivered. Their hopes were dashed to the ground when they realized that Nangutuuala had been tricked and that the new terms offered by the government amounted to the old contract labor system with one or two insignificant modifications. Two thousand workers had come to Oshikati by January 31, but came away again sadly disillusioned men. They saw that nothing was changed, and so they refused to take the medical test.

This new crisis was dealt with in the time-honored South African manner: General Joubert announced on the same day that the police (paramilitary) divisions sent to Ovamboland would be maintained there and, if need be, reinforced by units from the Republic of South Africa. "The reinforcements could follow to contain the situation and to give the necessary protection to the public who is entitled to it." If the workers refused to work, the whole violence of the state would be unleashed against them to make them work.

Minutes after Joubert released this statement from South Africa, Mr. Botha announced that, where necessary, units of the South African Defense Force would assist the police in the protection of international borders. He referred to the cutting of the border fence and admitted for the first time that a "serious state of tension existed in certain parts of the homeland."

In Windhoek, there was a feeling of increasing strain as employers decided to wait so that they could meet to "standardize" wages for Africans in the territory. Whites had no wish to pay their African workers a living wage—they had had it too good for too long, and they were afraid that the mines would set a standard that other employers could not reach.

Meanwhile in Gobabis, Jannie de Wet had come up with an all-purpose solution to allay the fears of the white farmers. There was to be a secret list of wage scales to be distributed to farmers. The 4500 white farmers of the territory were to agree to a wage scale by forming a "farm labor trust fund" for the protection of "white interest."

"Ovambo workers still working on the farms under contract would still go on working," de Wet said. What had changed then? Nothing.

A reign of terror then hit Ovamboland, with South African soldiers attempting to suppress any form of protest in that part of the territory. In the *Rand Daily Mail* Jannie de Wet said that the police operations were aimed at "protecting Ovambos who wanted to work from intimidators." The Defense Force was in the territory for one purpose only: to guard the international border with Angola—from whom or what, we were not told.

In Windhoek, the employers were still holding meetings to protect themselves from the unjust demands of the workers. The Divisional Inspector of Labour, Mr. J.J. Badenhorst, urged employers to accept a minimum wage standard, "so as to stop workers from drifting from one employer to another."

In Otjiwarongo workers who believed that they now had the right to negotiate their wages were sent back to Ovamboland. They had asked for one rand (U.S. $1.40) a day, and the town clerk, Mr. I. van der Vyver, said that eleven out of forty-one would return to Ovamboland.

On February 4 a meeting was called by the African strikers in the western part of Ovamboland at Ruacana Falls. Fifty-two workers had been sent back from Otjiwarongo; seventy miners returning for jobs at Berg Aukus had demanded higher pay. Trucks operating for the South African Railways, who hold a monopoly on all public transport into Ovamboland, were prevented from travelling to Ruacana. By the 7th of February, large detachments of police in battle dress arrived in Windhoek.

In the Legislative Assembly in Windhoek, the South African Administrator, Mr. B.J. van de Walt, said that while the loss of income caused to the mining community had meant a loss to the Administration, he was nevertheless happy to announce that the "erection of a youth center [of the Nederduits Gereformeerde Kerk] progressed faster than was anticipated and provision is accordingly made for the balance of the loan plus an additional amount of R24,500 which was approved by the executive committee." The center was for the use of white youth only. The Dutch Reformed Church had made no official comment on the strike.

Another climax came with the walkout of four hundred Ovambo workers from the Tunacor and Namib fisheries in Walvis Bay. The men demanded that they be paid overtime for working night shifts. Earnings from the factories exceeded forty million rand a year. The industry employs two thousand Ovambos.

Having declared all meetings and gatherings in Ovamboland illegal, the police spent much of their time driving up and down the country, especially along the border road between Ovamboland and Angola, attempting to prevent the people from gathering. This is how one African described it to me: "The people want to meet together to discuss their grievances, someone informs the police, who arrive with guns, and the people are shot and beaten. The people then blame the headman on whose land the meeting took place and they return to take their revenge on him."

An attack was made by strikers on sub-headman, Samuel Kaulinge. His wife intervened by throwing her body between them and was mortally wounded by a panga intended for her husband. Kaulinge himself was seriously injured.

With martial law effectively holding down the people of Ovamboland and with a succession of phone calls from the African personnel at my mission headquarters in Odibo telling me that the violence of the military and police was meeting with a violent response on the part of the striking workers, I felt it urgent that I go to Ovamboland to be with the people.

Chapter Thirteen

Bloody Sunday

Having decided to go to Ovamboland, I applied for a permit to the territory in the usual way. I was never sure why I was granted the permit, but the Department of Bantu Affairs issued it immediately. When I arrived in late January, Ovamboland looked like occupied territory. Heavy-wheeled Army trucks in convoy roared up and down the road from Ondangua filled with troops in combat uniform carrying automatic rifles. They were mostly young men recruited for national service from the Republic.

The most stringent laws were now in operation, and it was obvious that the strike was to be broken at all costs by smashing down the resistance of the people. At Oshikango, as I went through the police post, my car was stopped and I was asked to report to an officer in charge of the unit.

Cages had been erected all over Ovamboland to house the thousands who had been held while the emergency regulations were in effect. Into these constructions, men were herded in such numbers that it was literally impossible for them to sit or lie down. A single bucket was placed there for their toilet requirements. They were not let out except for interrogation, which was accompanied by beating and torture by electric shock.

I stopped my car at the police post; prior to this encounter with the military, I had never in my life been approached by a man with a loaded gun. I could well imagine, after that single encounter, the sense of outrage that must be burning in the hearts of the people as they saw their country invaded by such armed men. As the soldier approached me with the weapon held diagonally across his chest, I had the strongest urge to pull it out of his hands. The captain addressed a few remarks to me, demanded to know my business, and then let me proceed on my way unmolested.

At the mission, tension prevailed. Missionaries told me that the police had entered our mission and told the white staff that their lives were in danger, that reports had been received by the police that the whole mission station was to be burned down by the strikers. No one believed them. Police crawled on their hands and knees around the place at night spying and attempting to overhear conversations. It would have made excellent propaganda if the authorities had been able to declare to the world that white missionaries had fled. The missionaries refused to budge.

I travelled from the mission headquarters through rural Ovamboland to Oshandi, a beautiful place where our first seminary had started. The mission nestles among the soft leaves of a wood and is perhaps one of the most picturesque places in Ovamboland. From there I proceeded to Holy Cross at Onamanama, one of our strongest churches, where Anglicans cross over from Angola to worship on Sundays. The Kwanyama tribe still has two-thirds of its territory and many of its people cut off from it in Southern Angola.

Here the priest was frightened and had told the people not to come to Mass but to disperse, for fear that their service should be mistaken for a political meeting. Church services had not been forbidden, but the African priest here was old and intimidated by the state of emergency. He had good reason to be, having been previously beaten up himself by the South African police.

I addressed the people and pleaded that they remain nonviolent.

As I emerged from the church to the border road again, a score of trucks carrying troops raced past towards Epinga. They may have contained the troops who were responsible for Ovamboland's "Bloody Sunday," 30 January 1972, when my people, returning from Mass, were set upon by a contingent of military forces. Four Africans were shot dead and two died later. I was shocked and sickened at the account which was given me by my clergy, and I asked for a full-scale investigation, taking down all the particulars I could and checking the names of those who had been shot by the South African forces. Since the Pretoria government had imposed a blanket of silence over Ovamboland, I released a report myself to the world press. I quote it now to indicate the lengths to which the white troops were prepared to go to beat the people back to work and to crush their resistance. Later, the South African government released its own report saying that their men had met a howling mob of Ovambos who attacked them with spears, machetes, and sticks. I stand by the account given to me by the African clergy and people of my church, on whose evidence I based this report:

STATEMENT ON THE EPINGA SHOOTINGS

A peaceful crowd of Ovambo Anglicans, many carrying prayer and hymn books, were returning from Sunday church service at Epinga on 30 January. An armed patrol met these people near the church, which is just a short distance from the main border road. The congregation leaving the church saw the armed patrols, took immediate fright and ran away from them in all directions into the bush. The patrol then withdrew to the border road. Certain men from the armed patrol left their vehicles and hid themselves in the bush. The African people emerged from the bush and gathered near the church. The people were discussing among themselves why the armed patrols had come when the armed men emerged from hiding and surrounded them.

For the second time, the people, in fear, attempted to run away. Thereupon the police called out to them to halt. The people were searched for incriminatory documents and weapons. Eye witnesses said that the police found none.

One nineteen-year-old African youth was carrying a walking stick. A Captain approached him and asked if he had a knife. The youth denied that he had any weapon. The Captain said, "I know you men," and was alleged to have jabbed towards the youth's head with a stick. The youth took fright and attempted to ward off the blow and the Captain fired at him. The rest of the patrol opened fire and the youth's head was splintered by bullets. An Anglican priest, it is further alleged, has in his possession parts of the youth's skull.

The people then again attempted to run away and the police opened fire on the crowd and three other Africans were shot dead. Three were seriously injured and taken to hospital at Oshikati where one later died. Two are still in serious condition in that hospital.

The names of the people who were killed outright are:

Tomas Muasijange — Benjamin Helumani

Lukas Veike — Matias Ohainengena

The injured are:

Seimba Muixika — Phillipus Kotilipa

Kakaiube Nidinua

This account was given after a Church enquiry was held. I have written to the Adminstrator of the Territory and to the Prime Minister, Mr. Vorster, calling for a judicial inquiry into this incident in view of the conflicting police reports.

7 February 1972

Colin O'Brien Winter
Bishop of Damaraland

No one was safe in Ovamboland—people were arrested for the most trivial reasons. Even more, the slightest infringement on the emergency regulations brought terrible consequences. I was told of an Ovambo who was standing in his back garden in the cool of the evening and was shot dead from a passing police truck. People were told not to be out after dark.

One of the young ministers of my church was arrested and afterwards tortured. He had purposely decided to devote his life to the ministry of the church as he felt it had a vital part to play in bringing about peaceful change. He was a man of immense patience, a loving father to his young family, popular with his brother students when in seminary, and held in high esteem as a moderate among his brother clergy.

This is how his arrest was reported to me:

> STATEMENT ON THE REV. OLAVI NAILENGE
>
> On Wednesday 26th January, 1972, the Rev. Olavi Nailenge went to see the stock inspector to show his stock book to him. Many people went to show their stock books that day. There was a big crowd of people. They waited and waited for the inspector and he did not come. At last people decided to send someone to call the stock inspector from his kraal. They sent two young men to fetch him. After that, the police came and searched people. Unfortunately, in Rev. Nailenge's handbag, the police found a paper in which some notes were written down concerning America by President Nixon and some notes concerning contract labour system. Then the police arrested him.
>
> (Signed) Archdeacon
>
> Additional note:
>
> It appears that The Rev. Olavi Nailenge was arrested on 26 January 1972, and held for the first week at Oshikango, and then transferred to Ondangua on 2 February 1972 where he is now held.

Later, in August of 1973, a visitor to my diocese told me that she had met and talked with a very kind African priest, "an old man." Several times she stressed that he was an old person. When I said that we did not have an old African priest in that particular town, she told me his name. The "old priest" was Father Nailenge, who was thirty-seven. He was held by the police for one hundred and seven days and received torture by electrical shock.

A minister of the Lutheran Church has compiled a list of those who have been tortured in Ovamboland. The following is a statement made by Father Steve Hayes in the November 1971 issue of *Pink Press*, the official newsletter of the Community of Simon the Zealot. He writes as follows:

> Representatives of the Lutheran Church met with Mr. Vorster in Windhoek and the meeting went on much longer than was

> expected, keeping Ushoma wa Shiimi, leader of the Onganjera tribe (one of the smallest in Ovamboland) and chief councillor of the Ovamboland Legislative Assembly, waiting for two hours.
>
> One item which was discussed was the use of police torture. Mr. Vorster demanded specific examples, so Bishop Auala mentioned one case. Mr. Vorster said that this was an isolated case, and demanded to know whether the churches were accusing the police force as a whole of maltreating prisoners. Bishop Auala said that he was not accusing the police force as a whole, but that he had learned of a large number of cases where prisoners had been beaten and electric shocks were administered. Mr. Vorster said that any cases brought to his attention would be investigated, but that the action of individual policemen in these cases could not be condoned. The church should not make generalised accusations on isolated abuses practised by individuals.
>
> Pastor Gunther Reeh, secretary of the Evangelical Lutheran Church, then said that the church was not speaking of isolated instances, or of the actions of individuals. It was speaking of a machine, an apparatus, which was specifically designed for administering electric shocks and that the police force was equipped with these machines and used them.
>
> Mr. Vorster changed the subject.

From Odibo I drove over to Ondangua to meet with Johannes Nangutuuala, the leader of the strike in Ovamboland, to assure him of my support for the strikers and to ask if there were anything I could do in the present situation to help. An archdeacon of my church, The Rev. Lazarus Haukongo, accompanied me, along with a student teacher from our high school.

We swung off the main tar road, a road wide enough to take army trucks and to allow aircraft to land on it, and headed for the African location in Ondangua. I pulled up behind another car, which was standing outside Mr. Nangutuuala's door. Accompanied by my archdeacon, I attempted to enter the tiny house. A white official barred my path, and I had to force my way past him. I recognized that he was a member of the Security Police, but I was determined at whatever cost to speak to Mr. Nangutuuala about the strike and his plans for the future. Since I had nothing to hide, I did not demand that the Security Policeman leave us, so we held our conversation with the man glowering at us all the time from the doorway.

The house in which we met was typical of so many others in South Africa. It was sparsely furnished, with a scrubbed table top acting as a desk, on which there were many papers. The three cheap wooden chairs placed around it and a wooden bench were the only other furniture in the room.

Mr. Nangutuuala was completely calm, and I myself was tense and nervous, wondering if the Security Police would arrest me for being there. We stood as we talked, and he told me that he was going to Oshikati to make a broadcast for Radio Owambo. All the while, he was pushing papers into a battered old briefcase. He had previously been a magistrate's clerk in Ondangua, but was forced out of his job when he became the spokesman for the strikers.

I was now looking fully into the face of a strike leader whose people's actions had caused the world to hold its breath in amazement. The strength and calm of the man and his utter reasonableness are the abiding impressions I have of my meeting with him.

We spoke first of all about the strike, and I expressed concern over the killing of Samuel Kaulinge's wife by strikers when she went to defend her husband. I told him that such actions could only be detrimental to a cause which so far was entirely just and which carried the whole weight and sympathy of the world's opinion behind it. I further mentioned that as a churchman I stood with him and his fellow strikers in their grievances and was prepared to do everything I could to assist them.

He agreed with me in deploring violence, but added that the patience of the people had reached the breaking point with the brutality of the South African Police. He felt that it would be an excellent thing if I were to put out a pastoral letter, along with Bishop Auala, calling on the people to continue their resistance, but in a nonviolent fashion.

We then discussed his plans for forming a political party in Ovamboland. An opposition party was allowed in the Transkei and elsewhere in South Africa; why was such a party not permitted in Ovamboland? He discussed the frustrations the ordinary person in Ovamboland felt with the government-appointed chiefs and said all he wanted to do was to offer the people an alternative choice which would really face the government with the real demands and aspirations of the people.

Later, Mr. Nangutuuala was arrested and imprisoned for attempting to exercise his democratic right—and this immediately after Mr. Vorster assured the U.N. Secretary General's personal representative in Namibia, Mr. Escher, that total freedom of expression was allowed in Namibia. In October 1973, Mr. Nangutuuala received twenty lashes in a public flogging and was afterwards hospitalized.

I left Mr. Nangutuuala at his home, and he promised to send me details of his new political party. Expressing views held by the overwhelming majority of the territory's inhabitants, he later wrote:

NEWS FROM OWAMBO

1. The majority of the people of South West Africa rejected the South African policy of so-called homelands, but the South African government is always forcing his apartheid policy on us.

2. It is not only the laymen who are intimidated by the South African Police, but the African leaders are always told that they will be dismissed from their points [appointments] if they do not want to co-operate with the South African government.

3. It is clear that the majority of the people rejected the illegal administration of South Africa in Namibia, but they are afraid to say anything because they'll be punished by the South African government through the activity of the South African Police.

4. The people of South West Africa are now near to lose their hope about the independence of their country, South West Africa, because the UN is hesitating to give a favourable and final decision to take over the administration of South West Africa. Many of us are sure that we'll never get the true peace under the South African government.

5. At the moment, the South African police and soldiers are busy killing the Ovambos who are unsatisfied with the boundary fence between South West Africa and Angola. This boundary fence between Angola and South West Africa divided Owambo into two parts. There are still Ovambos on the side of Angola, namely, Onkwankwa, Ehingo, Ombandja, Evale, and one part of Oukwanyama. The original northern boundary of Owambo was the Kunene River. I think it'll be better if the whole Owambo will be put on the same side than to be divided into two parts, one on the South West African side and the other on the side of Angola. My suggestion is that this boundary problem has also to be discussed when the UN discusses the case of South West Africa at Addis Ababa this year.

6. We are very disappointed that the UN hesitates to improve the decision of the World Court on the 21st of June, 1971. South African government is not only illegal in Namibia, but the Namibians are very suffering from many ill treatments of South African government.

Johannes Jefta Nangutuuala

I returned to my car and drove off with Fr. Haukongo and the young African teacher whom I had promised to drop off at the house where he was lodging. He pointed it out to me in the distance and I drove into the drive. As he was getting out, I asked him whose house he was staying in.

"Herman ja Toivo's," he answered me.

I looked at him in total astonishment. For years, I had been trying to discover the whereabouts of the dependents of this man and had been fearful of asking too much as several Africans had become evasive when pressed about it. Quite by accident, I had now stumbled on the place myself.

I leaped out of the car as Mrs. Elizabeth ja Toivo came to meet us. She was the mother of the great African patriot, and I felt a surge of pride as she greeted me. She stood there in an old, threadbare dress and a short *doek* (head-scarf), her hands gnarled from hoeing and other hard work. Four or five children shyly stared at me from the security of the inner darkness of the small house, which had been the shop run by Herman when he was deported from Cape Town back to Ondangua.

I greeted her in traditional manner, "Wale lepo, Meme. Naua tu?" ("Good morning, my mother, how are you?")

She responded with warmth and great love. When I asked her about Herman, she broke down and wept. "They have taken my son and I don't know what they have done with him. They won't let me see him. I have one wish, Bishop. I want to see my son before I die."

I took her into the house and we sat down and talked. She was calmer now, and I took down from her, word for word, her story of how she was being prevented from visiting her imprisoned son. It was obvious from her statements that the local magistrate, a certain Mr. van Niekerk, was determined that she never be allowed to go to Cape Town: "Where will you get water from? . . . Where will you get the money for your trip and the ticket? . . . How will you buy food on the train? . . . Where will you stay in Cape Town? . . . Go away, you are a stupid old woman."

Like so many Africans, she had an accurate memory for dates and places. She had been given permission from the tribal authorities to go; the Robben Island[1] authorities had said she could visit; only a petty, half-educated government official stood in her way, and apparently delighted in so doing.

I read the statement back to her and asked if it were accurate and asked her again if this was a completely true account of events as they had happened. Since she could not read or write, I did not ask her to sign the document, but promised that I would see the magistrate personally the next day. I stayed on until the Monday morning to do this.

---

[1] Robben Island is a state penitentiary set aside for black political prisoners. It is off the coast at Cape Town. The inmates break rocks in the lime quarry, collect seaweed, and shift sand as part of their punishment.

When I entered the Magistrate's Court in Ondangua the next day, Mr. van Niekerk was in conference, so I asked if he could be brought out to speak to me. He was a thin, wiry man with a mousy moustache and a somewhat effusive manner. As he walked down the corridor, which was not well illuminated, he at first mistook me for a Roman Catholic missionary and, as he stretched out his hand to greet me, he asked, "Father who?"

I replied, "Bishop Winter."

His whole face contorted with annoyance. He thrust his hand forward and demanded to see my permit to be in Ovamboland. He used the African name for it. "Where's your pass? . . . Where's your pass? . . . Who gave you permission to be here?"

He was obviously relishing the thought of having me arrested for being in Ovamboland without permission.

I moved his hand away and showed him my permit.

"We'll see about this. . . . oh yes, we'll see about this," he threatened.

I asked to talk privately with him in his office and we entered it. He didn't ask me to sit down, so I asked if I might.

I told him the reason for my visit and he was immediately both defensive and evasive.

"I have come to find out whether you refused an old African lady permission to visit her son on Robben Island. She made a statement to me yesterday in which she says that she has permission from the tribal authorities and from Robben Island to see her son, but that you have refused. Is that so?"

He sneered at me and replied, "It might be."

I told him that he, as a magistrate, knew that his reply was inadequate and evasive and I asked him to answer my question with a simple yes or no. I put the question again.

"I might have said it," he replied.

I then cautioned, "Mr. van Niekerk, I am going to ask Mrs. Toivo to come and see you again and to put her request to you, which is a perfectly lawful and legitimate one. She has told me that she wants to see her son before she dies. There are many things which are cruel about your apartheid regime, but I find this aspect of it the most revolting: that you torture helpless old ladies who are totally at your mercy. I believe that I am speaking to a Christian, and I know that you will agree that to visit the imprisoned is considered a Christian act by our Lord himself. I want to warn you that I will inquire whether you refuse her again, and if you do so, I shall see that the matter is reported in the South African Parliament and brought before the United Nations."

I then left the office. I knew that my time was now limited but as I walked back to my car, I spotted the Rev. Peter Kalungula, the deacon who was under church discipline for his activities in attempting to split the church in Ovamboland. I went up to him and made one final attempt at conversation with a view to reconciliation. He was in no mood to talk to me. I asked him when he would come back to his senses and stop destroying the peace and unity of the church and cease working for the South African regime. As I finished my sentence, four members of the Security Police pulled up in a car and surrounded me. He had spotted them before I did and took advantage of the occasion to refuse to shake my hand.

They escorted me back to the magistrate's office. Van Niekerk was there with the Acting Commissioner for Bantu Affairs, as Jannie de Wet was out of Ovamboland holding discussions with the government. They spoke to each other and asked for my permit again. The one said, "Will you do it?" to which the other replied, "No, you'd better do it." My permit was taken and van Niekerk said, "I am cancelling your permit and you are to leave Ovamboland immediately."

I then asked, "May I know for what reasons and under what law you are removing me?" Van Niekerk beamed with satisfaction when he replied, "We never give reasons, Get out now."

I left the office and turned my car south for Windhoek. When I came to Mrs. Toivo's house, I stopped and went in for one final chat with the family. I left her some money for the children and promised I would try to see that she got something every month. I felt very tired when I finally got into my car, waved to the children, and drove towards Oshivelo.

The next day, I released the following communiqué to our friends in various parts of the world. I knew that my days were numbered.

BISHOP OF DAMARALAND'S PERMIT TO ENTER OVAMBOLAND WITHDRAWN

The permit issued to the Bishop of Damaraland, the Right Reverend Colin O'Brien Winter, by the Department of Bantu Affairs in Windhoek, 28th January, was withdrawn by the Magistrate in Ondangua, Mr. van Niekerk, on Monday morning, 31st January, in Ondangua. In an interview with Mr. Pieterse, the newly appointed Chief Bantu Affairs Commissioner for South West Africa, Bishop Winter was informed that this action was taken on instruction from Pretoria. The Bishop was further told that he may apply again for a permit to enter Ovamboland, but that the application, in his opinion, was not likely to be granted.

Bishop Winter issued a statement which reads as follows:

"This action on the part of the South African authorities is the culmination of what I consider to be a deliberate attempt to curb and weaken the ministry of the Anglican Church. Since I became Bishop, seventeen permits have so far been refused by the South African authorities. The present action is a deliberate one in cutting me off from the pastoral care of fifty thousand black Anglicans and those missionaries and other church leaders who serve them. The reasons for this are obvious.

"I have refused to accept the ideology of apartheid and have been outspoken about the suffering it is causing to the thousands in this land who are daily afflicted by it. I have chosen to act as the spokesman of those who are denied basic human rights and this the government will neither tolerate nor allow.

"I believe that the present situation in Ovamboland is critical and deteriorating daily. The government blames the missionaries for the present unrest and refuses to see that the Africans themselves are rejecting the contract labour system. The Church has a vital part to play in finding a solution. I have called for a dialogue between the government and the Church and the government and strike leaders. None has been forthcoming.

"There is a breakdown in human relations in Ovamboland which is critical and the government reports that things are calm in Ovamboland are false.

" 'The strikers hold a meeting. The police arrive in force to smash it. There is shooting—people are hurt or killed. The Africans retaliate by burning down the kraal or killing the person they think has informed on them,' is how one African described it to me.

"Here obviously is a case for the government to initiate talks with the strike leaders. So far, they refuse to meet with them, but how else can a peaceful settlement be arrived at? The result is bitterness and rising dissatisfaction.

"South Africa is unable to contemplate a change in the system of apartheid and its concomitant laws which the Africans reject. Its only answer so far is the dismissal of missionaries and violence to those who oppose it. For my own part, I shall continue to speak out whenever conscience, compassion or truth demand it."

Windhoek—2 February 1972.

The covering letter that went out with the report said:

The situation here in South West Africa as far as some Churches are concerned is deteriorating. I spoke to the Finnish missionaries in Ondangua just after the Magistrate had cancelled my permit, and they feel that their days are also limited. There is a rumour that the government's policy is to remove all white missionaries from Ovamboland. They themselves have denied this, but the rumour persists.

My own position is best summarised in the last sentence of the report. I shall continue to speak whenever Christian conscience, compassion or truth demand it. Effectively, the ban from Ovamboland restricts me in a sort of episcopal "house arrest," confining me to the south of my diocese. Ninety percent of my people are in Ovamboland and these will now be without a shepherd and will be barred from any of my episcopal ministry, except that which can be delegated through my clergy.

The effect the ban has produced is not immediately apparent. There will be the usual heated press campaign which continues to link what I am doing and saying as being the real "agent provocateur" in the strike. This is useful to the government because when you see a communist or an agitator under every pulpit, you have no cause to listen to the real grievances of the Africans suffering under the contract labour system.

I will continue to try and hold my own Church together under all this. Already, there appears to be a rift coming with certain white clergy who feel that we should not have a Bishop making statements to the press. These will draw ever further away and already one of my leading priests has expressed his "shock" that this has happened, shifting the blame from the government onto the bishop. In a Church which tries to be democratic, I must allow all people, clergy and lay alike, the opportunity of expressing their views. My position may well become a "scandal" in the New Testament sense, and if this happens, it remains to be seen how effective my ministry will be. It is noteworthy that not a single black so far has expressed anything but deep concern and sorrow.

What of the future? A high-ranking minister in a speech in parliament yesterday made mention of certain "clerics" whose activities have contributed to the violence in South West Africa. You will know that my own position is that of a committed Christian pacifist. I spoke to the leader of the strikers not from choice but because when I heard, whilst in Ovamboland, that a woman had been slashed to death with a panga and her husband critically injured, I felt that, as a Christian bishop, I had to speak to him. I had been told that this was a retaliation on the part of certain African groups who felt this man had betrayed them by calling the police to break up their meeting. You will know that the strikers are not allowed to hold meetings and also have not so far been met by the government. Frustration and violence were on the increase. During our meeting, I was asked by him to make a statement calling for peaceful negotiation.

My meeting with Mrs. Elizabeth Toivo, the aged mother of Herman Toivo, now confined on Robben Island, was equally fortuitous. Having heard what she said, I felt compelled to confront those who were responsible for debarring this old lady from meeting with her son. Time and again, I am placed in this situation here. I wish to continue my work as Bishop, but the nature of events here forces me to speak out for justice or for mercy. As you will know, this is nearly always misunderstood and I am accused of being an agitator. From the government's point of view, I should confine myself to what it calls "preaching the gospel." From my own point of view, I cannot confine myself to a Gospel which excludes the widows and the oppressed, together with the despised and downtrodden. In a word, there lies the Church/State tension, which is now a full confrontation. It was this which recently led me to appeal for funds to defend the twelve men accused of promoting violence in the recent strike.

My present position here as bishop means that I must not retreat from speaking out and show the people here and throughout the world the true position of those who suffer under apartheid. I know this leaves one wide open to the charge of sensationalism, rabble rouser and so on. Those who know me as a pastor know that my concern is for people and not for publicity. Those who don't will form their own judgements.

It is still too soon to see how events will go. I would value your prayers at this time. Many decisions concerning the future of this diocese still have to be made. Pray for the African leaders in Ovamboland. Events have thrust them forward into far greater responsibility sooner than we had planned. Pray that God's strength will sustain them.

My staff here have been wonderful and I don't think I could continue without them.

Love and peace,
+Colin Damaraland.

Chapter Fourteen

Trial

Twelve African men and one Coloured student were brought before the Magistrate's Court in Windhoek on January 25, 1972, for the role they were alleged to have played in the Ovambo workers' strike. They each had numbers hung around their necks and never once were they referred to by their names; each time, the magistrate called them "Accused Number. . . ." When Advocate O'Linn, for the defense, asked that the cards be removed and that names be used, the magistrate remarked brusquely that this was not necessary. The world took note that in South Africa these were black and therefore nonpersons in the eyes of the courts. They stood in court and were not allowed to sit down.

Through its official announcements, the South African authorities were quick to assert that the troubles were over labor disputes—yet right from the beginning, the evidence from the state was handled and presented by the Security Police, the very people whose appointed task is to protect the state.

Three charges were brought against the men:

First, that they had contravened the Masters and Servants' Act in that they, by means of violence, threats, or intimidation, incited workers at Katutura during December to stay away from or to desert their employment.

Second, that in December they incited, ordered, and caused Ovambo workers to stay away from their work.

Third, that the accused wrongfully deserted their employment in December.

There was an alternative charge to each of these counts; under count one they were charged under the Riotous Assemblies Act.

All of the accused were from Ovamboland except for one Coloured man, Harold Leonard Sam, who was a law student at the University of

Cape Town. They were a cross section of the men who came on contract, youth and age evenly dispersed.

This is the list of those accused:

Harold Leonard Sam	Coloured—22 years—not married—student for B.A. degree
Immanuel Mobili	Ovambo—36 years—married—education: standard 5[1]
Erastus Abet Shanila	Ovambo—20 years—not married—standard 1
Thomas Shepumba	Ovambo—25 years—not married—standard 6
Viliho Villiha	Ovambo—24 years—not married—standard 3
Cleopas David Kapapu	Ovambo—23 years—not married—standard 1
Maiakias Hiloohamb	Ovambo—51 years—not married—standard 2
Lazerus Shikango	Ovambo—21 years—not married—standard 3
Jason Nhituamata	Ovambo—27 years—married—education: none
Jonas Nduilihufa Nejulu	Ovambo—69 years—married—education: none
Matupang Shimuefeleni	Ovambo—26 years—not married—education: none
Leonard Nicodemus Nghipandula	Ovambo—28 years—not married—education: none

Windhoek's Magistrate's Court is an unimpressive, dull red-brick building, built around a courtyard in the center of which is a small, walled lily pond with goldfish in it. There is a stillness about the place, so much so that one almost instinctively catches one's breath and reacts the same way as when entering a church. The offices of the Chief Magistrate and Prosecutor are there. It was a place I visited occasionally to get marriage certificates, but a place most Africans fear, for obvious reasons.

The individual courtrooms themselves are quite small, divided down the middle by a wooden partition with blacks seated on one side and whites on the other. When seated, one could not see who was on the other side of the screens. A table was provided for the prosecution and defense counsels. A small dock of varnished brown wood stood on the right. A place was provided for junior clerks, who

---

[1] Standard 1 is the equivalent of three years' rudimentary education at primary school; standard 2 is four years and so on.

followed the proceedings on a tape recorder. A young policeman dressed in blue hovered around and from time to time menaced the blacks with threatening looks.

The magistrate, Mr. H.J. Kriel, a small, neatly dressed man, could easily have been a Dutch Reformed minister. His black gown was spotless and his shirt had a stiff collar. It was often difficult to hear him, as his voice was soft and he made no attempt to ensure that his words were heard by everyone, contenting himself with addressing the counsel. He seemed nervous, and with good cause, for on his courtroom were focussed the eyes of the world. Two observers—one from England and one from the United States—had arrived specially to see whether or not the justice which he administered was impartial and just. The one, Mr. Alex Lyon, was a British Member of Parliament who represented the constituency of York and was a legal expert and his party's spokesman on African affairs. The other was a judge from the criminal division of the New York Supreme Court, Mr. Justice William Booth, a black American.

The local press had reported the visit of these two distinguished men and their presence in Windhoek had a remarkable effect on the whites as well as the blacks. The whites felt threatened when faced with such men as Lyon and Booth, knowing that these two represented people and groups hostile towards the South African way of life. Both men had the bearing of authority, commanded respect, and went about their business speaking their minds openly. This was unusual in a country where whites are usually intimidated into silent acquiescence.

The local press made much of the fact that Alex Lyon had made contact with the Anglican Church. It was true that he had sought us out and had been a guest at some functions in my house and rapidly became a friend. He is a man of strong Christian convictions; in fact, he is an active Methodist lay preacher. The press tried to implicate the Church in some sort of international cloak-and-dagger plot to overthrow South Africa: "Sitting between two office bearers of the Anglican Church was Mr. Alex Ward Lyon." Lyon himself was direct and outspoken: "I am here to watch the trial to see whether it is conducted fairly—whether justice or injustice is being done."

Alex Lyon's comments were recorded and went all over the territory; they would be read by the white Karakul farmers on the fringe of the Kalahari Desert, who were left in no doubt as to the feelings of the Labour movement of Britain. Black peasant farmers in Welwitschia would see them. They would be devoured by the local black community in Windhoek's Katutura location, who would be quick to observe that the outside world was taking note of the struggle for human freedom which was being waged in that tiny courtroom.

"Apart from the Rhodesian issues, the Ovambo strike in South West Africa was the most talked-about subject in regard to the affairs of Southern Africa," Lyon told reporters in my home. He further pointed out to them that in Britain those who were opposed to South Africa's apartheid policies saw the strike as being the most effective way of breaking South Africa's stranglehold over Namibia. "People in Britain had been taken completely by surprise," he added, "for the Ovambo were regarded as placid people. The verdict of the World Court and this strike are as important as the Pearce Commission is for Rhodesia."

Back home in England, he gave further expression to his views, comparing the Ovambo strike to the early struggles of the labor movements in Britain for freedom. For such outspoken comment, Mr. Lyon was refused permission to re-enter Namibia in 1973 to act as an independent observer for the International Commission of Jurists at another trial.

The mood of the whites at the beginning of the trial was that the state should teach those blacks a lesson that they would never forget and that unless the government did this, there would be more disturbances. Most whites were looking for tough, long sentences; some wanted the men whipped. The opinion among my staff at the commencement of the trial was that the men could face sentences of up to five years' imprisonment. This thought was shared by the strike leaders themselves.

At the beginning of the trial, the men had no one to defend them. This was reported locally by the press as: ". . . The thirteen men returned a plea of 'not guilty' and did not ask for defence."[2]

Here we were up against a problem. We were determined to stand by the men at whatever price to the church. A group of American lawyers and others in England had told us that they were prepared to help with the cost of defending the men. Accordingly, a local firm of attorneys had been to see the men in the prison where they were being held near to the entrance to Katutura.

The attorneys were frustrated in their dealings both with the authorities and with the imprisoned strikers themselves. The prison authorities refused permission for the prisoners to be seen together, and would permit them to be seen only in small groups of two or

---

[2] All press commentary on the trial is from *The Windhoek Advertiser*, unless otherwise noted.

three. The strikers, for their part, felt—and rightly so—that this was an attempt on the part of the state authorities to weaken their case and to try from the outset to prove that their evidence was contradictory. They therefore said that they had no confidence in the attorney and would defend themselves. They expected the worst.

The Masters and Servants Act is a vicious, outdated piece of legislation. The mere whisper of insubordination from any black employee exposes him at once to its consequences in law—which can be flogging, fine, imprisonment, or banishment to Ovamboland. Without a competent advocate, these men were at the mercy of a system which was acting both as prosecutor and judge. It was vital that they have a defending counsel and the best that was available.

I consulted with Alex Lyon, and together we made our way to see the chief magistrate.

Our reception was civil, though frigid. I pointed out that South African justice was on trial and that in South Africa's own interests it was important that the Ovambo men be defended. Captain Tommie Thomasse, who was the investigation officer from the Security Police, said that he had no objections to my speaking with the men. The prosecutor, Mr. Johann Jaquire, said that he did not object either. I therefore asked the magistrate if I could see the men. The attorney asked for a break in the proceedings to allow me to interview the strike leaders. Thomasse said that he would accompany me to where the men were being held, and I followed him through the empty courtroom to a corridor between two buildings. The place was swarming with police. We were led to a narrow passageway between two buildings of the court. There was hardly enough space to stand side by side, and it was here that the Ovambo leaders were crowded into a confined corridor about ten to twelve paces long. It was airless and very hot.

I greeted them in Oshikwanyama and received friendly and warm greetings in return. They held out their hands to shake mine, several of them having to climb onto a small ledge on the side wall, and holding the shoulders of those in front, to reach me. I was deeply moved. I noticed particularly Leonard Nghipandula. He was a small man with a slight moustache, but his eyes were shining. I noticed this time and again as I watched him each day in the courtroom. So I addressed them:

> I bring you greetings, and I have come to tell you that I stand with you in what you have done. I want you to know that the church stands with you too. I believe that you have a just cause.

> I have not come here to make any decisions for you, but I believe that you cannot defend yourselves adequately. The South African state has a man who is skilled in the law and you are no match for him. There are friends abroad who have followed what you have done and who wish to help. They have told me that they are willing to pay for your defense and wish me to obtain the best lawyer possible. I come here as your friend, I stand with you in your struggle, but you must decide for yourselves whether you want legal aid or not. There will be no cost to you personally, but you must decide what you wish to do. Perhaps you will discuss the matter among yourselves and then give me your answer. The decision must be your own.

I looked across to where Captain Thomasse was standing, flanked by other white police officers. His face was deadpan; the other police looked at me with undisguised distaste. Throughout the trial, Thomasse was always cool and controlled. That speech of mine was a further step on the road to my deportation. I knew it, and as I looked at him, I knew that every word I said was being recorded and would be used against me.

The strikers did not hesitate for a moment. As Leonard Nghipandula took a quick look round, he was met with a chorus of "Heino" ("Yes"). I told them that I would try to get the best lawyer that was available, and this remark was met with smiles and thanks. Every single one of those men was a practicing Christian, and the eight who had any education had received it at mission schools. I turned to the captain and said that I would like to pray with the men and give them a blessing. He politely gave me permission and the men stood in that stifling corridor, heads bent in prayer, eyes closed, arms clasped. We concluded with the Lord's Prayer in Oshikwanyama. I shook hands with them all and was shown out.

The problem now was where to get an advocate in Windhoek who was sympathetic and who was prepared to handle the case. Such men were not easy to find. The judges in Windhoek were partisan to the regime and hostile to our church. The leading advocates were mostly the same. I knew one or two of them, and their attitude towards the African was at best paternalistic and usually hostile. Advocate Chris Nicholson, the one man to whom I would naturally have turned, had been forced to leave the Territory and abandon his practice because no one in the lower bar would refer cases to him. Among the others, there really seemed to be not a single person whom I could trust to handle the case with sympathy and conviction. I was wrong; there were two.

Karin Blum, daughter of Israel Goldblat, was a housewife and a lawyer who had recently taken sick. It was to her that I went seeking help. I was shattered when she told me that she could not handle the case herself, because I took her refusal to mean that she did not dare to be associated with it. She then said that we needed someone who was a fighter and that moreover she knew exactly the person: "Brian O'Linn is your man."

I left her office still feeling dejected and tense. Everything depended on getting someone of real ability. When we entered O'Linn's outer office, he was seeing a client and we were asked to wait. Fifteen minutes later, we were in his office explaining our needs.

I noticed first his cauliflower ear and a crop of dark curly hair. He had the look of a prize fighter about him as he sat at his desk with his arms folded into a heap of papers on the top of it. He was saying that he had just got back from his farm in the country, where he had been working with his cattle. He spoke easily to us, but there was more than a degree of caution as he looked up at me from time to time. One of his forebears must have been Irish, but he had grown up in an Afrikaans community, he had voted for Smuts' United Party, and he was politically cautious. He was not a Nationalist, but he was a firm believer in law. At that first meeting I did not get the impression that he was a man with a great deal of humor or imagination.

I noticed that he looked at me from time to time as though trying to size me up. I wanted to say that it was the Ovambos who were on trial and not I, but obviously he was having to weigh his decision carefully before making it. I explained what we wanted. We pointed out to him that there had been no time to get lengthy interviews with the men. We assured him that the church would be responsible for meeting the payment involved in the case as we felt that the men were victims of a corrupt system.

Our spirits were lifted at his comments. "This case should never have been brought against these men in the first place," he growled. "It just won't stand up in open court."

He agreed to take the case for us, said that he would ask for a postponement because he was handling another case at the moment and would need time to prepare his brief. He added that there would be no problems. He had the air of a football player who has surveyed the ranks of the opposition, tensed his muscles, and readied himself to burst through their ranks. "I'll tell the prosecutor that unless he drops the charges, I'll make him look stupid in court."

We left that office as reassured as we had ever felt in our seven years in Namibia. Though O'Linn kept us at a distance, always maintaining a professional attitude towards us, we were inspired by his professionalism. This, in turn, was conveyed to the prisoners, who arrived at the Magistrate's Court each day singing hymns.

As I looked across the courtroom at the accused standing there in various positions by the side wall, the first thing that struck me was their poverty. Some came in coveralls which were buttonless down to their stomachs. Others wore rubber boots such as are issued to men who work in the local slaughter houses. One young boy of about eighteen wore an old pair of tennis shoes, the hand-me-down of some white employer. Many were without socks. One glance at these men should have revealed why the strike had happened.

I have sat and watched Africans many times in similar courts in South Africa. It is a painful experience. Usually, they are part of the million blacks a year who are tried under the Pass Laws. They stand bewildered, look very frightened, and grip the edge of the dock or nervously lick their lips. Looking on such men on these occasions, I used to remember cattle rounded up for slaughter in the slaughter houses in my home town. There was nothing of that look about the black strikers in that Windhoek courtroom. Fire blazed in their eyes. They were clearly not helpless souls standing alone and naked facing white man's laws and mute with fear and guilt. It was South Africa and her exploitative laws which were being judged, and though Magistrate Kriel may not have fully comprehended the truth, it was manifestly reflected in the bearing of these men, in their answers, and in their obvious solidarity. Separated from them by a wooden barrier, I sat and watched them and felt proud and humble.

The whole balance of the courtroom procedure was swung from defense to attack the moment O'Linn stepped into action. The first thing he asked for was a seat for the twelve accused: "My clients have a right to be comfortable as this trial proceeds."

Two benches were immediately brought in, and the men were seated on them. O'Linn then demanded that they be provided with paper and pencils so that they could take down notes or make memos to pass to their counsel as the trial progressed.

Referring to the cards around the men's necks, he asked the magistrate that these be removed and that the accused be referred to by their names. Magistrate Kriel refused this request, perhaps feeling that he had already been criticized too much in the handling of the trial.

O'Linn asked for and got a postponement in order to prepare his brief, even though the prosecutor said that he was due to take up the post of magistrate in Rehoboth and delay here would cause inconvenience to himself and to his future colleagues.

Looking at those powerful shoulders leaning forward as though pushing against some invisible object, I saw Brian O'Linn as a last bastion of hope for men whose cause previously had seemed so hopeless. Prosecutor Jaquire immediately reacted to O'Linn's presence in court, became unsure, groped for words, often let points slip by without rebuttal. At the beginning he seemed menacing as he gathered his academic robe around him, rising to establish a point. O'Linn never used his robes and had an untidiness about him as he hunched his shoulders and seemed to weave his body from the accused to the judge, gesturing with his hands and blocking arguments which seemed trivial to him. His presence transformed the accused as they listened to his Afrikaans and watched his face and gestures fixedly. They clearly sensed that O'Linn was fighting for them and they knew that hope had reappeared in that courtroom.

Four state witnesses had spoken before legal aid was granted the accused on 25 January, at noon. After the recess, Warrant Officer E. S. Laubscher was brought in to give evidence. He was described as a "finger print expert and police photographer." Under cross examination from O'Linn, he admitted that the photographs of the accused had been taken when they were held in custody in the local gaol. There were no photographs to link the men with the scene of the strike. The pictures of the "mob" in the compound were no more revealing. He thought he could perhaps recognize one or two of the accused, but he wasn't absolutely sure. His evidence collapsed under O'Linn's cross examination.

Perhaps one of the saddest witnesses was an Ovambo, Gideon William. He looked frightened and strained when he entered the witness box to give evidence against his own people. He never looked at his comrades on the opposite side of the court, spoke in a near whisper and had to have questions repeated to him. He said that he had seen a poster in the compound on the 7th of December and handed it to the police.

A brief statement followed by a member of the Security Police, one Daniel Olwagen, who reported that he had gone to the compound and found a note stuck to a telephone pole there, "written in Ovambo," and twenty Ovambos were round the pole reading what the note said.

After the twelve accused had been arrested, he had found notebooks on "Accused Number 12" (Leonard Nghipandula) with certain names in them. The accused also had in his possession a copy of the Universal Declaration of Human Rights. He also found the document of "a certain church."

He had found a cowboy book on the person of "Accused Number 1" (Harold Sam) on the back of which were the words "Organisation SWAPO Education." Inside this book were written a number of names.

Olwagen identified three of the accused as some of the main speakers who had addressed the massive crowd just outside the compound a few hours before the strike materialized.

Magistrate Kriel then addressed the accused, and impartiality was swept aside. The influence of the Security Police and their near-infallible status as being above the law and beyond suspicion immediately revealed itself. Kriel said that bail would be refused the thirteen because the police had found "certain documents" in which the accused were mentioned; a proper translator had to be found to make a "thorough" translation of these documents, and, he added, "Industries and other businesses are hit by the strike action and the state will use this as part of the evidence . . . in the pending trial." He went on to say, "Many of those trapped in the Ovambo compound in Katutura will be called to testify. The Court realizes the freedom of the individual and does not intend to break this meaning or interpretation. Justice must prevail and bail is refused so that the accused cannot make contact with the state witnesses."

"Accused Number 11" (Matupang Shimuefeleni) complained that he had been assaulted by the police. The Magistrate asked the prosecutor to "Take note of this complaint," and that, if necessary, "an investigation should be carried out."

A brother of Harold Sam, the law student, was brought forward, and he told the court that he had "cautioned Sam several times about his profligacy," telling him that he would get in trouble if he did not find work. The accused were then held in custody until 12 January.

The intervening period was one of marked uncertainty. The press was clearly trying to implicate the Anglican Church in some sort of massive conspiracy to undermine peace and order, and somehow to work up the "Natives" ("the part of certain clerics should not be overlooked"). Basically, this was a failure on their part to credit the Ovambo people with the capacity to organize and pull off a strike which had caused such devastation to white property and to white morale. The newspaper reporters, often taking their lead from the Security Police and, on their own admission, clearing their stories with these men before publishing them, heavy-handedly emphasized the part the Church was playing in hosting Alex Lyon and Bill Booth, and the fact that one of the accused had a certain Church document on his person (this document was never identified by the Court or the Press).

Every attempt was made to divert public attention from the bona fide grievances of the strikers, and a witch hunt started in which the church leaders and missionaries were to be dubbed agitators.

O'Linn caused the greatest sensation of all in cross-examining a witness called Frans Voigts. Voigts worked for a firm called Pupkewitz, which ran a sub-agency for Volvo cars and sold farming equipment and building materials. "Accused Number 8," Lazerus Shikango, a twenty-one-year-old Ovambo, who had had five years' education, was in his employ.

Voigts was shown a contract form, marked with Shikango's thumbprint, and was asked to identify it and also to identify the accused, which he did. All this was carried out in a matter-of-fact way by O'Linn.

"Could you tell the court how much the accused was paid?" Voigts was asked.

"One rand, fifty-four cents a week," he replied (U.S. $2.15). There was a cry of astonishment from the black section of the court, and Magistrate Kriel reacted angrily saying he would clear the court if people on that side interrupted or made comments on the proceedings.

O'Linn waited for the comments of the courtroom to subside and put the question again, apologizing for his bad hearing.

"How much did you say you paid him?"

To which the same reply was given, "One rand, fifty-four cents a week."

"Did you ask him what his qualifications were?"

"No."

"Did you ask him whether he had a wife or family to support?"

"No."

"Did you ask him what he was paid in his previous job?"

"No."

"Why not?"

"I didn't think it mattered," came the bland reply.

The court was seething with anger. Blacks on the benches opposite were passing back the information to the crowded corridors outside, where people could not hear the proceedings.

In that one piece of interviewing, O'Linn had revealed the hardcore reasons behind the strike, the sheer callous indifference of the whites to their labor force. "I didn't think it mattered" was so typical of what lay behind whites' attitudes to black people.

In drawing out his witness, O'Linn had received the following information from Voigts: Shikango was paid twenty-six and a half

South African cents a shift, which was a whole day's work. After working for Pupkewitz for one hundred and fifty-five shifts, he would receive a slight increase in pay. As it was, he worked as a general laborer putting in forty-five hours a week.

Every newspaper in South Africa took up this point, and the curtain of silence which had covered Namibia was lifted, showing to the outside world that conditions for migrant laborers there were decidedly worse than anywhere else in the Republic of South Africa.

One of the directors of the firm, Harold Pupkewitz, phoned me at my home that evening. He was deeply distressed, he told me, at what had transpired in the court that afternoon. He further explained that the white foreman was not empowered to speak as he had done and that Voigts had done the company a great deal of harm by what he had said. He wanted Judge Booth to go away with the right impressions.

"Was what he said then inaccurate, Mr. Pupkewitz?" I asked him. "Do you, in fact, pay your black employees more than that figure? I will be happy to give Judge Booth the correct figures."

He hesitated and said, "I don't wish to white-wash the situation, but I am not the only employer in this territory who pays the basic rate as laid down by the authorities."

I pointed out that this was the minimum rate, and that there was no maximum rate.

He told me that, of course, he paid his "houseboys" several times that figure, but for "raw, untrained labor" he couldn't offer the same amount. He then asked me to be fair to him and said that although that was the basic wage, and he did not wish to deny it, yet the African could earn much more than that with overtime.

Again, I asked for figures, and he replied that with three hours overtime a day, an African could earn three rand a week (U.S. $4.20).

"Mr. Pupkewitz," I said, "you come from a race which has been persecuted and exploited throughout its history. I am ashamed for you. Having been oppressed yourself, I cannot believe that you could have learned nothing from the experience. I'll pass your message on to Judge Booth." Quietly, I put down the telephone.

Momentarily, throughout the territory, there was a certain swing in white opinion as people admitted that these wages were outrageously low. The fact that Mr. Pupkewitz had telephoned me was significant in itself; such an attempt at self-justification had never before been made to me in the whole time I was in Namibia. A number of whites who paid slightly higher wages were conspicuously self-righteous. But the overwhelming majority were silent about how much they paid their "boy" or "girl." There were always excuses appealing to how much they were given in old clothes or to the cost of the room they slept in.

A manifesto of the strikers was found in the possession of Leonard Nghipandula, and an African named Petrus Omakali was brought in from the Bantu Education Department to translate the contents into Afrikaans. The first document exhibited was a letter written to the compound from Walvis Bay. "We are having trouble with the white man, Jannie de Wet, who says that we want to be on contract. But we must talk about ending this system. . . ."

The second letter, translated, said that blacks should come to an agreement. They were informed that there would be a meeting outside the compound on 11 December, starting at 2:00 p.m., and that all were invited.

The third letter said the following: "You have all heard what our people are doing and have said in Walvis Bay, Oranjemund, and Tsumeb. When are we going to be able to talk to each other? We must try and alleviate the suppression of our friends in slavery under the contract labor system. Write to me. We are going to break down the gates in the compound and we will do the same to the office in the perimeter."

Another letter said: "The contract system must be ended now, and we command our friends not to go to work on Monday. Everybody—the cook, the bus driver—must not go and work. Nobody must work, and those who do will be punished. We must decide now to break this contract labor system by not working. The white men's wives accompany them when they go away for a month. We stay away for longer than twelve months and our families' lives are ruined and our wives stay behind. M.C. Botha says we want the contract labor system ourselves. We do not want it anymore. We want to be able to move and work in Namibia as we please. We want to be seen as people and not as slaves. We must have rights to come and go as we please."

The heat in the crowded courtroom was intense. Though the door was open and an occasional gust of wind came through the open door, for the most part the atmosphere inside the courtroom itself was stuffy and oppressive. The Security Police came and went, often gathering in a small group outside. They had a swagger and a triumphal look about them. The court interpreter stood next to where the Africans were seated and often assumed an aggressive air as he put questions to the accused, translated from the Afrikaans of the lawyer.

The questioning droned on: Magistrate Kriel's pen scratched away, as he kept his head down, shoulders hunched over the vast leather-backed court record book, hardly ever looking at the accused men.

"Who told you to strike?" the interpreter passed on the question to the African accused.

"God did!" came back the answer.

Kriel's head rocketed back on his shoulders and he blinked with astonishment.

The next day, the headlines of the newspaper read: "Man said God spoke to him in Compound."

Chapter Fifteen

Judge Booth

William Booth, the American jurist, hit the headlines from the moment he flew into Windhoek's Ondekaremba Airport. A black man himself, he was by background and experience used to the massive tension which had built up around us. He is a dedicated Episcopalian, a vestryman of Trinity Church, Wall Street, he had been an active campaigner for the Civil Rights cause in the states and, above all else, he was an experienced and highly qualified judge. His coming evidently alarmed everyone from Magistrate Kriel to the Security Police, who watched him closely night and day. A more genial, lighthearted and happy person one could hardly hope to meet. Bill Booth wisecracked, laughed, joked, poked fun, cajoled, and teased his way around Windhoek like a fencing master toying with a novice; yet underneath the playful asides, here was a man sensitive to the suffering he saw all around him. He was a model of gentlemanliness, and before he left, he even found time to thank Magistrate Kriel for the courtesies which had been shown him. Yet, he was fearless and shouldered up to his tough assignment with complete candor.

The press asked for a conference with him, and this was given over drinks in my home. It was obvious from the start that the local reporters found Booth intriguing. For the first time in their lives, they were meeting an educated, sophisticated black who was perfectly composed and who dealt with their questions in a masterly fashion, but who turned the tables on them by proceeding to interview them.

The South African Press Association representative asked him if he had dined in one of our hotels and if he had been politely received. Booth replied to both in the affirmative. A smug look spread over the questioner's face, and someone commented, "We are not as bad as we are painted."

Though it was Bill Booth's interview, I could not allow such a remark to pass unchallenged and said, "You know very well, Mr.

Davies, that if Justice Booth were a national from this country and a black, the nearest he would get to the dining room of the Grand Hotel would be the kitchen, unless he were waiting on table suitably uniformed."

Bill's influence on my own family at this time will never be forgotten. He has a young grandchild whom he adores and whom he obviously missed. My youngest daughter, Catherine, was home during his visit, and they became close friends. On Valentine's Day, she shyly set at his place at the table a card she had made for him that day at school. He loved it, and when he left, he presented Catherine with a transistor radio which was the envy of the rest of the family, who had been away at school during his visit.

For Mary and me, his coming into our home was a tonic. Surrounded by an increasing tide of hate and suspicion, with friends and church people moving away from us, it was splendid to have the loving support, no matter how fleetingly, of a man who had suffered more, had conquered, and was so devoid of hate and meanness. What he did in bringing hope and courage to the hearts of Africans, he certainly did for us too.

He told us of an experience in the Deep South of the States when he had demonstrated with a group of blacks and marched on the home of the local mayor to tack on his door a list of civil liberties which were being infringed upon as far as the blacks in the community were concerned. Bill was marching at the front of the crowd when they came to a dip in the road where the local police blocked their path, carbines in hand. Called on to stop, the marchers momentarily did so, but those at the back began pushing, so that those in front were forced into the ranks of the police and thought they were near to death. The commanding officer accidentally dropped a shell from his cartridge case and, instead of bending down for it, began to feel for it in the dust with the toe of his shoe. Booth laughed, slapped his knee and said, "Man, I knew if I was scared to death in that front rank that night, I wasn't the only one." The crowd surged forward, the police ranks broke as if by magic, and a sort of Red Sea happening occurred in which the people passed through to the other side.

This story and several more like it put our problem in its world context. We were not the only community who had to suffer for the sake of righteousness, nor would we be the last. Booth saved us from fear by showing us that it is the most natural thing to feel at such moments, but has to be overcome. He showed us his poise by his very presence among us and also by his indestructible sense of humor.

Racism is so ludicrous and so often can best be dealt with by laughing at it.

Mary and I were under considerable strain at this point, knowing that sooner or later a way would be found of removing us altogether. Our phone rang and insane laughter would crackle through the wires, bells would jangle, or the person at the other end would just breathe hard into the phone. All this sounds insignificant enough, and most often we dismissed it as the work of cranks, though it was certainly the intention of the people doing it to harass and worry us. During Booth's visit, we had a phone call every night exactly at 6:30. The man had a thick Afrikaans accent and used foul language, always beginning his diatribe by asking, "Is the Communist pig in?" One evening, Mary beat me to the phone, anticipated the identity of the caller, and before he could begin his onslaught, said in a voice dripping with sweetness, "This is the wife of the Communist pig." He hung up routed. Booth had taught us to face violence with a smile.

Bill Booth achieved what no white could have done. He slept the night in an African location, and he went into the African compound at Katutura, saw where the men were housed, and what they ate. This experience shattered him. The next day, the local Afrikaans newspaper reacted in a typical manner to his comments about the food. In so doing, they revealed the total unwillingness of whites to see even the most glaring evils in their system. Booth had complained that the food was served to the Africans on a shovel, that their ration of meat was largely fat, and that it was often only a hunk of bone with no meat on it at all. The men had told him that they would not serve such food as that to their dogs in Ovamboland. Here was a chance for the editor of a government newspaper to admit that things in the contract labor system were wrong and cry out for reform. Instead, he wrote a nasty, sneering attack on Judge Booth, asking if in America such an advanced technological state had been reached that cattle were produced without bones.

Bill Booth held two meetings in Katutura. Upon only a half-hour notice, the word spread like wildfire that the American judge was going to speak, and over twelve hundred black people packed the Lutheran church which was set aside for him. Using two interpreters, he spoke for well over three hours. The people would have kept him there all night. As he looked up from the rostrum, he could see the Security Police standing at every exit to hear what he was saying to the people. A roar of laughter went up from the crowd when he cordially invited one officer to sit up in the front row, where he could have a better view. His offer was declined. What Booth could not see from where he was standing, but realized when he left the building, was that the whole place was surrounded by armored police cars.

I stood at the back listening for a few moments to part of his address.

" 'What can you do about racialism in South West Africa?' a questioner asks me, 'What can you do?' Well, I'll tell you." Booth was hoarse now and looking hot and tired. He'd been hard at it all day and it was almost eleven at night. "I'll tell you what you can do: you've got to put your body where your principles are . . . you can always say no. Say it."

"Say no to slavery; say no to serfdom; say no to contract labor; say no to expressions like 'boy' and 'girl'; say no; say no." I looked from Booth's face to where the police stood with their guns at the ready.

What is it that really fightens them about men like Booth? He'd be gone in a few days; he had no guns; he couldn't lead a resistance movement. Why were they so scared? Words of T.S. Eliot flitted across my mind: "Human kind cannot bear too much reality." They were terrified of him because he spoke the truth and they could not bear to face it. That is why they were harassing him, accusing him of this and that, and wanting to remove him physically out of that location. "You can say NO." The blacks listened in Namibia that day, and they are still saying it now.

The meeting finished and Bill Booth was surrounded by dozens of Africans; they mobbed him, pressing forward just to touch his hand, to be able to boast to their children and grandchildren that they had once been in the presence of a good and a brave man. Bill, though obviously strained and tired, knew what he had to do and delighted in being so warmly welcomed and loved by the gathered throng. As he stood there, dripping wet with sweat and near to exhaustion, I quietly walked out of the vast, barn-like church, climbed into my car and drove home, welcoming the cool evening air that poured in through the open windows of my car. I went straight to bed.

About one o'clock in the morning, Fr. Stephen Hayes came stumbling into my bedroom. We rarely locked doors in our home, and so he was able to enter quite freely. He made his presence noticed only when he stumbled over a small table in the hall outside the bedroom. Mary went to see who it was before I was fully awake, and she returned looking frightened and tense. "Bill Booth has been taken by the police in Katutura. They think he's been put in prison."

I leaped from my bed, now fully awake. Steve was standing by that same table assuming a quiet air. He spoke without emotion, though he was obviously deeply disturbed.

He had made all the arrangements for the judge's meeting in Katutura, had taken him to the meeting and introduced him to the leading members of the Herero community, and was to have brought him back. After the meeting, the judge was to have gone to the house of Chief Kapuuo for further discussion, because well over three hundred people—the chief's advisors, headmen, local political figures—wanted to meet the judge privately. Worn out though he was, Bill Booth had agreed to talk with each of them and had left the church with a party of Hereros, Father Steve following in a second group.

When they got outside the church, confusion reigned. The Secret Police surrounded them and Booth was pushed into a car, so that Steve lost all contact with him. After searching the Location fruitlessly for over an hour, he had returned to fetch me, as he feared that the judge had been arrested by the police and taken into custody.

In our two cars, we raced through the deserted streets to the Location. I had slipped into a white cassock and a pair of open-toed sandals. The Hereros who were with Steve suggested that we make another turn by the home of Chief Kapuuo first. This we did. I leaped out of the car and raced up the steps. Sitting on a bed in the corner with a paraffin lamp giving a warm glow sat Judge Booth calmly writing postcards home to his wife and little granddaughter. He brushed aside our inquiries and treated the evening's drama as light entertainment telling us that he had enjoyed it all immensely.

As soon as he had left the church, the Hereros accompanying him realized that the Secret Police would follow and hound them, so they quickly pushed him into a van, opened the driver's door at the other side, dragged him right through the first vehicle into the second which was parked next to it. The two cars set off at the same time, followed by a whole group of waiting police vehicles, and all roared through the darkened streets of the Location. The two cars separated at the end of a narrow street and Booth's van was driven at breakneck speed into the garden of a corner house. He was taken through the garden, down some steps, then along a darkened street where another truck was awaiting him; off they went in a totally different direction. He said that cars were flashing by in all directions, making the place into a miniature Indianapolis Speedway. Booth was quietly deposited at his destination—Chief Kapuuo's house—while the Security Police were chasing a van out onto the Okahandja road, some fifty-five miles north of Windhoek.

When I entered the room, Bill Booth greeted me with a calm and serenity as though he were a monk contemplating in his cell. I left him with Chief Kapuuo to spend the night with his new-found friends who were honored to have him in their community, the first American ever to have slept the night in an African location in Namibia.

Each day after the court sessions, Bill and I stopped and chatted with hundreds of Africans who had come to watch the trial. Among them were messengers from local banks and American-owned mining firms. Newspaper vendors, urchins, old men from the country in wide sombrero-style hats—all stood and conversed with local black businessmen and political figures from Windhoek. Namas spoke to Hereros, Ovambos chatted away with Damaras as they went over the morning's or afternoon's events. What was clear to all was the friendly and open way they greeted us, always responding to the proffered handshake of the judge and gathering around him with great affection and warmth.

One lunchtime, as I was waiting to drive him home to lunch, a young man dressed in very shabby clothes came up to the judge and pressed ten cents (US 14¢) into his hand. The judge looked at the coin, shaken.

"What's this for?" he asked in astonishment. The young man smiled back and said, "For bread, Judge, for bread." All this in heavily accented English. "But I don't need it. I have enough for bread," the judge replied not knowing what to do.

The African replied: "Take it. Use it for our brothers in America."

I watched the whole event and then walked with the judge to the car. "Did you see what that guy did?" he said. "He gave me ten cents. He couldn't afford that. Why, he needs that for his own dinner. He gave it to me. . . ."

I drove on and said, "That's a sign that you are his brother, his friend; that gift is a token of love and kinship. He wanted you to have it to show you what he felt about you and your coming here."

In the mirror, I could see tears streaming down the judge's face. We drove home in silence.

On the last afternoon of his stay, he sat as usual in court next to Dave and Steve at a table which had been specially set aside for him. When the magistrate had adjourned the court for the afternoon, Bill stood up and asked if he could be allowed to address the court. Kriel was startled. I don't think he knew what to expect or how to handle the situation. He sat tense and nervous, looking at Bill with wide eyes.

"Before returning to the United States of America, I would like to address the court, through you, Sir, and to thank you for the courtesies which you have personally extended to me as I have been an observer here. I shall return and make my report to the International Commission of Jurists, on whose behalf I have appeared here. I want you to know before I go that I am grateful for the provision of a special table set aside for me which has allowed me to follow the proceedings more closely than otherwise would have been possible from the body of the court. Thank you for this courtesy."

As I watched Bill Booth, the dignity of the man overstrode the pettiness and hate that surrounded the whole trial proceedings. The Afrikaans press had put out the usual smear campaign against him: America was told to put her own house in order and to keep her nose out of things which did not concern her, and Booth was often reminded to go back to Watts or the Deep South and not to meddle in matters which were of no concern to him.

The South Africans bombarded the American Embassy in Cape Town with protests that here was a distinguished visitor who, once allowed into the country by the goodwill of the South African government, was abusing his accredited status as an impartial observer and making political statements and addressing public meetings. Accordingly, the American Embassy phoned him at my office to ask for an explanation and to rebuke him. I have always considered this a failure to stand up to South Africa. Booth had committed no breach of the law; no conditions had been laid down for him to observe when he came into the country. In the addresses he gave, and in the contacts he made, he neither preached insurrection nor violated any code of etiquette which his profession demands. He did, however, refuse to be straight-jacketed and muzzled by the regime itself. Justice Booth was not the only distinguished visitor who came to Windhoek and used the contacts and facilities of our church, but he was one of the few who refused to hide behind a cloak of silence. When asked, he gave his opinions without fear or favor. I believe that even those who were hostile to him at least responded to him as a man. They knew where they stood with him, knew what he thought; he listened to their point of view and gave honest, straightforward answers in return. It was obvious that they differed, but they did not respect him any the less for that. His comments were reported every day in the Windhoek newspapers, and yet ordinary private citizens from the white community flocked to meet him and were cordial.

Where American Embassy officials erred, as do so many others when dealing with South Africa, was in being intimidated by one of the toughest regimes in the world. Diplomats appear to be just plain scared. When the American Ambassador went grouse shooting on Robben Island and used black convicts to beat the bushes for himself and his hosts, the Nationalist Party ministers, no protests were forthcoming from the American Embassy. Yet, when a man like Booth enters the country and is criticized by the South African government, the American Embassy officials become rattled, demand caution, and want an explanation. Any wonder that blacks in Namibia laugh and ask, "Are America and Britain afraid of Mr. Vorster?"

Much is spoken today in America and Britain about the need to maintain contact with South Africa and not allow her to be isolated in a laager of her own devising. It is said that such contacts as are possible through governments, members of industry and trade, student exchanges, tourism, and sport—these will work for peaceful change from within. I find this all just so much talk when men like Booth are challenged by their own embassies for speaking their minds openly about apartheid. African opinion in Namibia sees the West's so-called "diplomacy" as a hollow sham, understands our ambivalence as proceeding from a desire to cling on at all costs to our massive profits, and looks with contempt at our seeming inability to take a strong line against the racism which underlies the greater part of South Africa's constitution and legislation. South Africa is a mirror of Western diplomacy. Booth is one of the few ambassadors from his country who could look into that mirror and honestly say, "I did not compromise either my moral principles or those my country holds sacred."

Here are some extracts from the report he made in March, 1972, for the International Commission of Jurists on his visit to the trial in Windhoek:

> The court-room procedure was most proper. The magistrate, prosecutor, and defense counsel were all diligent and fair in their various efforts.
>
> Defense counsel were able to procure a bench for the accused and note paper for them as well. The trial was recorded on dictaphone belts. Daily copy was made available to me. My host, Bishop Colin Winter, Bishop of the Anglican Diocese of Namibia, made a staff assistant available for translation. There were, however, differences in procedure that struck me as a jurist and long-time defense counsel.
>
> First, the accused were wearing on their clothing large numbers making identification (by number) easy but unreliable. Second, the advocates rarely objected to the introduction of opinion evidence and hearsay explaining that they would reserve objection on this until the closing argument. Third, the court-room audience was divided racially, and the overcrowding (150 black people packed into a space reserved for 40-50 persons while about 15-20 whites sat in a similar-size space) one day

caused the afternoon detention of several black Namibians by the magistrate. Since the accused spoke several, varied tribal languages and the trial was in Afrikaans, the interpreter throughout the trial was not well able to convey to them all the gist of the testimony. Finally, all the accused but one are held without bail. Accused Number One, Mr. Harold Sam, has been freed on R200 bail, but must report to the police twice daily.

These are the men who are charged with causing 15,000 Namibians to strike on 13 December, 1971. In addition to the testimony of an informer, the other evidence of *inciting* the strike consisted merely of testimony that one or two of the accused stood on an oil drum inside the compound and said something to the workers in their tribal language—the police witness gave the opinion that the workers were told to strike! The evidence of *intimidation* consisted of testimony by the police that some of the accused had sticks, about three feet long and the size of a broom handle in circumference and that with these sticks being used in a jousting position, they held back about 1,500 men inside the compound. This, together with testimony that one man knocked a piece of bread out of a worker's hand, is the total evidence of intimidation.

After a couple of days of testimony, the prosecutor withdrew the third charge since police witnesses all testified that they had kept all workers inside the compound in accordance with their orders. Thus, the accused *could* not carry out their labor contracts and so the prosecution announced that no further evidence would be offered on the charge of contract breaking.

Something must be said of the background of the country in which the trial took place. In the U.S.A., where unions have developed to such sophistication that it is not even considered anti-social to strike, it must be difficult to consider a country where such actions may be criminal. However, one must realize that South West Africa (Namibia) is a country where the mere existence of several black tribes has been used to keep disunity among the black population. That this is a country where there is constant police surveillance of black movement; that black "informers" are paid to inform on other black people; that the press twists all news to suit its own ends; that a man can be classified as "Communist" because he is "active in America in Civil Rights"—to quote a South West African Dutch Reformed pastor about me.

To illustrate the official attempt to keep all tribes dis-united, let me relate one of my visits to the Ovambo compound. The compound is the place where workers are put up by their employers while in town under labour contract. The employers pay for the housing and feeding of the workers. The cost runs to about R12 a month, of which it was estimated by the court that food cost is about 20¢ per day for each worker. The men are housed in barracks-type buildings with only a concrete locker-type bed for each man. The kitchen is quite unsanitary with flies all over the place and cats chasing each other throughout the place. The food is served through openings in a wire fence separating the cooking area from the dining area. Porridge is slapped in a bowl with a shovel, a conglomeration cf liquefied vegetables is poured over the porridge and a piece of bread is also given to each man. For meat, a hunk of bone is given on which there is a slight bit of beef. When I noted this at a press conference, it was reported in the local newspaper. Later, a letter to the editor inquired if I thought research could develop boneless cattle. It is local knowledge, though, that at stores there one can buy meat for whites, meat for blacks, and meat for dogs, all in descending quality. The men also get free beer at all times. This is a specially-prepared brew which tastes not at all like our beer. It is said to be a major source of their protein. These workers come from far-off (500 miles) Ovamboland where their families must remain while the men are at work. There is no conjugal living in the compound. The area used is a fenced-off part of the black township, Katutura, six miles out of Windhoek. This township is the area designated for all black people to reside in. Interestingly, by the way, the "Coloured township" is on the exact opposite end of Windhoek!

Inside the compound, I asked our official guide why the Ovambos were kept separated from the rest of the Katutura township and, particularly, separated from the Damara workers, who are kept in hostels on the far side of Katutura. He said that if they were permitted to live together, they would naturally fight each other to the death! Later, representatives of all the black tribes heatedly denied this allegation, pointing out that Damaras, Ovambos, Hereros, and all other tribes do live together in peace and harmony in the township. I couldn't help reminding myself how white America has always driven wedges in the black community by separating the "Field boys" from the "House boys," and now by separating dark from light Negroes, northern from southern Negroes, and West Indian from American Negroes! I thought, too, how convenient to make a white minority superior by lumping together under the category "white" the warring Irish, German, French, English—there, as here, creating a "majority" which in fact does not exist.

Two more observations on background should be noted: surveillance and the low base pay of black workers. At the airport, we noted a non-newsman snapping pictures of me. He showed up at many places where I happened to be throughout the trip, even in the courtroom. No newsman knew him, so it was concluded that he was working for the Secret Police. When I visited the people of Katutura, and was driven to various homes of black people, we were always followed by car and on foot. When I stayed overnight at the Katutura home of the Chief of the Hereros, Clemens Kapuuo, police in unmarked cars followed us and circled the house all night. There were police (black) in all my audiences in the churches and police (white) were always seen at the open church doors during my speeches.

The main impression I gained from the people of Katutura is

their blind faith in the United Nations. They believe that the U.N. Declaration of Human Rights is self-fulfilling, that the Security Council is all powerful and that the resolution adopted at Addis Ababa will end the reign of South Africa over Namibia. Thus, they looked to the proposed visit of Secretary-General Waldheim with great anticipation. I felt compelled to be realistic in my discussions with them. Being careful to avoid at all costs "advising," I did nevertheless suggest that they ought to prepare alternatives to United Nations action. I tried to inform them that the U.N. documents were meaningless unless the Great Powers used their resources to gird these up.

The shortness of my stay in Namibia provides little evidence for far-reaching conclusions. But some of the flavor of the South African way of life cannot but rub off. The blind faith of the black Namibian in the United Nations must head the list in this respect. Only time will tell, of course, if that faith is earned.

Next, the fear of the white population is strongly expressed. There is fear of losing their good life if the black majority ever gains strength. There is also the ever expressed fear of the possibility of a Communist take-over of the African continent with all the violence and instability that can be augured up by such a takeover.

Finally, there is the expressed (by whites) idea that things are changing for the good of the black man. When a representative of the American Embassy called me to warn that the government felt I was "interfering" in the trial instead of observing, he said that any such interference might upset the delicate efforts being made at progress for the black South African. By the way, all persons on the scene in Windhoek denied the allegations of interference by me. The sadness is that the American Embassy should deign to give credence to them and should walk on eggs for fear of crushing the so-called progressiveness of the South African government.

It is my firm belief, though, that the human indignities imposed on so many by so few cannot but arouse the many sooner now than before since there is some communication between them and the outside world.

At the press interview for Justice Booth held in my home, I indicated to the Afrikaans reporter present that the Anglican Church, because it felt the demands of the strikers to be just, believed in the right of every person to legal representation when brought to trial, and wished to assert its solidarity with the workers, would meet all legal expenses of the accused strike leaders out of our church funds and would appeal to people of good will throughout the world to contribute.

The newspaper carried banner headlines to this effect, and a smear campaign which had been going on for some time was intensified. This was all that the state needed to prepare the way for my deportation.

Chapter Sixteen

Violence and Nonviolence

"Preach the Bishop must; not permitting himself to be silenced by merely human fears or temporal considerations; not watering down his message for the sake of spurious peace or loss of friendship with any worldly authority, or possibility of being misinterpreted by wicked men. . . ."

Bishop Donal Lamont, the Roman Catholic Bishop of Umtali, spoke these words in 1959. Bishop Lamont is a strong Christian leader who has met the crisis the church is facing in Southern Africa and is one of the few Christian leaders honestly to have attempted to face that situation in the light of the gospel. Lamont's words have a sting to them and an honesty which ought to cause the church to emerge from her holes in Southern Africa and really begin to live by the gospel and not by expediency. Lamont wrote:

> The hour is not far off when the Church may have to take such a firm stand, dissociating herself from the action of the civil authority so that she maintains her credibility and is faithful. It may mean the loss of material assets, the closing of institutions, the deportation or imprisonment of spokesmen, but the Church will have to be true to its mission.
>
> That is what people tend to forget: the Church has a mission, not merely a message. It has both, of course, but unless the message is not words only, unless the message of doing unto all men as they would be done unto themselves is the aim and the concrete achievement of the mission, the whole thing is a farce.

When the Namibian strike occurred, I was on holiday with my family and heard the news broadcast as we sat gazing out over the placid waters of the Indian Ocean at Gordons Bay. Though I remained with my family until the end of my vacation, I kept in regular contact with Dave de Beer in Windhoek. The utterances of the Prime Minister and others made it clear that South Africa was looking for scapegoats who could be blamed, thus diverting public attention away from the real causes of the strike. In previous meetings with my senior clergy, which were held about four times a year, we had discussed the deteriorating situation in Ovamboland. The feeling of both the black and white priests who advised me was that I should keep away from Ovamboland at all costs; otherwise, the government would seize the opportunity to remove me or act against me in some other way. Reports by the South African government alluded to the work of "certain missionaries" who were provoking the African people.

Pastor Hans Ludwig Althaus, a German youth pastor of the Evangelical Lutheran Church, was served with a deportation notice on 2 December, 1971. He had been in the country only since the middle of 1970, and the news came as a terrible shock to us, especially to those black students whom Hans Althaus had befriended. One of the black students at Augustineum College, where the pastor took services, said of his ministry: "It was always a pleasure to call at the pastor's home. One was not treated there on the basis of colour, nor was one offered a soft drink in a separate, cracked glass. One could drink from the household's glasses."

The government consistently denied that there was any church/state confrontation in South West Africa, yet all the while moved to prevent missionaries from continuing their work or to stop them from coming into the country. Earlier in 1971, Sister Irene Noh, one of the Evangelical Lutheran Church workers, had been refused a reentry visa to teach in the church's Bible School of Otjimbingwe. All this was in flagrant violation of the League of Nations mandate which South Africa had sworn to uphold as a sacred trust. Even more ironic to notice is that all those who believed in and strove for peaceful, nonviolent change were being systematically removed.

The state's power to remove clergy was an effective weapon, intimidating the churches into silence. A spokesman for the Lutheran Church in Windhoek at the time of Pastor Althaus' removal would say only that the Mission Board of the Church had "no comment to make." The same responses had been given by other churches in Namibia when missionaries were acted against. We were informed by the Roman Catholic hierarchy that the cancellation of a visa of a Roman priest was a "mistake." Well-informed circles in the Roman Church said he need not have been deported; it was some sort of "clerical error." The Administration had told them as much.

At the time of his deportation, Bishop Ambrose Reeves was told by leading Anglicans, rather reluctantly, that it would be better for the Diocese of Johannesburg if he resigned. When Bishop Mize was ordered to leave Damaraland, he was told by Anglican Church authorities to keep quiet for six months while back-door maneuvers were being attempted by the Anglican Church authorities with the state. The Church has always believed that it can achieve more without provoking the authorities by protests in the press. In actual fact, its record is dismal. Bishop Mize, like so many others, was thrown out anyway. In all these instances, the church was backing away from confrontation with the state, so much so that when a member of the Christian Institute staff in Cape Town was asked by a distinguished South African journalist what he thought of the church/state confrontation in South Africa, he replied, "What confrontation? The church is back-peddling so fast that the state can't catch her up."

In their short stay in Windhoek, the Althauses had become very dear friends to us all. They had three small, attractive children; their home was bright and cheery. Elizabeth Althaus was a perfect hostess, friendly and warm; and Hans Ludwig was full of humor, with a quick mind. Trained in the post-war school of German theology, he delighted in ecumenical contacts. He had won the hearts of his African students and it was obvious that the church could not allow such a man to leave without suffering great loss to itself.

At times like these, the local churches were desperately divided in their policy. At the farewell service called in Katutura to say good-bye to the Althauses, only a sprinkling of whites were present; yet the place was packed with blacks, even though it was hazardous for them to show their loyalty in this way. A new spirit was moving among them: they were not prepared to take the matter lying down. Here was the state unjustly removing a beloved pastor from their midst, and the blacks were determined not to let him go without protest. One always realizes that protests at such a time could only be tokens; but to have let the Althaus family go back to Germany without saying a word would have been cruel to them as fellow Christians and a denial of the gospel. How one yearned at such times for the church to take its stand on the gospel, for "when one member suffers, all suffer."

As I entered the Lutheran Church in Katutura, the atmosphere was tense. A reporter from *The Windhoek Advertiser* was present, and I looked around to see where the Secret Police were sitting. I had been to several services in this particular Lutheran church before, when the congregation was as relaxed as it would be in any other church at service time. This time it was different: the congregation was animated and the speeches of the young black pastors, which were made in the form of sermons, were passionate. In some instances, it was hard for the speakers to control their emotions. They loved this pastor and his family; they were tired and frustrated at seeing Christian missionaries—one after another—flung out. They wanted action.

I sat back and listened to Pastor Althaus deliver a controlled address on Ecclesiastes 3:2-9. He spoke in Afrikaans—a language he had mastered in six months—from a small portable lectern which was beneath the larger pulpit. Despite the old liturgical trappings, I knew we were listening to a new style of missionary. On my last visit to that church, I had listened to preachers speaking on Bible Sunday. The sermons were pietistic and remote from our struggles; I recalled one sermon which had consisted of a sentimental rendering of the conversion of a little girl of ten in England in the 1870s. The people squirmed with boredom in their pews and found no message in it for them in their day-to-day sufferings.

Hans Althaus's sermon was not in that category at all. I felt for the man and wondered if I could show the same degree of self-control when it came my turn to preach a farewell discourse to my own people. Though clearly moved by the occasion, his voice was measured as he expounded his text. "The time to keep quiet is gone," he said.

I looked from where he was speaking to watch the reactions of the older white missionaries, who sat still and quiet; their faces gave nothing away. I wondered what they felt about his candor.

His words caught me again: "Teachers have told me that no one can live at liberty here. This is a terrible thing resting on our shoulders—that we have a time to keep silent, but no time to speak. The young have told me many things. They have said that bridges should be built. I ask those of you in Windhoek to realize this ideal and to have dialogue with each other."

I thought of the increasing sense of frustration among the black youth. I then caught a glimpse of the face of the passionate black minister-in-training who had once called out to his white confreres, "Take away from us your sugar-coated Jesus." The older missionaries were shocked by what they felt was blasphemy; the younger ones were equally shocked at the blasphemy in the attitudes of whites.

Althaus's sermon was nearing its climax and I was to speak next. "Was the truth spoken too little? Did we all keep silent too long? Have we acted sufficiently for the good of the country? The gospel drove the church not to keep silent any longer." Althaus was done: pale, but smiling, he sat down.

I wondered what would await the Althaus family in Germany. Would the church authorities really understand the cost to them personally in the stand they had taken? Or would there be the usual friendly gestures, a mere token of concern which was really a veneer covering the deeper resentment that they had failed, blown it, let the side down? An act of violence had been committed against him, against his wife and family, against the blacks around the world. Would the church in Germany see that and protest against it? Or would they be lulled by South African propaganda into believing that he was guilty of some crime? Such is the effectiveness of South African propaganda that he and others like him were found guilty by the church back home. The reason is easy to see.

South Africa spends millions of dollars a year on propaganda in an attempt to sell to the world the delights and merits of the country. This campaign has taken on new approaches as in newspapers in America, Scandinavia, and Britain a counter offensive has been launched against the liberal forces in those countries which find apartheid revolting. Advertisements are placed there by local people who are in sympathy with South Africa's apartheid policies.

The Club of Ten is such an organization in Britain. It exists to discredit the World Council of Churches and any other organization which attempts to support the African cause. Half-page advertisements in the London *Times* and the *Guardian* are costly. The Club does not divulge its membership, and the whole group is shrouded in mystery. Its spokesman and one of its leaders, Judge Sparrow, is known for his right-wing views and his writings on the regime of the colonels in Greece, which he favored as well.

An advertisement appeared in the *Guardian* on 24 August, 1973, under the heading "No Dealings with Diabolos." Then followed an attack on the World Council of Churches in an attempt to discredit it as being more interested in violent revolution than in working for peaceful change through the improvement of wages paid to blacks. So, their argument continued:

> The Church of England as well as the Swiss Protestant Churches is beginning to have grave doubts concerning the support of the 'Programme to Combat Racism' organised by the World Council of Churches. Churchmen in Switzerland discovered to their dismay that the campaign was in the hands of people "who have lost all meaningful contact with Church life."

The advertisement went on to say:

> This profound and growing doubt is attributable to three main causes:

> 1. It is a fact that the victims of terrorism in South Africa are mainly innocent and peaceful Africans butchered in remote villages by terrorists indulging in murder orgies.
>
> 2. The instigation of the terrorist movement, its main finance, and its arming, comes almost exclusively from communist (and, by definition, atheist) sources.
>
> 3. The 'Programme to Combat Racism' seems more concerned with revolution than with raising the African standard of life and living.
>
> So what was originally supported under the title of Freedom Fighters has become something very different, a campaign from which peaceful Africans suffer most, their only crime being their reluctance to give sanctuary to murderers.

The advertisement then calls on the Archbishops of Canterbury and York to terminate support for the campaign at once on the grounds that it is un-Christian and indefensible.

There can be no better refutation of Judge Sparrow's ad than the words spoken by the SWAPO leader Herman ja Toivo at his trial. Namibian blacks have told me repeatedly that they do not wish to replace one foreign regime in their country with another. They want domination by neither South Africa nor Russia. What they want supremely is freedom, without which life is intolerable. For South Africa to claim that freedom fighters in Namibia are murderers is not only a lie, but seeks to divert world opinion from the facts.

Who is murdering whom in Namibia today? Were I to read out Judge Sparrow's words to Africans in Namibia and inform them that they are supposedly terrified of the SWAPO freedom fighters, they would greet that piece of specious propaganda with the same amount of ribald laughter as they do the outpourings from Pretoria.

I leave Herman ja Toivo to deal with the so-called Communist threat:

> Your Lordship emphasised in your judgement the fact that our arms come from communist countries, and also that words commonly used by communists were to be found in our documents. But, my Lord, in the documents produced by the State, there is another type of language. It appears even more than the former. Many documents finish up with an appeal to the Almighty to guide us in our struggle for freedom. It is the wish of the South African Government that we should be discredited in the Western world. That is why it calls our struggle a communist plot, but this will not be believed by the world. The world knows that we are not interested in ideologies. We feel that the world as a whole has a special responsibility towards us. This is because the land of our fathers was handed over to South Africa by a world body. It is a divided world, but it is a matter of hope

> for us that it at least agrees about one thing—that we are entitled to freedom and justice.

Three approaches to the matter of violence are discernible in Namibia at present. One view, taken by Africans as well as white churchmen, is that bloodshed is to be avoided at all costs. Instead there must be meaningful dialogue. Older blacks usually subscribe to this view. They are afraid of the consequences to their people of armed struggle. At the same time, I am bound to point out that they do not vigorously repudiate those of their people who have opted for the armed struggle; in fact, many tend to recognize this as a valid and honorable reaction to apartheid.

Second, the overwhelming majority of the blacks are silent on this whole issue and when questioned will make guarded remarks, afraid of being incriminated if they speak out for armed struggle. The reason is obvious: life imprisonment or death result from such talk in Namibia today.

Third, the overwhelming majority of students and young people honestly believe that they themselves will have to fight to obtain their freedom. They see no solutions being offered at the United Nations. They accuse the Western countries of connivance with South Africa in her policies. They regard their leaders at home who seek dialogue as being unable to achieve anything through it. In fact, the leaders are finding their position increasingly difficult to maintain, as there has been no effective dialogue at all with South Africa so far.

Africans who take the line that armed struggle is the only alternative now left to them are often ridiculed as being naive and stubbornly refusing to face the fact that South Africa is the most powerfully armed nation on the continent. These arguments are usually from whites who are trying at all costs to avert suffering to themselves. Whereas this attitude is understandable, it is vital for the outside world to appreciate the feeling of Namibian blacks on this subject as they themselves see it.

Their first feeling is that South Africa has got to be withstood. They are not, in the first instance, concerned about victory or even South Africa's overthrow. They do believe that there will be no dialogue or interest in their point of view until an armed struggle forces South Africa to the conference table. They are quick to point out that the whites in South Africa have never had it so good, and because this is so have never shown the least inclination to discuss with the blacks their sufferings. It is in the light of the need to remove this complacency that the armed struggle is seen as vital.

Western minds react to discussions on armed struggle pragmatically by pointing out that no coup d'etat has ever been successful unless certain conditions obtained. These include control of the army and the existence of a middle-class intelligentsia. They are quick to say that attempts under any other circumstances would be virtual suicide for the blacks engaged in the struggle.

The best thing I can do is to allow Africans to speak for themselves. An exiled African informer gave me the following interview in London after I too had left Namibia.

I began by asking him: "Critics of those Africans who feel that the only way their country will be liberated is through armed struggle are quick to point out that this, in fact, is courting suicide. What is your own assessment?"

"Of course, from one point of view, it can be regarded as suicide, for, after all, South Africa has one of the best equipped armies with the best weaponry on the continent. But it isn't just a question of resisting arms with arms. People must try and see what lies behind our decision, what motivates and drives us on. Look at the Warsaw ghetto. Can you not see a parallel between them and us? The Jews there knew full well that they were all going to die, but they said, 'Let's do something. Let's at least go down fighting.' Sure, they knew that Hitler ruled the world and that they wouldn't last more than a couple of shots against him, but the genocide that he was plotting against their nation so outraged them and they knew they would all die sooner or later. There's no difference between our thinking and theirs. What future do we have as a people under apartheid? We have suffered under the Germans; they exterminated us like flies. We have suffered under South Africa; we have suffered cruelly under this Vorster government. Does the world really think that we love freedom any less than those Jews in their Warsaw ghetto?"

He went on: "For an oppressed people to give up the hope of fighting is to commit racial suicide. We have one thought and one thought only: that is, the liberation of our country from everything that is evil and from South Africa itself.

"We wanted to establish the notion that we, as an oppressed people, have the necessary courage to face our oppressor in one way or another. The consequences of our actions are not the main concern in the present situation. After all, we are not like bank robbers who say, 'Okay, my chances of getting away with the money are slight.' There is a principle at stake: in our instance, a man is prepared to offer his life to obtain freedom for his fellow man. We are not robbers; we are the ones who are being robbed. Doesn't the Bible say somewhere,

'Greater love than this has no man, that he lay down his life for his friends'? Well, we have prepared to lay down our lives for Namibia.

"That principle had to be established by the Namibian people in one form or another. It had to be done by a political organization. It just doesn't come out of the rain, an idea like that. It is wrong when people say that innocent people were sent to their slaughter because they didn't know what they were doing, that they were just dying like sheep. Can't people see it as we see it? It just isn't true in our struggle to say that a man is going to take up a gun and offer his life without first thinking about what he is doing. Not even a mouse would do a thing like that."

He asked: "Can't people understand that any Namibian who says, 'I am going to take up a gun and go back into my country and die' is not being sent there against his wishes? He goes because he believes that this is required of him. That's a lie when people tell us that such a man is blind or doesn't understand what is being asked of him.

"Would our critics say that those Jews in the Warsaw ghetto didn't know what they were doing, that they were just dupes. If they were, so are we.

"It isn't a matter of victory either. It really is that we have this overwhelming desire to do something against the oppressor."

We discussed the attitude of Archbishop Helder Camara of Recifé, who says that he felt equally impressed with the courage and integrity of Martin Luther King, Jr. and that exhibited by Che Guevara: one was prepared to die for freedom with a gun, the other without. In *Church and Colonialism*, Camara asks:

> How long will nuclear bombs be more powerful than the poverty bomb which is forming in the Third World? Allow me the humble courage to take up a position on this issue. I respect those who feel obliged in conscience to opt for violence—not the all-too-easy violence of armchair guerrillas—who have proved their sincerity by the sacrifice of their life. In my opinion, the memory of Camila Torres and of Che Guevara merits as much respect as that of Martin Luther King. I accuse the real authors of violence: all those who, whether on the right or the left, weaken justice and prevent peace, following the example of Paul IV; personally, I would prefer a thousand times to be killed than to kill.

I said to the African: "Camara himself once said that he must follow the path of non-violence, yet he could not condemn a man as a patriot who felt the only option left to him was to die for the freedom of his country."

We then spoke of what Camara calls the "spiral of violence." I asked my informant what effect he thought violence had had on the Boers themselves. He thought carefully before offering his reply.

"From the very beginning, we expected the 'enemy' to react very harshly because they would not succumb to our violence. Obviously, they were not going to give up just because some Namibian freedom fighters had planted a mine in the Caprivi Strip. We anticipated a very strong reaction; but, on the other hand, we also felt that finally there would be a change in their attitude in that they would be forced to respect us, a thing which under the present system of apartheid never happens. The white racist dominates, bullies, oppresses, exploits us, and we, the people, cower and do nothing.

"Even *The Transvaler* [an Afrikaans newspaper] has to admit that now there is violence on their own doorstep, so now they have to meet force with force. When we first made our protests, they could ignore us, sweep us aside with contempt as a man brushes off a fly that is irritating him. But not anymore. Now, the human spirit which they thought they had crushed forever through their oppression begins to reappear. This, at least, is what I think it proves to them: that we, the downtrodden and despised of the earth, can also take up a gun and meet our oppressor face to face at that point as an equal. Maybe not now, but he foresees what is going to happen.

"This psychological reaction within the enemy, I think, is very important. He sees there is a day of reckoning; he knows that ultimately it will overtake him."

I swung the approach to another angle and asked whether there was an inner need within him as an African to respond in this way to those who were denying him his manhood and treating him so contemptuously. Did he need to take up arms to prove his own manhood?

I queried: "You have said that the Boer will now respect you, but is what you really mean that you feel there is a need for a man to respect himself, and that no oppressed people can really find this respect if they meekly lie down under the jackboot? Are you saying that as an African the freedom struggle is vital to your self-respect as a human being?"

"Right, Bishop. It has been very violent to us as a people. It has gone beyond that too. For instance, we get letters from people in Windhoek, little African girls who have no political sophistication. They write to us: 'We hear the Ovambos are shooting the Boers up there in Ovamboland. Ain't that great news?' The fact that this is taking place in another world—it's not involving her yet, she doesn't know what the hell it's all about—but just that she hears that Africans are reacting like men, are not prepared to tolerate the daily insults to their persons—well, this moves her deeply and she risks a large fine or imprisonment if her letter is read by the police and she writes to encourage us in our struggle.

"No, we don't think for a moment that we will make an immediate breakthrough. You have to understand how we have been marked mentally; in fact, it is vital for us to make a breakthrough. Mentally, it is intolerable for a man to be black in South Africa today. It is a process of mental torture that we live through daily. Violence is not the only way, of course.

"Education, religion, both have their part to play in our struggle, a vital part too. Violence is not the only thing in the resistance of the people."

I wanted him to say something of what happened to him as a human being under apartheid. So I put the question: "What is it, in the end, which is going to move a black in Namibia to resist to the extent of laying down his life?"

"The thing that I very starkly remember about apartheid is the police. The policeman is the all pervasive symbol of the apartheid society. The power that a policeman in Namibia has over another human being's life is my strongest recollection of the whole system.

"It was all so illogical: no matter how far a black had progressed, no matter what standard of education or culture you had attained, no matter how nicely you were dressed, you could never escape him.

"You would just be quietly walking down the street, peacefully going about your business. He stops you, asks to see your pass, then throws you into a cell, if you had forgotten it or mislaid it. You are beaten up, cursed, insulted.

"You were just quietly going about your business, or going to meet your lover, and suddenly this little guy pounces; he has total power over you. You can do nothing. The next day they may release you. They may not even ask you to pay a fine, because your pass had been produced, or your boss pays the admission of guilt for you and you are free again, but each day, every time you pass him on the street, you say to yourself: 'He's going to call me back *now*.'

"It's the way he looks at you. He can disrupt your whole life at whim. It's the eyes of those Boer policemen—they still haunt me even now. He was always looking for trouble, here was the great big monster of an aggressor. You couldn't win; you couldn't reason with him, simply because you could never reach out to him as a person. He was not a person; his personhood had been destroyed, consumed by the hatred he felt towards you."

It was clear from the tone of his voice, from the agitated way he gesticulated with his hands, that he was still tortured by this memory.

"I myself don't believe that I could kill a man; at this moment, I don't believe I could kill anyone, no matter whether he was white or black, but I agree with the armed struggle and I see why SWAPO decided on this course of action. I was there and took part in the discussions which preceded the decision, and I still haven't changed my mind. I believe it's the only way. We may not always articulate it too well to the outside world, but I understand and respect fully the motives which lie behind it.

"There are some things that I, from time to time, don't agree with—in this case, I think they could have taken more time before letting people know their feelings about violence, become better established as an organization maybe, but that is a small point. On the main issue of the necessity of violence to free our country, I am entirely behind them.

"The principle of facing an enemy who is out to sit on your neck, of not retreating from him, but responding to his force with force, this I accept as inevitable in our struggle. I just don't think that there is another way for us."

We then discussed those black leaders within Namibia who felt that they still wanted to work for peaceful change. I thought also of some of my black priests, some of whom had suffered greatly, but who were still prepared to teach the people that the way ahead, as far as they were concerned, lay through peaceful methods. I phrased the question like this: "I feel there are many in Namibia today who are still looking for ways of securing peaceful change. I will not call them 'moderates,' for that would imply that you are immoderate, and I don't believe that that is so; I would be slandering you. Where would you see the peacemakers in the system?"

"We have the highest admiration for men such as the black Lutheran Bishop of Ovamboland, Leonard Auala. The moral force that Auala can confront the enemy with is a hundred times more effective than any gun that is being used in the country today. Auala is untouchable as far as Vorster is concerned. Vorster cannot possibly throw the Bishop into gaol at the moment, not because Auala is strong physically; but the moral position he maintains makes him untouchable. Vorster cannot touch him with a ten-foot pole. So, speaking of the moral aspect of the struggle, it is in this that lies the germ of ultimate victory. It is this that will bring the victory. It is not guns that will do it. Guns are just a small pressure point, one small aspect of the whole struggle. The force that lies behind men like Bishop Auala is that which, in the end, I believe, will bring the victory."

I asked what he felt held Vorster back from incarcerating men like

Auala and for how long such men would be allowed to remain free or relatively unmolested.

His reply was: "If Vorster imprisons Auala, then everything the Boer prime minister claims that he stands for will have been demolished. Not only would it be difficult for him to face the outside world after doing such a thing, but he could not even face himself. He would be exposed as the great liar.

"Herein lies the great difference: when Vorster gets up in Parliament in Cape Town and says, 'We have shot fifteen terrorists today,' then his supporters all over South Africa will stand up and cheer, but if he gets up and says, 'I have put the black Bishop of Ovamboland in gaol because he does not like my apartheid policies,' he knows he hasn't got a leg to stand on."

I then turned the question about and asked how long men of peace like Bishop Auala could maintain their position among young black leaders who were tired of being told to turn the other cheek and to be patient, when they had been born and grown up under the devastation that apartheid wreaks on the black psyche. Black consciousness is sweeping through Ovamboland. Everyone who returns from working there now speaks of the growing impatience of the black people. I was told that whites from the outside world are hardly tolerated. He pondered the question and this is how he dealt with it:

"Black power forces seen in the overall picture are very temporary things—necessary, no doubt, for the moment, but bound in the long term to give way to other things. They are born as the children of utter frustration and, naturally, who can blame them if they become impatient—impatient with their leaders, most of all impatient with the whole system?

"I must emphasize that what Bishop Auala stands for is not a thing of today or tomorrow; it is an eternal something. It is not even of Auala himself; it is, rather, an all-pervasive thing, for even if Auala died tomorrow, there would be someone who would replace him, who would, no doubt, offer his life in the same way, say the same things, uphold the same principles.

"Today, we are living in a frustrating period when black people are hurt and very confused and don't know where to turn. I know the Ovambo people, as I know the other Namibian people; there is simply no place in their hearts for abiding hatred. They are a gentle, a soft people, and what is happening today is the result of a terrible situation; once that situation is relieved, they will then go back to loving again as they should.

"No, I am full of confidence, full of hope. I would never think of what is happening now in Ovamboland as being lasting. Once the Vorster regime is removed, they will once again become the people who show all the splendor of love. This is the kind of people that I know the Ovambos to be.

"Never think of what is happening in Ovamboland in the short term. I have hope that our country will one day be the land where all people will live together in harmony and peace. This place has all the potential for achieving this racially liberated atmosphere for our children to grow up in."

I asked him finally what effects living in exile had had upon him personally. He replied, "The first effect, of course, is the terrible feeling of frustration. It is a depressing feeling of never being allowed to work according to your merit.

"The first thing people ask when they meet you is, 'Where are you from?' When you reply, 'Namibia,' their whole attitude towards you changes immediately. You are no longer a man then, you are just a refugee, someone who has come to make demands upon them. You are obviously someone who has come to them looking for assistance. You are never in a position of equality with them, but because of your circumstances, you are forced to go through life asking, asking, asking.

"This has a terribly demoralizing effect upon anybody. I couldn't take it anymore, because I know the motives of the people I am forced to appeal to for help all the time, the Super Powers. They are not genuine; they really don't care a damn about people as people. They see people as something to be manipulated. They see me as a little cog in a great big international wheel. Exile has been a very frustrating period; I will never get that time back, nor will this generation of exiles ever recover from its effects.

"My own way of coping with the situation is to try and deal with people as individuals. That's my escape out of it."

I refuse to see these men as murderers. I respect both their integrity and their courage, and though I myself must go the way of a pilgrim of peace, I wish all who read this book to have the same sympathy for these men. White Afrikaners in South Africa fought Britain in order to preserve their own culture, language, and customs. American colonists fought Britain to achieve their own independence. How is the struggle of the people of Namibia different? The Afrikaners have never experienced, nor had the Americans, the misery and oppression that the blacks face daily under the apartheid system. If men could only reach back into their history and apply its lessons to the problems of others, there would be no need for armed revolution in Namibia today. Unless they do, it will continue unabated until all my black countrymen are free.

Over the six-month period from December 1959 to June 1960, some of the country's most politically active leaders—about a dozen of them—decided to leave Namibia, believing that by so doing, they could speed up the process of their people's liberation.

"The people were being victimized. Men who were politically active were refused jobs in Windhoek and were sent back to the reserves accused of vagrancy. In this way, the government was attempting to immobilize the people's political resistance."

Hopes were high and the great Mecca that they headed for was New York.

"Everybody scampered for New York City. They all wanted to go and petition the U.N. We came through Botswana and Southern Rhodesia (which was then part of the Central African Federation), from there into Tanzania, which was still not yet independent, but had a tunnel organization there which was very strong politically. When we reached Dar es Salaam, they would help you get a ticket to New York. The U.N. would send a cable to Dar and this enabled us to get in to petition, even though we did not have a passport. The cable would say that this man is a petitioner and has the right to enter the country to do that."

The exiles' feeling at this time was one of euphoria. They felt that independence was merely around the corner and was bound to come. All that was necessary was for them to keep the needs of their people before the U.N.; sooner or later it would, it must, act against South Africa.

"My God," we thought, "now that we are telling the world like it is, our freedom will come. We just had to tell the world our story."

"To whom did you tell your story?" I asked.

He laughed, throwing his head back and rocking to and fro on his chair. "Nobody. Nobody. Nobody was interested in our damned story, really, basically. The Fourth Committee met and said, 'Well, we are very sympathetic with your cause, and our governments pledge to do everything in their power to help the people of South West Africa' and they then went on to the next item on their agenda and forgot us." (Note: It was always some of the Western powers—not the Fourth Committee—who frustrated any action.)

These Namibians had overcome insuperable odds first to obtain an education, so that they could articulate to the world at large the sufferings of their people; next, they had overcome poverty and one of the strongest and most vigilant police states in the world to organize the resistance of their people. Having faced police bullets and Saracens and realizing that more was needed if the situation were to be remedied, they willingly faced voluntary exile to speed up the process of liberation.

"We pleaded, talked, debated, discussed; meanwhile, the people back home were being tortured and killed. For two years, we went on like that until, my God, we thought something more has to be done."

A look of utter disillusionment spread across his face at the prospect. If there were anything more that could be done, he would willingly face it.

"There was a great deal of interest at that moment in the United States. This was Africa's big moment, as more and more countries in Africa were being granted independence. The early sixties saw the focus of world attention on our continent. We felt that the smell of independence was in the air, and although we did not altogether agree with Prime Minister Macmillan that the 'wind of change' was actually rushing into our part of Africa, yet we were sufficiently encouraged by everything that was happening elsewhere."

They decided to return to Dar es Salaam, hoping to organize there a center from which they could launch a campaign to mobilize world opinion.

To further their education, many of the group remained behind in the United States, and some went to Germany or Scandinavia. For all of them, education has been one of the strongest motivating forces. Deprived of it in the country of their birth, they have developed an intense thirst for it, knowing that when freedom finally comes to Namibia, their main hope for the future, as far as the modern world is concerned, will be in producing their own trained leaders, scientists, and technologists who can lead a modern state to self-dependency.

"Many went to study, but a small group went back to Dar with Nujoma. This was already around 1963 when we gathered there once more to plan our own strategy. We felt that we had been misled, taken in by a dream not entirely of our own making; but we felt strongly for it on our own. No one, least of all the United Nations, was going to hand our country over to us on a platter."

They had travelled the world speaking about their country's struggles, but the overriding sense now hit them that this was a waste of effort which could be put to more profitable use elsewhere. In 1963 it finally dawned on them that they were embarking on a long struggle and that they had to plan accordingly. They felt that neither the West nor the East was prepared to step in to do anything really effective to help them. Accordingly, they opened an office of SWAPO in Dar es

Salaam. Immediately afterwards, they were enabled by the Egyptian government to open another office in Cairo. I asked why they chose that city.

"Dar es Salaam was the only English-speaking city in independent Africa at that moment. Cairo was one of the most sympathetic. Financially speaking, the Egyptians were our mainstay." Nasser, my companion thought, had a sound political strategy for Africa.

"I met him with Sam Nujoma. He had a particularly shrewd assessment of what was going on in Africa. He was a very open, a frank kind of guy. He wasn't a political wheeler-dealer. There were no smiles, no nothing. He'd just say very bluntly, 'We can do this for you or that and we're going to do it.' If he said, 'We are going to give you a thousand pounds to help you with your struggle,' you would get it. It was he who gave us the money to set up our organization abroad. Nasser was kingpin, because there was no money at that time from Dar. They just didn't have it to give. They were poor politically as well as financially. They were struggling as much as we ourselves." The Egyptians gave them their first help to obtain their headquarters and purchased a couple of Land Rovers for their transport.

Two things were to be enshrined in the constitution of SWAPO, to which they were to dedicate their entire struggle. They wanted to do everything in their power to assist with the education of the Namibian people within and outside the country. Secondly, they pledged themselves totally to the armed struggle to liberate Namibia.

Chapter Seventeen

The Birth of a Nation

One of the greatest leaders and patriots that Namibia has produced is Herman Toivo ja Toivo. Herman ja Toivo was born in 1924, the son of an African teacher who had worked on a Finnish mission in Ovamboland. He himself had received his higher education at the Anglican High School at Odibo, which had given him a fair degree of fluency in English. At the outbreak of the 1939 war with Germany, he had volunteered for service with the South African forces, who used him as a guard for one of their ammunition dumps. He had travelled extensively outside Namibia, observed other countries and their political systems, and returned home convinced that before him lay the massive task of helping to unite the blacks of Namibia into one coherent whole in order to overthrow the yoke of apartheid. Fired with this ambition, he returned to school in 1950 in order to complete Standard Eight. This meant that he was a high school junior at the age of twenty-six.

Eventually he became the leader of the contract laborers who were working in and around Cape Town. At that time, Herman was working as a checker in a white grocery business in Green Point, a seaside suburb of Cape Town. As a highly valued and trusted employee, he was given a post of great responsibility by the white man who employed him. He succeeded in establishing a headquarters in a barber shop which was the central meeting place for Namibians in the Cape. It was here that a revolution was born—conceived, directed, encouraged, and guided in that Namibian diaspora community in Cape Town by a man of genius who is today regarded with the same reverence as a prophet. Though these Africans were 1500 miles from their home, they were being politically awakened by his teaching and by his example. I asked a friend who had been among them to describe to me how the Namibian settlement looked and how ja Toivo went about his task.

The first thing that impressed him was their solidarity and their capacity to share.

"They were holding regular meetings in and around Cape Town at this time, and when one Namibian managed to get a house, he took in others also. For example, there was a hotel in the Strand, a seaside resort near Cape Town, and this had been entirely taken over and staffed by Namibians. One black had managed to get a job there, and he was such a good worker that he prepared the way for the others. So you see, there were these colonies of Namibians scattered throughout the Cape peninsula which kept in regular touch with each other through the care and oversight of Herman ja Toivo.

"Those Namibians who worked in this hotel in the Strand would let other Namibians share their rooms and living quarters there, so others who didn't have a job or who had no pass could come and stay there and were looked after. The great thing was the hotel was never raided by the police. The Africans who worked there received fifteen dollars a month plus their food, and because they were so communally minded, they survived probably better than any other group.

"They had a deep sense of humanity, and they had this knack, this real gift, of getting very close to one. You suddenly found that they were winning your heart very gently, without pressure, without pushing, just by sharing."

He went on to describe their meetings. "At that time, I had no idea what meetings were for and how you could get people to communicate with each other and discuss their problems. Two things were done in their meetings: first, each one talked about his own problems and needs, and then they discussed the needs of any fellow Namibians who were in trouble or who needed help. This was followed by a general discussion to decide how much money each person at the meeting should give to help those in distress. The amounts donated were small, maybe just twenty cents, but there was this strong corporate sense of sharing among them. The money was then given to Toivo to distribute. He didn't keep any books, but then he didn't need any because they all trusted him completely."

Herman ja Toivo was using all the resources available to him in Cape Town to help educate and politicize the Namibians working there. At this time, African political spokesmen from such parties as the African National Congress would hold meetings on the parade in Cape Town. From these men, Toivo learned which whites he could turn to for advice in acquiring educational skills. Barred from attending the University of Cape Town through lack of funds and educational qualifications, he used every conceivable contact which would prove useful to advance his people and himself. Professors at the University of Cape Town respected him, and he became a constant visitor to their homes. He discussed his country's problems with them, borrowed their textbooks, and then explained them at the regular Sunday meetings which took place in the barber shop in Sea Point. One marked characteristic of Toivo was that he never acquired knowledge or friends for his own advantage but shared them all with his fellow Namibians.

"I always felt that this man was a very Christian human being who lived his religion. I'd never seen this before, neither in black or white. He shared everything he had with me; I used to wear his shoes and even his clothes. Sometimes I got scared because I wasn't an Ovambo, but he never gave me a feeling of rejection and always accepted me as a brother Namibian. I remember, too, the great love he had for his mother, who was a very old woman. He used to write to her often and send her money and I suppose you could consider him to be a model son. His mother meant a lot to him.

"I never got the impression that he was trying for political leadership. He had the role of the prophet and I saw him as a kind of Mahatma Gandhi figure. He also had a real abhorrence of violence."

So the picture emerges of Toivo as a dedicated Christian leader with a manifest lack of hatred for whites and an ability to turn every conceivable contact into something by which he could help his people but also a man singularly lacking in political ambition. Stirred by the hope that if only the outside world were in possession of the actual facts, the U.N. would act to remove South Africa from Namibia, Toivo prepared a tape-recorded message which he dispatched to the United Nations hidden in a copy of the book *Treasure Island*. By today's standards, it was not a strong statement. It said that South Africa's presence in Namibia was illegal and that the United Nations must come to the rescue of the people.

Toivo knew the risk he was running and his fears were fulfilled when the Security Police arrested him in Langa, and he was ordered to be deported from Cape Town and returned immediately to Ovamboland. The effect on the group of Namibians in Cape Town was traumatic.

"We had this empty feeling. Toivo had been the pillar of our existence, and with his going, there was nothing to keep us in Cape Town. As we left, we formed a political organization called OPO (Ovamboland People's Organisation). It was strange that we chose this name, as most of our group felt it was a harking back to tribalism, but I felt strongly that we were right to stress the part that the Ovambos had played in our struggle, and I told them so. As far as I was concerned, they could rename the whole of South West Africa Ovamboland if they wished to, and I told them that we could be proud to call it by that name. We had a small constitution, and so it was the forerunner of SWAPO came into existence." Having done this, the group disbanded and returned to Namibia. The Namibia they came back to was not the slumbering country they had left.

In the South, the white state was about to move in to crush the resistance and determination of the people in the Old Location who remained there. This was to culminate in a shoot-out which took place in 1959. My companion reminisced about the courageous determination of the people to hold out. They hated Katutura and the prospect of moving there appalled them; but the alternative of moving out to the African reserves was even more appalling.

"I left Namibia soon after that myself, and all the way as I travelled there were the carcasses of dead cattle strewn on the sandy wastes. The country was in the grip of one of its worst droughts, and the beasts and animals were dying all around us. The reserve called Aminuis was just a windswept wilderness; it could sustain nothing. This was the choice the people were accepting: rather than move to Katutura they preferred to face slow starvation on the reserve. It may seem strange to say this, but given this choice, a drought-stricken reserve for them meant freedom."

Raids and beatings increased in the Old Location as the white community demanded that the political activity there be suppressed. As for the blacks, this was the time when many decided to leave the country in order to continue the struggle from abroad. They yearned to get their message across to the outside world, still believing that they could rouse the conscience of the United Nations into activity. They really believed in 1959 that freedom was just around the corner.

"We felt that if we told the world, that there was bound to be some action. That was our great motive in leaving. Everyone who was really involved in the political struggle came out except Toivo. Toivo and Kapuuo stayed behind."

Back in Ovamboland, the feeling was now overwhelming that South Africa would never give in to the Africans' cries for justice and for freedom unless physical force were used against her. There was therefore a growing sentiment, which was at first resisted by Toivo, to engage in an armed struggle, to take weapons and to go into the bush to train as freedom fighters. This decision was made in 1965, and in 1966 the freedom struggle was launched.

Toivo, like so many other African patriots before him, had tried to follow the path of reasonable patience and dialogue but found by so doing that he was losing credibility among his own people. It was no easy decision and was taken only when every other avenue had been closed to them, but having once taken it, those engaged in the struggle were determined to offer their very lives for the freedom so long denied the land of their birth.

South Africa responded to the activity of the freedom fighters by launching a massive manhunt with troops and helicopters. Paid informers were used. A SWAPO arms cache was unearthed, and thirty-seven Africans were rounded up and placed for six months in solitary confinement, where they were beaten and tortured. Among their number was Herman ja Toivo.

In his testimony before the Fourth Committee of the United Nations, Mr. John ja Otto, a member of SWAPO's National Executive, gave the following account of the torture he underwent during his confinement before the thirty-seven were tried in August 1967:

> I am a teacher by profession and was among the thirty-seven SWAPO members tried in Pretoria in 1967-68.
>
> I have spent months and months in solitary confinement, surviving merely on meagre penal diet. I have been tortured a lot by the South African Security Police on numerous occasions during my political life.
>
> On December 1st, 1966, while teaching my pupils at a Primary School in Windhoek, two white Security Police agents entered my classroom and arrested me on the spot. I was taken to my house, which was searched thoroughly for at least four hours. There were looking for documents and anything they could use against me as evidence.
>
> I spent the night in jail in Windhoek and moved to Pretoria the following day, December 2, together with my colleagues Jason Mutumbulwa and Nathaniel Mahuilili and an escort of not less than thirty-two armed police on the plane.
>
> However, before we took off from Windhoek I was assaulted even before I got on board. While I was still standing on the ground, about to board the plane, Lieutenant Ferreira of the South African Police kicked me with his right foot on the head, aiming at my jaws. He hit me so hard that I bled from my mouth as a result—and this occurred simply because, according to Ferreira, I whispered something in Mutumbulwa's ear.
>
> I was also beaten several times on the plane, and the policemen who were supervising this were Captain Erasmus, Sonnekus and Captain Van Rensburg.
>
> On arrival in Pretoria, the five of us were immediately taken to the Pretoria Central Prison and locked up. I was ordered to

strip and instructed to enter my cell; my trousers, shirt, etc. were thrown in after me. At this particular moment, the police did not assault me except for the prison warden who insulted me several times.

On the 6th December 1966, two white policemen, Erasmus and Ferreira, accompanied by two African policemen, Simon and George, all of them from Pretoria, came to fetch me. They took me to a certain building known as Compol and presented me to Captain Swanepoel and a certain Gericke. Gericke asked my name. I told him and he then smacked me hard across the face.

Sergeant Simon ordered me to undress, and while in the process of doing as he said, he grabbed my shirt, pulled me, and then the shirt was torn into several pieces. Sergeant Zulu, one of the African policemen, was present and he used a hose-pipe to beat me continuously on my back. And since I was naked, all the policemen, African as well as white, were beating me simultaneously.

Captain Erasmus fetched a broomstick from somewhere while I was unconscious from the beating. I only regained my consciousness when they poured a bucket of water over me. They ordered me to stand up immediately, gave me the broomstick and instructed me to hold it above my head with both hands. I was then told to run as fast as I can around the table. Eight Special Branch men were surrounding me, and each one of them had an object to hit me with, a stick, a hose-pipe, etc., they were all hitting hard as I went around the table holding the broomstick above my head.

Captain Erasmus was sitting on the desk and each time I passed near him, he used to give me a very painful Karate chop between my shoulders. Due to fatigue and pain, I could not go on running. I fell down and pretended to have fainted, but all in vain—the policemen kicked and hit me in concert. Then Captain Swanepoel, who had gone somewhere, came back and asked "whether the kaffir is not yet dead." He made a remark that I should witness and experience what several others have already gone through.

Following Captain Swanepoel's remarks, Eino Johannes, one of the African policemen, blindfolded me and handcuffed me to a pipe—up on a pipe with the total effect that my feet could hardly touch the floor. Then I felt something being fixed to my penis and then electric shock penetrate into various parts of my body. They did this with short intervals of about one and a half minutes. They were continuously telling me that I must remember that I have sent a number of people for military training—and because I refuted their statements repeatedly—the process of torture I have described before was continued for some time.

Captain Swanepoel arrived on the scene and found me suspended, and instead, he ordered me to open my mouth widely and when I did, he spit into my mouth and the others followed suit—spitting into my mouth and instructing me to swallow their saliva. After three hours in this position, they removed me from there; because it was lunch time, the handcuffs were also removed.

After a break of about twenty minutes, I was handcuffed again, my hands were handcuffed against my ankles with the effect that I could feel them penetrating into my flesh and causing so much pain; two desks had been placed a few inches from each other and a strong stick was used to suspend me between these desks, and I was upside-down in this position—Eino Johannes, one of the African policemen, went on kicking me on the head, several times, that is. This went on for about two hours before a change of method. It was not until eight o'clock in the evening that they took me back to prison.

On the following day, Ferreira came to fetch me and handed me a heap of blank papers to make a statement—about anything pertaining to SWAPO and how our members were military trained, etc. The papers were later torn by him because the statement as written by me did not please him. The routine of torture followed: electric shock, beating me and so on mainly because, according to Ferreira, I was arrogant. This way of torturing went on for several days, and at times they used to ask me questions in between.

At one time while the South African police were torturing me, they had a revolver on the desk—I could not stand the pain anymore, it became most unbearable to say the least—that was when I went for the revolver in an attempt to commit suicide instead of more and more suffering at the hands of the brutal police. I failed in my attempt though—Ferreira wrestled with me and managed to take the gun away from me, and torture continued more and more.

I was kept in solitary confinement for about five months on end. They used to let me out at least once a day for about two minutes—and I had to run to and fro in the corridor as part of my physical exercise during those two minutes.

Food: they served me mainly hard cooked porridge and black coffee without sugar in the morning—and at times, hard boiled mealies. For the five months that I spent in solitary confinement, I was not allowed to go outside and have some fresh air. I had a bucket for a toilet and I received no visitors, and was thus held incommunicado far away in Pretoria where I hardly knew anyone. On Sundays, the prison authorities forced me to drink a certain liquid, and the purpose for doing that was never satisfactorily explained.

Just a few days before the trial, we were at least allowed to be three in a cell. The trial started in August 1967 and ended on the 9th of February 1968. I was found guilty under the terms of the Suppression of Communism Act and given a five year suspended sentence. I could no longer teach nor live in Windhoek because the authorities did not allow me to. Thus I went

> to live in Ovamboland where I have from time to time also suffered at the hand of the South Africa Security Police—until a few months before my departure about a month or so ago.

Before being tied along with his fellow Namibians, ja Toivo himself suffered terrible torture and was suspended in a room for four days and four nights at Compol, the Security Headquarters in Pretoria. The South African government paid out to one of the accused, Jacob Mbindi, the amount of 4200 dollars as indemnity for injuries sustained during captivity, a tacit admission by them of their use of torture.

The trial itself lasted from August 1967 until 9 February 1968. In his summing up, the judge mocked these patriots as "cowards" and misguided "dupes" and sent them to the notorious prison on Robben Island. In language marked by its emotional character, Judge Ludorf found thirty of the men guilty of the main charge of terrorism, for which the death sentence could have been passed. Nineteen of the Namibians were sentenced to life imprisonment; nine—including Herman ja Toivo—received twenty years imprisonment; two were given five years; three were found guilty under the Suppression of Communism Act and were sentenced to five years, of which four years, eleven months was suspended for three years; and one had died in custody, allegedly from a tooth infection which was supposed to have led to encephalitis.

The judge did acknowledge that all the accused had been held in prison before the Terrorism Act had actually been made law: "It also weighs with me that all the crimes whereof the accused have been convicted on the main count were committed before the Act was passed by Parliament and that this is the first trial in which persons who are charged with the contravention of an act appear before the Court because of the retrospective effect thereof."

For his part, ja Toivo was allowed to address the court before sentence was passed on him and his comrades. South Africa has heard many such speeches during the course of political trials which have gripped the attention of her people and that of the outside world for the astonishing courage shown by those who have been prepared to resist apartheid at the cost of their lives. Ja Toivo's speech, made in that courtroom in Pretoria, must rank in the forefront of such statements. It is clear from what he said that he spoke not only on behalf of those standing trial with him, but for all Namibians who yearn to see their country rise from the shackles of South African bondage to take her rightful place in the world community as a free nation. The text of ja Toivo's address is reprinted in the Appendix.

Chapter Eighteen

Profit or People?

The South African Press Association (SAPA) official, immaculately dressed in a stone-colored linen suit, looking like some retired American Southern Colonel, kept an impassive face when he answered Judge Booth's questions about how white people in Namibia reacted to the United Nations' statements about South Africa's occupation of that country.

"We are more concerned about the drought, the price of sheep and issues of that kind. What goes on at the United Nations is a matter of complete indifference to us." In a word, white residents were more concerned with profits than with people.

This man could have been speaking of the whole of white South Africa. This blind indifference on the part of whites is a cause for consternation to Professor John Dugard, who lectures in law at the University of Witswatersrand. It is a combination of seeming contempt for the world body on the one hand, and on the other a stubborn refusal to see South Africa as part of the world around it, responsible to that world for the sufferings its policies are causing the black people of Namibia and answerable to that body for its refusal to comply with United Nations' resolutions. Professor Dugard sees the whole Namibia question as South Africa's Achilles heel, exposed and vulnerable and leaving the country open to international criticism and, perhaps later, to concerted international action against her. He writes, "The South West African dispute is a major threat to South Africa on the international scene. This is a topic about which most South Africans are largely uninformed and abysmally apathetic." The professor goes on to point out that in South Africa the white government has allowed the Namibian affair to be discussed only in armchair, legalistic jargon. He believes this to be a deliberate attempt by the South African authorities to keep the issues out of day-to-day party politics and, therefore, away from public debate and concern.

South Africa has fought an intensive campaign at the United Nations, supported by certain Western powers, and has striven to hold on to the territory of Namibia at all costs. In 1950 the South West Africa case was first referred to the International Court of Justice at The Hague for an Advisory Opinion. After their deliberations, the Court made four rulings:

1. that the Mandate for South West Africa had not lapsed with the termination of the League of Nations.
2. there was an obligation on South Africa to account to the UN for the way she was administering the Territory.
3. there was no legal obligation for South Africa to place South West Africa under trusteeship.
4. that any modification of the Territory's status could be done only with the approval of the UN.

This Advisory Opinion was accepted by the UN General Assembly, but not by South Africa.

Such opinions, though legally authoritative, are not legally binding since there is no machinery to enforce an Advisory Opinion. No one knows this better than South Africa, and throughout this period she has made certain gestures in an attempt to buy time. Pretoria suggested that the territory be partitioned, the barren reaches of the North being put under trusteeship and the South incorporated into the Republic of South Africa.

There is always the possibility of the Security Council's being asked to intervene when an Advisory Opinion has been delivered, and this she can do by ordering economic boycott or by military intervention. Through Resolution 1142 (XII), the General Assembly recommended that member states institute proceedings against South Africa. This recommendation was acted on by Liberia and Ethiopia, the only two black African states which had been members of the original League of Nations. In their application they asked the International Court to confirm the four rulings of the 1950 opinion. For her part, South Africa objected to the competence of the Court to hear the dispute. After legal debate, the Court finally decided that it did have competence to hear the case, basing this decision on Article 7 of the Mandate, which allows a member state to act against a mandatory when there is a question of the latter's interpretation or application of the mandate. The Court also found that the two African applicants had necessary legal standing and therefore could bring an action against South Africa even though their own nationals were not involved. This was in 1962.

In 1965 the International Court of Justice at The Hague heard the case, and in July 1966 it gave its verdict, obtained by the deciding vote of a white judge, the Australian Sir Percy Spender. In this judgment, it reversed its findings of 1962, claiming that the applicants did not have the legal right to petition on behalf of the inhabitants of Namibia, but only on behalf of the interests of their own nationals, who were not here involved. In so doing, the Court dismissed the findings of 1962 as not binding upon it. Professor Dugard's comments are telling here: "This decision can only be explained by an examination of the composition of the Court. As the result of the death of one judge and the recusal of two others, it avoided having to pronounce on the dispute at all."

South Africa was jubilant, although her lawyers had not pleaded this position; but the overwhelming majority of international lawyers took the position that the Court had no competence to reverse the earlier decision.

The General Assembly took action in response to this decision and by a vote of 114 votes to 2 (South Africa and Portugal) passed Resolution 2145 (XXI) declaring that the Mandate had terminated since South Africa had violated its terms. (Three countries abstained from voting: France, the United Kingdom, and Malawi.) In 1967 the Council for Namibia was established, whose function was to administer the territory until it became independent.

South Africa reacted sharply by rejecting the findings of the General Assembly. By thus defying the world body, South Africa made the situation explosive. The first result was that black Namibians were driven further by frustration and took up arms against those who illegally occupied their country, believing that only if they did so would the world at large and South Africa in particular see that they meant business. South Africa's response to this was the arrest and imprisonment of the Namibian patriots, their illegal detention without trial, and the enactment of the savage Terrorism Act of 1967, which was made retroactive to the year 1962. What South Africa had not anticipated was the world reaction to her policies which resulted in the dispute's being taken to the Security Council for the first time since the United Nations had come into existence. Thus, in 1968 the Security Council condemned South Africa for its conduct in holding the trial of the Namibians in Pretoria and followed up this condemnation by a series of resolutions. In March 1969 it called on South Africa to withdraw from the territory. In August of that same year, it repeated its request and demanded that South Africa withdraw from Namibia (so named by the UN in 1968) before October 1969. This was followed in January 1969 by the further declaration that South

Africa was illegally occupying Namibia. In July 1970 it called on all states to isolate Namibia by ending diplomatic and economic relations with South Africa whenever she acted on behalf of Namibia. Finally, the Security Council asked the International Court for yet another Advisory Opinion on South Africa's continuing occupation of Namibia.

The situation had deteriorated considerably for South Africa, and although she could see that world opinion had turned dramatically against her, yet she agreed to appear before the World Court, and then made the startling offer of a plebiscite for the whole territory, confidently believing that the black races would be confused and vote for her continued occupation. Justice J. van Wyk, an ad hoc judge on the International Court in 1962 and 1966, said, "It has been claimed by experts on South West Africa that possibly 80% might prefer South Africa's administration to that of the United Nations."

The Court refused to be drawn into this and rightly so, for it would have reduced the whole Namibia problem from a question of international law to a matter of party politics. Consequently, the Court ruled that since South Africa's presence in Namibia was illegal, it followed that all her acts concerning Namibia were similarly illegal.

In June 1971 the Court decided as follows:

1. South Africa must withdraw from Namibia immediately.
2. Member states of the United Nations are under legal obligation to recognize the illegality of South Africa's presence in Namibia and the invalidity of its acts on behalf of or concerning Namibia, and to refrain from any acts and in particular any dealings with the Government of South Africa implying recognition of the legality of South Africa's presence. (Security Council Resolution 276—1970)

Harassed as she is by world opinion, South Africa pursues her policy of multi-nationalism. In 1968 the South African Parliament had declared that it was desirable for the "native nations" of South West Africa to develop in an orderly manner towards self-government and independence. Local councils were authorized to be created giving power to the existing council of headmen to make laws on local matters. Seven tribal authorities were recognized by the South African government in Ovamboland. The legislative council thus created was not elected by the people themselves, but by the South African government. Many of its members were entirely illiterate, and the majority of them had never been out of Ovamboland nor experienced the humiliation of working under the savage apartheid laws in the South. There was no semblance of democracy in the procedure, but

South Africa was quick to tell the world that democracy had come at last to Ovamboland.

The same procedure was followed in the eastern part of the country, with legislative councils created in the Kavongo and Caprivi. The amount of money spent on the centers for these councils is a cause of alarm and shame to thinking blacks. South Africa was prepared to throw in vast sums of money for buildings for sham operations merely to impress the outside world with her backing for democracy. What in fact was happening was that certain peasant stooges were being frightened and intimidated into playing political games defined, controlled, and supervised by the South African henchmen. In 1972 the Damaras rejected the offer of a homeland, contemptuously dismissing the area allocated to them as a chicken run. Only 7,700 of a population of 65,000 Damaras live in the homeland at present.

Professor Dugard sums up the whole struggle as follows:

> Suffice it to say that events like the 1971 Ovambo labour strike, the unrest in Owambo which has resulted in the imposition of emergency regulations there, the declared opposition of the major churches to separate development, and the emergence of a number of groups which favour South Africa's withdrawal, have completely transformed the nature of the dispute. No longer is it simply an international dispute between the United Nations and the South African Government; it is now a struggle for decolonisation with United Nations backing. South Africa is no longer being urged to account to the United Nations and to place the Territory under Trusteeship. Instead, she is being pressed to grant independence, both by groups in South West Africa itself and by the United Nations.

People who adopt a cynical attitude towards the struggle the United Nations had been engaged in against South Africa often point contemptuously to the dozens of resolutions and the endless debates, and are then inclined to dismiss it as inept and hairsplitting. Certainly in South Africa itself, the UN is widely ridiculed by whites. It is important to remember, however, that the United Nations has succeeded in keeping the issue alive and that the South African government itself, despite the violence of its protests, recognizes the weight of the world body and continues to negotiate with it. Granted such negotiations often go in South Africa's favor, in that as long as there is dialogue, she is able to maintain her grasp on the territory. Even so, the United Nations has not retracted from the struggle; on the contrary, the struggle has become a demand for South Africa's total removal.

On 11 December 1973, the Security Council voted unanimously to discontinue the negotiating efforts made by the Secretary General to persuade the South African government to give independence to South West Africa. Dr. Waldheim said that "no useful purpose" would be served by continuing the dialogues. It remains to be seen what action the UN will take next.

The repeated failure of the United Nations to implement its decisions was ably criticized by Mr. Chiao Kuan-hua, China's Deputy Foreign Minister to the United Nations, on 2 October 1973. "Frankly," he remarked in a speech characterized by blunt language, "what we have experienced in the United Nations has caused us to become worried. Speeches are multiplying and resolutions are piling up in the United Nations. Yet it has not been able to look into matters which it has been asked to investigate. If things continue this way, what future is there for the United Nations?" He concluded his speech by suggesting a Charter revision that would give a greater voice to the smaller countries so that the United Nations would "cease to be controlled by the superpowers" (*New York Times*, 3 October 1973).

When the United Nations came into existence in 1945, it wrote into its Charter certain binding legal obligations which it was determined to see fulfilled. Article 73 deals with non-self-governing territories and states:

> Members of the United Nations which have, or assume, responsibilities for the administration of Territories whose people have not yet acquired a full measure of self-government . . . accept as a sacred trust the obligation . . . to develop self-government, to take due account of the political aspirations of the peoples, and to assist them in the progressive development of their free political institutions, according to the particular circumstances of each territory.

The effect of Article 73 has been to change the map of the world. It caused Britain to change its empire, then the greatest in history, to a commonwealth of free-governing nations. General de Gaulle admitted when he turned eighteen former French colonies into independent states that he was accepting the necessary decolonization of the world. The same could be said of Belgium, Holland, Italy, and Japan. Now that Portugal's empire in Southern West Africa has collapsed, South Africa and Rhodesia stand together in resisting what the UN clearly set out to achieve: the abolition of colonialism. The very foundation principles of this great world body are set in contempt and defied by South Africa. Enshrined in the UN Charter is the determination "to achieve international co-operation . . . in promoting and encouraging respect for human lives, and for fundamental freedoms for all, without distinctions as to race, sex, language, or religion."

When one studies the effects of foreign investments in Namibia, it is immediately apparent that the Vorster regime uses such investments to strengthen its hold on the country. Here is a double alliance: Vorster provides the cheap labor without which the vast profits of these foreign firms would be decreased; they, for their part, provide him with the capital needed to implement his apartheid policies. The investments have a further effect: they prevent those states which have investments in Namibia and South Africa from abiding by UN resolutions and cause them to block any action attempted at the UN to give Namibia its freedom.

On the surface, American policy towards Namibia seems reasonable enough. In 1970 the Nixon Administration made the three following points through Ambassador Charles Yost. He said that American investments in Namibia would be officially discouraged; that export-import credits would not be available for American firms trading with Namibia; and that in the event of an African government ousting firms when the country gains independence, those firms could claim no assistance from the government of the United States. Yost asked that other governments do the same.

The United States' position on Namibia seems more definite than that of the United Kingdom, which, along with France, does not accept the findings of the World Court. William Rogers, when Secretary of State, went on record as saying that America does accept the decision of the International Court.

Strong action has been called for by the black caucus in Congress. In March 1972 they asked that those U.S. firms trading in Namibia not receive credit on U.S. income taxes for taxes paid to the South African government. Though this action was backed in a letter from several leading senators, it is unlikely to be passed.

Direct U.S. investments in Namibia, according to estimates from the Commerce Department, total about $50 million, of which 90 per cent is invested in the Tsumeb Corporation.[1] A glance at the trading figures and profits of this American-controlled company reveals the following: from the three mines operated by American Metal Climax and Newmont Mining, the controlling U.S. companies, astronomic profits have been received. The Tsumeb mine was bought in 1945 for

---

[1] David Newsom, Assistant Secretary of State for African Affairs, in *Hearings before the Subcommittee on Africa of the Committee on Foreign Affairs House of Representatives*, Government Printer, May 29, 1970, p. 175.

just over one million British pounds.[2] Total dividends paid by AMAX to its shareholders since 1952 amount to $78,882,483, whereas their original investment was $840,000.[3] Newmont made an original outlay of $1,151,400. The total dividends they have received amount to $85,737,676—an average annual return of 372 percent.[4]

The South African government has found such gains greatly to her own advantage. Mr. J. P. Ratledge, manager of the Tsumeb mine, has gone on record as saying that the present tarred road which runs fifteen hundred miles from Cape Town to the Angolan border—so vital for the speedy deployment of troops and military supplies—could not have been constructed had it not been for the $140 million in taxes paid by the Tsumeb Corporation since its inception.[5] In 1970 the company paid $14 million[6] to South Africa in taxes, amounting to 8.6 per cent of Namibia's budget. The Tsumeb Corporation has laid deeper stakes in the country by spending over $1 million a year in excavating for new deposits of ore.[7]

Far from helping the black people of the country attain a better life, such companies as the Tsumeb Corporation pay near-slave wages to their black employees. Rates of 67¢ per shift were what black surface workers received before the strike. Those blacks working underground received 73¢ per shift (per day, that is). This gave an average wage to a black surface worker of $17-$19 a month. The average wage received by blacks in the mine was $28. The company claimed at this time that their highest-paid black employee was earning $134 a month—this in a country where the cost of living equals that of the U.S. Wages for white workers ranged from $270 to $440 a month.[8]

At the end of the strike, Tsumeb Corporation made much of the fact that they had raised their rates of pay for black workers by 24 per cent for surface workers to 94¢ a day. Those working under-

---

[2] Reed Kramer and Tami Hultman, *Tsumeb—A Profile of United States Contribution to Underdevelopment in Namibia*, Corporate Information Center of the National Council of Churches, April, 1973, p. 17.

[3] 1970 Annual Reports, AMAX and Newmont Corporations.

[4] *Ibid.*

[5] Advertisement in *Wall Street Journal*, September 5, 1969, Tsumeb Annual Report, 1970, and company data.

[6] G.M.E. Leistner, "South West Africa's Economic Bonds with South Africa," in Lejeune, Anthony (compiler), *The Case for South West Africa*, London 1971, p. 213.

[7] J.P. Ratledge, General Manager of Tsumeb, interviewed by Tami Hultman and Reed Kramer, *Namibia*, 9 March 1971.

[8] The preceding data comes from the interview with Ratledge.

ground had pay raises of 27 per cent, giving them $1.06 a day.[9] The final pay received by black workers was still only $24 a month for surface workers and $28 a month for those blacks working underground.[10]

Any wonder that the official organ of SWAPO made the following comment on the effects of overseas investment on the Namibian situation:

> Foreign capital from the United States, West Germany, Britain and France has joined in a criminal alliance with South Africa to fight our people in their struggle for national liberation and world peace. Continued South African misrule is made possible by the ready support and encouragement she receives from overseas exploiters, for whom apartheid is a corporate insurance policy guaranteeing the perpetual exploitation of Namibia's wealth and people.

I cannot believe that such corporations have the interests of the blacks at heart, as so often they claim at their annual board meetings. Their very trading figures show their total indifference to the legitimate grievances of their black employees. On December 14, 1971, the manager of the Tsumeb mine, Mr. Ratledge, said, "All our Ovambos are working and there is no sign of unrest."[11] Three days later, 4,000 blacks at Tsumeb downed tools to protest slave labor.

Because I know that the overwhelming majority of white managers and the firms they represent reflect the same prejudices and indifference to black suffering as is revealed by the South African government, I am convinced that international pressure must be brought to bear to have these firms removed as speedily as possible. With their modern machinery, it is conceivable that they could extract most of the country's mineral wealth within twenty-five years.

At the annual meetings of AMAX and Newmont in New York City and Wilmington, Delaware, respectively, in May 1972, the Episcopal Churchmen for South Africa filed identical resolutions asking for a full disclosure of the companies' activities in Namibia and South Africa. Newmont opposed the resolution for several reasons, arguing that it was not relevant for stockholders to arrive "at an informed business judgment on the retention or evaluation of the worth of mining properties."

---

9 Plato Malozemoff, President and Chairman of Newmont, in a letter to the Editor, *Wall Street Journal*, April 19, 1972, and further detail supplied to Kramer, *op. cit.*, by company officials.

10 Interview with Ratledge.

11 *Windhoek Advertiser.*

In 1973, ECSA asked the company to remove itself from Namibia in accordance with the UN resolution. It added the caveat, "Such co-operation presents a danger to the Corporation by involving it in direct support of an illegal regime and the use of forced labour."

In 1973, the United Church of Christ filed a stockholders' resolution with Newmont calling for fair employment practices and programs which would ultimately ensure equal job opportunity. Newmont responded that the UCC resolution would, in fact, mean that the company would have to contravene local laws in South Africa, with which the company did not necessarily agree, but with which they had to conform.

My own thoughts on foreign investment in Namibia were made clear in a statement which I wrote to be read at the AMAX and Newmont 1973 annual meetings.

> "We do not believe in a system which sells people." When 13,000 black men struck in Namibia, this was their manifesto. From the hundreds who spoke to me, it was obvious that their grievances were basically that they understood that two things stood in the way of their freedom: first, the illegal occupation of their country by a white foreign regime which maintains its presence there by force of arms, torture and imprisonment; and second, the collusion of certain foreign business concerns who are systematically stripping the natural resources from their country, offering the Vorster regime taxes from these proceeds to further implement policies of the hated apartheid system, and securing for their own enterprises returns of vast profits in the process.
>
> I believe those responsible for the policy decisions of AMAX and Newmont Mining know in their consciences that what they are doing is wrong. When 75% of a country's labour force rises up and declares a belief in freedom, any but the most insensitive will listen. When leaders such as the Chief of the Hereros call out to such companies to stop the wholesale removal of their country's wealth, freedom-loving people all over the world take note.
>
> We are at present powerless to remove AMAX and Newmont from assisting in plundering the peoples of Namibia. We do not accept their excuses and we accuse them of being among the bandits of the 20th century.
>
> It is not sufficient for the government of America to call on firms to desist from entering into trading agreements in Namibia; a truly democratic government in this land should forcibly remove such firms as being a blight on the name of the American nation.
>
> +Colin O'B. Winter
>
> Locust Valley, N.Y.
> 22 April 1973

One interesting outcome of the above was an action brought by children and grandchildren of the original founder of AMAX, Max Shott. The suit, a complaint for injunction and damages of one million dollars, was filed in San Francisco. Section X of the legal document claims:

> The defendant directors, Newmont and South Africa, have lawlessly deprived the legal and lawful authorities of Namibia of the public revenue from the operation of Tsumeb and have caused that revenue instead to be delivered to South Africa, which has no legal right thereto.

Section XVI states:

> AMAX has not paid, and is not now paying, taxes to the United Nations Council for Namibia, the legal administrative authority of Namibia.

The claimants then argue that AMAX has been damaged as a company because certain stockholders and potential customers have threatened to sell AMAX shares "and thus depress the market":

> Defendant directors, by their conduct, herein set forth, have damaged and injured AMAX to the extent of many millions of dollars, and threaten to continue the same damage and injury.

The whole object of the suit was an attempt to obtain a legal precedent for American corporations to follow United Nations resolutions. A spokeswoman for the plaintiffs summed up the whole reason behind the action by saying, "It's essentially a moral suit." In ruling in favor of the corporation, the judge said, among other things, that an American court had no jurisdiction to rule on the overseas activities of American firms (Johannesburg *Star*, 5 Jan. 1974).

Such litigation against overseas firms may be doomed to defeat at present in America, but the moral indignation of individuals, churches, legal experts, and others is bound to increase. It might well happen that the Council for Namibia, which has assigned to it the task of legally administering the territory (from outside, since South Africa refuses to allow it to enter Namibia) until independence is asserted, will decide to begin writing laws for the territory itself which could challenge the positions of such firms as AMAX and Newmont, who could then, in terms of international law, be guilty of violating its tenets as applied to Namibia.

Foreign investors have played a vital role in the economy of South Africa since 1946. The country faced her worst financial crisis after the shootings in Sharpeville in March 1960, when sixty-nine Africans were killed and nearly two hundred injured. Foreign capital fled the country, so much so that by 1961 half the country's foreign reserves were withdrawn. By 1964, however, the white regime had demonstrated to the outside world that by arresting thousands of Africans and delivering massive assaults against those who resisted her, she was capable of maintaining a stable economic order. She was fortunate to have foreign allies who were able to stand by her with massive loans and propaganda stunts. One such person was the American mining magnate, Charles Engelhard. He had launched a company called The American South African Corporation, which sought to attract American capital back to South Africa. As a result of his confidence, and together with a huge advertising campaign, ten American banks came up with a loan of $40 million.[12] So effective was this campaign that by 1970, foreign reserves in South Africa had quadrupled, British investment had increased by 677 per cent, and U.S. investment had risen an equally astonishing 400 per cent.[13]

Because of the massive profits to be made out of such investments, which are vital to South Africa's stability and have been estimated as giving from 17 to 21 per-cent return, these continue to be made. Mounting pressure by church and other groups protesting against the alliance between Western capitalism and South Africa has had the effect of making banks and other corporations reluctant to reveal their connection with the South African regime. This is obviously a tribute to the effectiveness of such campaigns as have been launched against these enterprises as well as an indication of the feelings of guilt that such companies feel in continuing to do business with South Africa.

More and more facts come to light. The Corporate Information Center in New York obtained confidential internal papers known as The Frankfurt Documents originating within a U.S. multi-national banking firm, the European American Banking Corporation. These reveal that a group of forty banks from the U.S.A., Europe, and Canada have made secret loans to the government of South Africa and its agencies since 1970. Of the $210-million total, $70 million came from eleven American banks. Due to mounting public pressure, several of these eleven have withdrawn from participation in the loan.

South Africa has recently stepped up her propaganda campaigns in an attempt to ward off criticism of international investments in her repressive economy. Advertising space is bought in leading news-

---

[12] Ruth First, *The South African Connection.*
[13] *Ibid.*

papers, and attacks launched on those who, like the World Council of Churches, are leading a campaign for disinvestment. The campaign on the part of the South African authorities is as subtle as it is effective. Western newspapers, dependent as they are upon advertising to keep their papers running, accept such advertisements without any qualms.

One of the most effective is the advertisement headed, "DO NOT KILL US WITH KINDNESS." It shows the face of Chief Councillor Gatscha Buthelezi and quotes him as saying,

> Those who advocate trade sanctions and economic withdrawal to help my people and punish the whites in South Africa may be killing us with kindness. What we need is not disengagement, but full foreign participation in South Africa's overall economic development to create more jobs, higher wages, and better training opportunities. I am no apologist for apartheid, but a realist who knows that a job may make the difference between living and starving for many black families in South Africa.

As far as the last part of his statement goes, no one would deny that the first group to suffer from trade embargoes or the removal of capital from South Africa would be the black people themselves. It is worth noting that in a similar embattled position, where a black nation is fighting for its freedom and survival, the exact opposite has been called for. In Rhodesia today, the black leaders of the people are complaining that those countries, mainly in the West, who are breaking the sanctions policy advocated by the United Nations are thus impeding their chances of liberating their country. It is not sufficient, therefore, to quote one or several black South African politicians, but rather to attempt to see the problem in a world setting. Such eminent men as Nobel Peace Prize winner, Chief Albert Lutuli, believed strongly in the use of sanctions against South Africa. In his autobiography, *Let My People Go*, he wrote:

> The economic boycott of South Africa will entail undoubted hardships for Africans. We do not doubt that. But if this is a method which shortens the day of bloodshed, the suffering will be a price we are willing to pay. In any case, we suffer already; our children are often undernourished, and on a small scale (so far), we die at the whim of a policeman.

Would South Africa ever do what Buthelezi is asking of it? Would it allow foreign capital to be invested in any large sums in the Bantustans? I seriously doubt it, as by doing so she would remove the incentive to any black to leave the tribal area, where he is subjected to the humiliation of the pass laws, job reservation, and the thousand and one other harassments in the white man's cities. By increasing investment in the reserves, white South Africa would slow down or cut off its labor supplies to the white cities and thus the bastion of apartheid—a cheap, flowing labor source—would fall. There would be no incentive for blacks to leave their so-called "homelands." The South African economy would be threatened and might easily collapse.

It is clear that Chief Buthelezi is fighting hard to win something better for his people, and one would not quarrel with him for that. But there are African leaders in Namibia equally determined never to accept the homelands policy at any price. His call for investments in the homelands must accordingly be balanced by what others currently struggling for the same liberation for their people are saying. It would be an insult to their country and integrity to claim that we must take the one view because the man propounding it is a black African leader. Commenting on the request from South Africa's Minister of the Interior, Dr. C. Mulder, that the UN should recognize the Bantustans, Buthelezi said: "It seems to me that if Dr. Mulder means what he says, then he must give us more land so that our homelands can become proper countries. If he means what he says, the Government must allow development agencies of the UN to assist the homelands. *I have asked for this, but I have had no response from Pretoria* (italics mine)."

SWAPO of Namibia today is not prepared to see the struggle in terms of the allocation of more land. For them, there is only one objective in the whole struggle and that is complete freedom from the white man's racist regime. They are not prepared to take even the first step in leading their people into the Bantustans. For them, therefore, the whole issue of boycotts and trade embargoes takes on a different meaning. They suffer already and are prepared to suffer more if the ultimate independence of their country can be so achieved.

It is because I feel that South Africa has been allowed to violate everything that was sacred in the Mandate and holds down the black people of Namibia with every ruthless weapon that I find myself in agreement with Arthur Larsen in his concluding remarks in "South West Africa: Testing Ground of Human Rights." I quote from that paper:

> The most interesting possibility for direct international action, if we rule out military action by the United Nations as unrealistic, would be all-out application of measures short of military force by the United Nations under Chapter VII of the Charter to compel compliance with the General Assembly's directive in

respect of South West Africa. I realise that when this sort of thing is proposed, the first reaction will be that we have tried various kinds of embargoes and economic sanctions against South Africa and they have been notoriously unsuccessful. One crucial distinction must be observed, however. All of these prior sanctions against South Africa were directed towards the ultimate object of inducing South Africa to change its internal apartheid policy. A substantial number of U.N. members who went along with these measures either by voting for them or abstaining were anything but enthusiastic about the actions, the reason being there was always the lingering reservation that this constituted interference in the internal affairs of a sovereign country in violation of Article 2 (7). But, as to South West Africa, there need be no such reservations. A much more general consensus of United Nations members, including the principal trading partners of South Africa, ought to be possible when the objection of interference is removed.

Larsen concludes with this statement, with which I agree fully:

The effort is doubly important, because in addition to the necessity for undoing this specific example of man's inhumanity to man, the overall success of world-wide promotion of human rights must surely be affected by the success of the society of nations in dealing with a case where both the international character of the problem and the severity and extensiveness of the violation of human rights are probably as clear as they will ever be in any human rights case.

A week before I was forced to leave Namibia, I wrote the following open letter to the Prime Minister of South Africa and to the Administrator of South West Africa:

Honourable Sirs:

Very few Christian democratic countries can lay claim to the distinction of having deported two Christian Bishops within four years, without following the due process of law, as understood in the West since Magna Carta. Further, at a crucial time in the history of South West Africa, when the eyes of the world are focused on it, this action can only be interpreted by impartial people as yet another sad attempt to muzzle the Church in this land, to intimidate its members and to suppress criticism of a régime which has now, so far as Ovamboland is concerned, abrogated the due process of law.

I am very conscious that I speak to two men who are Christians, and I claim your indulgence to address you as a Christian Bishop.

You have separated me from the people I love and whom, I believe, God has called me to serve. By removing the Rev. S.T. Hayes and Mr. David deBeer, the Diocesan Treasurer of this diocese, you have effectively attempted to destroy the organisation and the work of the Anglican Church here. In the past you have claimed that there is no Church/State confrontation in this country, and yet this action is the end of a process which included the refusal of eighteen permit applications for missionaries to do humanitarian and healing work in Ovamboland and your action in debarring me from ministering to 90% of my people. I believe this is the culmination of the policies of panic on the part of those who rule here. Nothing I have said or written can be questioned in truth by those who are in touch and aware of the feelings of the Africans who are the overwhelming majority of people in this Territory. The Church, which must always give expression to the voices of the poor and afflicted, has warned you time and again of the deteriorating human relations in this land. Your Government has totally ignored our attempt to secure consultation with the effective leaders of the blacks and has failed to initiate conferences on such things as the migratory labour system. We see in their place torture, extended imprisonment without trial, violence and shootings in an attempt to suppress the feelings of the Ovambo people.

As a Bishop and also as a Christian pacifist of long-standing, may I draw a comparison from the history of your own people. At the turn of the century, the Afrikaners were a minority group in South Africa. History records that you were exploited and your land appropriated when gold and diamonds were discovered in South Africa. You felt that you had a just cause and you were prepared to fight to the death for the right to be free men in your own country. Your people withstood, in a long and bloody campaign, the greatest power in the world at that time, and you won the admiration and respect of those who fought you for your bravery and dedication to the cause in which you believed.

At the conclusion of the war, you dedicated yourselves, as a people in a free, democratic country, to promote your own language, culture and your way of life. Since then you have resisted every attempt to superimpose another language and another culture upon your own. Since 1948, you have been the effective leaders of this land and now control the lives and destinies of a multi-racial nation of some twenty million people.

It seems to me ironic and tragic that you cannot look into your own history and learn lessons which would cause you to avoid the mistakes you are now making in your attempt to suppress the African groups within your country and within South West Africa.

The life surge which is now in Ovamboland is the desire of a people to be free from state laws which have reduced them to virtual slavery, and have restricted them from free travel in the land of their birth. These laws have been superimposed by you upon an unwilling majority in this land. You must know that the vast majority of blacks in this country groan daily under the indignity of apartheid, reject totally your concept of Bantustans, yearn to live and develop as free men and, as this last strike has clearly indicated, will never lie down under your laws which now oppress them.

Church leaders in South West Africa know that the strike is not "communist-inspired," but is a courageous gesture of freedom-loving people to break the yoke of the oppressor and to claim those basic freedoms which were described in "The Open Letter to the Prime Minister" by the Evangelical Lutheran and Ovambo-Kavongo Churches.

You can continue to deport those who speak out on behalf of the suffering people. You can put on trial those African leaders in our nation who are seeking a juster and saner society; but you will never silence the voice of truth in this land. In the end, you yourselves will be forced to implement those very changes for which we are now calling. A solution to our country's problems based on discussions with effective African leaders will have to be found. The abolition of all racist legislation will one day be effected. Justice based upon the worth of every soul in the sight of God will one day be granted to this territory. As my family and I are forcibly removed from this country, we wish you to know that we will continue to work and to pray for peace, justice, and freedom in South West Africa.

Faithfully in Christ,
+Colin O'Brien Winter
Bishop of Damaraland

28 th February 1972:
Windhoek, S.W.A.

Since I wrote that, my family and I moved to exile in England. It is because I am firmly committed personally to seeking a peaceful solution to the Namibian question that I am determined to do all in my power to work for the implementation of sanctions, the withdrawal of investments in Namibia, and the removal of foreign firms working there as offering one important contribution to the country's ultimate freedom.

Once before in its history, the Christian church was confronted with the massive challenge to human freedom and dignity in the form of slavery. History, I believe, will expect of this generation that we see the Namibian issue in the same light as we viewed the freedom of the slaves. The church today is not called to ask the question: "Is it safe, expedient or politic?" But with Martin Luther King, the church is called to ask "Is it right?" and from there to make its stand with the oppressed people of Namibia.

Chapter Nineteen

The Cost of Discipleship

South Africa is a Christian country. As far as church attendance is concerned, the church scene is healthy by comparison to what pertains in the countries of Western Europe. Whereas they face rapidly declining congregations, in South Africa thousands flock to church Sunday after Sunday. Church business is booming.

Having said that, one has to face the appalling fact that the Christian religion has failed miserably to change the plight of the ordinary black citizen. After three hundred years of Christian teaching, the church has not succeeded in removing a single piece of repressive legislation from among the thousand or so racist laws. It has failed even to have law tempered by Christian concepts of mercy and compassion. Supremely, it has failed to impart to the thousands of the country's white citizens, who throng the churches Sunday by Sunday, the need to express in their daily lives such concepts as the blessedness of sharing, the obligation to pay just wages, the need to see all men and women equally as children of one heavenly Father. The church in South Africa has failed to be the conscience of the nation.

It has failed also to promote among its members the need for honest self-examination. As a church, it has not yet emerged from the 19th century. Such movements as the "Honest to God" and the "Death of God" debates have swept past it largely uncomprehended by the overwhelming majority of its people and its clergy. And though it is in a situation where it has God-given opportunities to produce such a challenging theology as that which is emerging currently from Latin America on the subject of liberation, most synodical and church agendas in South Africa today would, at best, pay lip service to such concepts and, at worst, retreat from them with paranoid fear—and for obvious reasons: "liberation," when used in the South African context, as far as whites are concerned, can only mean Communism and is therefore a dangerous and dirty word.

Certain churches do, from time to time, make grandiloquent utterances condemning apartheid, or the government, or the removal of freedoms in South Africa, but these are dismissed with contempt by those who rule. For, at heart, the churches in South Africa are geared to white power and white finance, and most often are content to spend their time playing church games, dabbling with liturgical reform here or dispatching a bishop or dignitary to a unity commission there, but failing hopelessly to implement a theology which would enable them to grapple with one of the gravest threats that Christianity faces anywhere in the world today. If Nero fiddled while Rome burned, the lasting impression made by the churches in South Africa is that they are playing an incredible game of "ring-a-ring-a-roses" while the state outmaneuvers them, blocking their effectiveness, intimidating their members, and destroying their credibility while they cower in their sanctuaries and watch.

This is not to say that South Africa has not produced some of the world's greatest Christians. But these have been individuals who, so often, have been left to stand and witness alone. They form a distinct and hallowed minority, and it is they who have given the church in South Africa a reputation which it hardly deserves. The outside world reads with wonder about and it is uplifted by such men as Albert Lutuli, Nelson Mandela, Herman ja Toivo, Ambrose Reeves, Trevor Huddleston, Michael Scott, Alan Paton, to name but a few, and it would be natural for the world to conclude that a church which has been able to produce such men and women must carry the mark of sanctity in its courageous stand in the face of oppression. Yet, the tragic side of the picture lies concealed and obscured. The church is, in fact, following a policy of appeasement which neither impresses nor forms an effective witness against the state. It is certainly creating frustration and increasing alarm among discerning Christians in the outside world, for the sad fact is that South Africa's martyrs are, for the most part, an embarrassment to the churches from which they come. Worse still, the church in South Africa is losing the support of thousands among her black adherents who, in the past, have been so loyal to her.

In the face of massive state intimidation, the church clings to a policy which is not only outdated, but which has proved, time and time again, to be ineffective.

Alan Paton writes about the courageous scholarly Archbishop of Cape Town, Dr. Geoffrey Clayton,[1] and summarizes his episcopate

[1] *Apartheid and the Archbishop.*

by saying that the Archbishop above all else "sought to stave off direct confrontation with the State." Great man though Clayton was, he saw this policy of nonconfrontation in tatters when in 1957 the state threatened the very life of the church by passing a law in Parliament called the Native Amendment Act, which sought, among other things, to make compulsory segregation of worship the norm for South Africa. Clayton signed a letter warning the Prime Minister that such an action on the part of the state would force him to lead the church into open defiance. The strain on the old man, who was then seventy-three, was too great, and after signing the letter of protest, he died in his sleep that same night. With great sadness, he had confided to Bishop Ambrose Reeves, "I am an old man. I don't want to end my days in prison, but I'll go if I have to."

In a speech in England, Clayton had laid down the pattern which is still followed today. He asked for the prayers and remembrances of other churches in the Anglican Communion, but stressed that Christians in South Africa must solve their own problems. "We Anglicans in South Africa need the prayers of our friends in England and we need help in men and money to deal with the new problems with which we are faced. . . . Our work goes on and we look forward to the future with confidence."

This confidence is not shared by many, for those who love the church in South Africa and who have served with similar devotion are yet today among her severest critics. When Oliver Tambo, a brilliant African patriot, was banned by the South African government for his work for the African National Congress, Bishop Huddleston, who had been Tambo's friend and parish priest in South Africa, wrote an article in *The London Observer* (Oct. 10, 1954) with the title, "The Church Sleeps On." It is a powerful and devastating criticism of the church's lethargy by a man whose own life and witness had inspired the outside world and had kept Christian hope alive in the hearts of millions of the church's black adherents. His criticism is just as applicable today as when he wrote it:

> The Church sleeps on. It sleeps on while 60,000 people are moved from their homes in the interest of a fantastic racial theory. It sleeps on while a dictatorship is swiftly being created . . . so that speech and movement and association are no longer free. The Church sleeps on—though it occasionally talks in its sleep and expects (or does it?) the government to listen.

A fair summary of the attitudes of white churchmen in South Africa today could be described as follows: Hands off; we are fighting a tough battle in South Africa, and any interference from outside, however well intentioned, will only make matters worse for us, resulting in the whole fury of the state being unleashed against us. Be assured we are working for change in our own way, using our own methods, but our situation is unique and only we on the inside can understand and cope with it.

Like a man who has learned to live with cancer, white Christians have learned to live with apartheid and follow a course of action which can only be described as "safety first." This is not true of the emerging black leadership in the church. Just as there is massive ferment in the black political community at large, this is now reflected in the writings and actions of young black Christians. Nothing shows this more clearly than the startling book on black power edited by Basil Moore called *Black Theology: The South African Voice.* The Uncle Tom attitude of older blacks has been replaced by a new, active, black outspokenness. Young blacks are no longer prepared to keep quiet and remain docile. Their voices are heard in the synods of the church challenging and rejecting alike the white hypocrisy and timidity as well as the acquiescence that older blacks have often shown in the past. Whereas the white churchmen wish to move ahead slowly and cautiously, blacks are prepared to take risks in South Africa today. These risks are terrible in their consequences and often result in the young black's losing his freedom by banning or in his being constantly harassed by the Special Branch, who hound his every move and frequently cause his imprisonment and torture. Today in Namibia young black Christians are showing immense courage. Black resistance to apartheid is spreading in the churches and is a force to be reckoned with. Further, because they have had the advantage of education, young black Christians are able to learn from the freedom struggles taking place in other parts of the world, especially those in which black Americans are currently involved. These actions are eagerly interpreted and then applied to the Namibian situation.

This quotation from James H. Cone, professor of theology at New York's Union Seminary, certainly reflects the position of young black Christians in Namibia today:

> Black power is the recognition that black freedom becomes a reality only when the victims of white racism declare that the oppressors have overstepped the bounds of human relations and that . . . it is now incumbent upon black people to do what is necessary to bring a halt to the white encroachments on black dignity. The willingness to act on this conclusion means that blacks accept the risk of defining themselves like our forefathers who rebelled against slavery; we know that life is not worth living unless we are fighting against its limits.

In summary, while most church leaders in Namibia and South Africa today are fine, God-fearing men, their approach to the apartheid problem, together with their opposition to the government, is blunted because, at heart, they reject the theology of the cross and have accepted expediency in its stead. With sad monotony, the majority of white Christians turn away in fear of the consequences when they come into head-on collision with the numerous daily sufferings their black fellow Christians endure. Backing away into silent acquiescence, they leave the black man alone to take the brunt of government violence. The following illustrates what I mean.

I was having a discussion in my home with a group of black and white priests. I could sense strongly the mounting opposition and resentment that the whites were feeling towards the things I was saying and doing on the race issue, but I could not get them to express their hostilities openly. Basically, they felt it would be better to be quiet and get on with their job as pastors rather than "meddle in politics." In the hope of drawing them out, I asked them a question: "What would have to happen in your parish to cause you to speak out against the policy of the state?" A white priest replied, "If any of my people were hurt or tortured, then I would most certainly protest."

Before I could carry on the conversation, an African priest addressed his white colleague: "Father, you were speaking earlier about X, a catechist who worked for you for fifteen years. I went to see him last week in the hospital."

"How was he?" the white priest asked. "Had he had an operation, or was he sick?"

The African replied, "No, Father. He hadn't had an operation and he wasn't sick; the police had beaten his feet. He is now crippled; he can't walk."

At this, the white priest flushed and replied heatedly, "I'd need to speak to witnesses and have evidence that the police actually did that before I could accept it as being true."

Another incident occurred when I had finished confirming in a remote part of Ovamboland and was setting off for home. A young man stood in the shade of a maroola tree. He smiled and motioned me to stop, so I pulled the Land Rover over to the side of the track and he asked for a lift to Tsumeb. He was well dressed and spoke perfect English, but I had never met him before and knew nothing of his background.

We travelled through the tracks of the woods, hit the bumpy, dusty road that leads to Ondangua, and then sped down the main military road to Tsumeb, some three-hours' driving time away. I shared some food with him and suddenly noticed that he had a scar the size of my fist on the right side of his face. The flesh was pink over the wound and no beard grew over it.

"How did you get that mark on your face?" I asked him. "Did you fall into the fire when you were a child?"

He laughed, struck his thigh with the palm of his right hand and said, "No, Bishop. A white man did this to me. I was imprisoned in Pretoria Prison for six months and they tortured me. A white man pulled out my beard with a pair of pliers. We had held a meeting and they caught us. They said we had Chinese arms, but we didn't."

"Why did they arrest and torture you, then?" I asked, feeling sick at the thought of the torture inflicted on him.

Again, he laughed outright. "These whites are very stupid people, Bishop. The only weapons we had that day at the meeting were our tongues." He stuck out his tongue and pointed to it for greater effect. "We're not Communists, Bishop. I don't even know where China is." He burst out laughing and said no more.

There is a cost to discipleship which has so often been lost sight of in countries like the United States and Britain. In today's South Africa, it is often dangerous to try to live as a genuine Christian. Some Christians there can say with Saint Paul: "I bear in my body the marks of the Lord Jesus." They have dared face up to the demands of the gospel and suffer the consequences: banning, house arrest, deportation, imprisonment. The outside world, together with the ordinary work-a-day Christian in it, can hardly conceive what words like "banning" or "house arrest" can do to people and the state of mental torture into which they are driven as they are forced into an imposed solitary confinement while working in the world without being allowed contact with it. The state allows them to go to work, but bans them from the simplest interaction with their fellow men. They have been convicted of no crime, brought before no court of law, neither have they had a chance to defend themselves or provide answers to their accusers, but they are regarded as enemies of a state which uses them to intimidate its citizens into silent acquiescence. Banning is a sophisticated form of psychological torture used, with so many other methods, by South Africa to break the back of resistance.

These men and women will never be silenced; their very presence in South African society is a living reproach to a regime which can never break them. I salute them; I yearn for the church to stand by them, to see them as the spiritual children of Isaiah, Amos, and Jeremiah.

John is a white South African candidate for ordination whom I wanted to have work in my diocese, where he would have been part of the Community of Simon the Zealot; he is still not yet ordained. He was active in the Liberal Party in South Africa before it was disbanded. For me, he typifies the hopes of the young everywhere in their yearning for the church to regain the vision of her early self and, if necessary, to face martyrdom, but never to come to terms with oppression. John is one of South Africa's brightest lights, and yet is daily hunted and watched over, with hundreds of others who have been placed under house arrest and have been declared banned persons by a state which brands their Christianity as diabolic.

John is engaged in a study of Bonhoeffer, yet is refused permission by the state to enter the university library, is confined to his small town, and may not meet or speak with more than one person at a time in his home or elsewhere. This restriction means that he cannot attend his young daughter's birthday party.

Further, he may not be quoted in South Africa; he may not write. To support himself and his family, he has taken various jobs as a sales clerk. Yet, he resolutely refuses to leave South Africa, the country where he was born and which he loves.

This is what he wrote to me after my exile:

> Dear Bishop Colin,
>
> I must confess that my first week in the shop was a bit morbid. It is not exactly mentally stimulating. In slack periods, for want of anything better to do, I pace up and down the counters, weaving elaborate figures of eight round the stands and underpant displays. Objectively speaking, an edifying experience. This is how the bulk of the population live their lives. Most people, black and white, live meaningless, boring, working lives. I can articulate my discontent because this is imposed on me. I know of a different way of living. But for the bulk of the working people, there is no alternative. They are unconscious of the burden they bear, or of the wrong done to them, for they have never known different nor expected it in the future. It's forty-five years behind the counter and (with luck) a gold watch at the end of it all. No wonder they get sloshed stupid at weekends and talk sexual fantasy during the week. As I said, it's edifying. The average university-educated person is very segregated from people of a different class. These others are generally looked down upon as the uneducated, the thickies, the crunchies, the yaps. Whereas in fact, they are very good people, many of them unpretentious, and, in many cases, far less racialist than their educated betters. So whenever yours truly thinks to himself: "My God, what am I doing here selling shirts and dusting jerseys, when I could be writing the great South African novel, preaching on beauty, goodness and justice, practising my super superior talents, etc.?" then he is suitably edified by the people around him. Who am I to complain?

Perhaps what I mean to say is that I am not getting all bitter and twisted because the church won't give me a job. Bored perhaps, but not despairing. I rather like the image in the New Testament of "Causes of stumbling are bound to arise, but woe to him responsible."

"As a good soldier of Christ Jesus, be prepared to take your share of hardship" (2 Timothy 2:3)—my confirmation text chosen for me by the Bishop of Natal. The fact that by God's grace one can and should find all experiences edifying does not let the South African government off the hook.

I do know that if I crawled, I would be ordained. If I crawled, I would probably be given some sort of a job. If I promised to be a good little obedient priestling, the heavenly diocesan doors would undoubtedly open. Stubborn sinful pride may be at the root of it (it probably is), but I don't feel like crawling. I prefer to be banned and selling shirts.

As Ivan Illich says somewhere, one can only love the Church as She; the Church as It, the ecclesiastical body which we deal with so often, is unbearably corrupt. I think, perhaps unfairly, that you have probably had a bellyful of the Church as It by now. I am sure that you grieve about your people and the projects in SWA which had great possibilities and which should have meant the world to the universal church, but didn't. You must be very lonely in exile. The trouble with the Church as It is that it has the wrong priorities. In theory, the Church as It has all the right ideas. It would be hard to fault the Church as an It organisation on its theology, its adherence to nonracialism, its support for the down-trodden and oppressed. But all these correct and laudable ideas are shuffled away in inaccessible portions of its brain. I have no doubt that the Archbishop of Cape Town thinks about a diocese whose bishop has been torn from his flock—for how many minutes a day, a year? I have no doubt that the Anglican Church will think about banned people like Steve, Dave and myself. FOR A FEW HOURS A YEAR. I have been banned for over 3,000 days. Did the diocese in the person of the bishop devote as much as one day to doing something about it? It was never a priority. Steve's temporary job expires at the end of this month. Although I am assured that there are plans, no one has bothered to inform Steve of them. They do not see him as a priority. The whole question of racialism in the Church is explained not by inadequacy of ideas—Church theory on race is sound enough—but by a refusal to make racism and its attendant evils a priority. Maybe I have a twisted temperament. But when I saw powerless Africans having their homes demolished and when I actually saw children die of starvation, it meant to me that I would spend most of the rest of my conscious life thereafter thinking and doing things (however ineffectual) about it.

Anyway, sorry for the long-winded ravings. You must be thinking that these banned people are interminable talkers/letter writers about themselves. I just want to say again: Thank you for being an encourager. Thank you for revealing to me something of the Church as She. John is really happy (or perhaps in joy is a better word) because he cannot think of a better place to be than where he is. He chose it. And there, by God's grace, he will stay as long as necessary.

A common experience of Christians who resist the Vorster regime in South Africa is the new light in which they are able to see God's ways through Scripture. Texts which have been recited dutifully but without evoking response suddenly become the very voice of God, strengthening, sustaining, calming.

The dimensions which have separated Christian from Christian down through the centuries lose all significance and seem petty and irrelevant. The things that the church was struggling to defend, the dignity of every man under God, the sanctity of home and marriage, the human freedoms which were being stripped away from Africans, these gave an urgency and vitality to the gospel which often seems to be lacking in the West.

This is how David de Beer, who was himself banned in South Africa after being deported from Namibia with me, described the cost of discipleship:

> It is difficult to describe what the banning felt like, what this destruction of a way of life meant. It is as if you suddenly have all the flesh blasted off your body, and you are left with only the skeleton of what you were before. In the first few weeks, I found it very important to find out exactly what this skeleton was, what it was made of, what bones were left, and how they functioned. "Who am I?" was a question continually on my mind. It took about two weeks for me to reach my lowest depths, but it was also there that I found my strength. Stripped to the bone, you cannot become any weaker, and so in fact you are at your strongest, you have nothing to lose. But then came the temptation to close myself off from everything that was around me and almost hibernate. The effect it took to resist this was well worth-while though. Giving is still more blessed than receiving, no matter how weak you are, no matter how little you are allowed to give.
>
> Almost immediately, I felt the need to "have control over something," to prove I could still do something no matter how small. So I spent a lot of time being creative by cooking exotic meals and cleaning and polishing everything in sight. I probably have not lived in such a clean house either before or since.
>
> In one way, being restricted was a new experience for me. My past experiences of Government action were expulsions; being restricted is certainly a different experience from being expelled!
>
> Just how quickly I had adapted to being with only one

person at a time was brought home to me when the Magistrate granted an application for me to have lunch with the rest of the office staff. It was almost unreal to sit down to a meal in a room filled with people talking to each other and having "social intercourse." Even now, it is sometimes a strain being at lunch with others rather than alone.

Another thing which takes some getting used to is the monotony of life. There are few real milestones to mark off progress anymore. Now there seems no real reason why each day should pass, because there isn't exactly much to look forward to. This sort of permanent state of suspension is still around in terms of work, and outside of it, I have to create my own special landmarks to show the passing of time. It is what is known as groping your way through a murky kind of life. But, at least, it is onward.

And so slowly new and different flesh is put on the bare skeleton. But it is often a painful process. One pain is that just as you seem to be creating some sort of new identity, you come up all the more forcefully against some or other restriction and frustration once again boils over. Or else, your memory is jogged perhaps by an encounter, a phrase, a song, a glance and your wounds are brutally opened and the healing process has to start anew. The trouble is that you almost become masochistic about it. The joy of experiencing a friend relating to your past experience is almost a new birth. The trouble is that it is so quickly followed by a new death as, after a hurried escape, you re-enter the world of the banned.

In many ways, being banned is a security. You know what you are in for, but you can become fearful for those whose fate is still undecided, for those who are still involved and exposed. Because of this, the banning of the NUSAS [National Union of South African Students] and SASO [South African Students Organisation] leaders hurt me deeply, for here are yet more of my friends with whom I may no longer communicate.

This is one of the most spiteful restrictions, not being able to communicate with people who have been almost like brothers to you. Like when John's daughter was born, the news was broken to me by someone saying, "You've become an uncle." An uncle, yes. But I may not communicate with someone close enough to be called a brother.

There are all the other frustrations, too. Like people not being able to understand the strains of being banned. What is it like to have to think "Is that legal?" before you do anything; to make sure that you are never in a gathering; to explain that you cannot go to dinner or go away for a weekend; to refuse a well-meaning invitation to tea after church; to know that you cannot get away from the concrete jungle for five years; the pain of seeing the sea on the cinema screen as it reminds you of the last carefree jaunt to the beach a month before the banning?

The "No Gatherings" restriction has another annoying corollary: seeing your friends one at a time takes up a lot of time, and I am finding it difficult to give as much attention to my study as I feel it should be given. Especially as this is one of the few creative things I am allowed to do.

However, in all this, the word "integrity" has taken on great meaning. My actions may have been drastically curtailed, but the quality I give to my life is inviolate. This knowledge has been very sustaining and has made meaningful two further concepts. The first is that all these trials are purely man-made. We cannot escape the sin of the world, but we do share in God's victory over it. And the more we share in the sufferings of Christ in this world, the greater our ability to participate in the glorious triumph of His Resurrection. My first reaction to the banning was one of liberation.

The second concept should possibly have come first, in that all life is given to us and we must live it out in an honest and integrated way. We must never expect success, and if it comes, we must thank God for such a blessing.

My final thoughts are these (and I am sorry to have gone on for so long): Bannings are meant to negate and destroy and so our primary reaction must be to avoid these negative sides and to turn the whole thing into a positive force and so nullify the destructive effects. New strict discipline has long been accepted by the Church as an aid to personal development, and looked at positively, all banning does is give you restrictions/disciplines within which you must live your life. Not many people have such an explicit set of rules by which to live. And so I hope that my first year of being banned has taught me just how much more I can learn in the next four by taking the forces of destruction and using them as the tools of construction.

It has been very good being able to share all this with you, because we have shared so much in the past. But then, we share in the communion of all men, and in the unending love of God.

Much love as always, and I remember you all very closely (even Catherine).

As ever,
David

Chapter Twenty

The Yearning for Home

In a church synod which was held in Windhoek in December 1972, the clergy and laity of my diocese met and passed a resolution in which they asked me, by a two-thirds majority, to continue to be their bishop, though in exile. This was a costly and courageous thing for them to do. In so doing, they were passing a vote of confidence in me and the things I had stood for, and were showing to the world at large their determination to resist the Vorster regime whose supporters had removed me. It has been a costly decision for them as well as for me.

I am often asked how I manage to maintain contact with them and what I can now do for them. Briefly, I am kept informed by letter and through telephone and tape-recorded messages of what is happening in my diocese. I am still one of their chief fund raisers and spend much of my time raising money for our various needs at home. I travel the world speaking to governments as well as to churches about what is happening in Namibia, and in the process I have become identified with thousands of exiles from South Africa who yearn for freedom to come to their country so that they can one day return to build a juster, saner society.

There are three parts to the freedom struggle in Namibia: the workers' strike, the role played by the Freedom Fighters, and the role played by the church. This book has been an attempt to show what the church's part has been in that struggle.

As bishop, I send in, from time to time, pastoral letters to my people. I do this to let them know that they are not forgotten, to keep hope alive, and to remind them that I still stand with them in their struggle. This was my Christmas message to them all.

London
12 December 1973

Though I am writing this letter six thousand miles away from the diocese, I do not find it hard or difficult to picture you all. Perhaps it would be a good thing for us all to remind ourselves what is the Anglican Church in Damaraland. This letter will be read to congregations in the compounds of Oranjemund and to the faithful in what is still one of the smallest cathedrals of the world. It will be shared with contract labourers, hundreds of miles away from their wives and children whom they love, as well as to the young servicemen in training in Walvis Bay. It will be read to those who are leaders in industry, as well as to those who hold the most menial positions there. This year it will also be sent to those who live in the Territory as well as those who are forced to live outside its borders. It will be read, I hope, by refugees outside our country, as well as those who still live in it; by those who dwell at home and by those whose thoughts at Christmas are naturally drawn to home. It will be read by those who are banned—we share this in common: we all call this country "home" and we share the Christian faith. So whether you hear this letter being read in the mud and thatch churches in Ovamboland, or in the South; whether it is being read to you as you are in exile or in prison, I remind you of the startling fact, we share the same faith; we all worship the same Christ; we are all part of the same mystical body of Jesus. I have the same greeting for you all: "Grace and peace to you from God our Father and from the Lord Jesus Christ."

Whatever your job, whatever your social position, whatever your political outlook, wherever you are and whoever you are, the message of Christmas rings out throughout the length and breadth of our world. You are loved by God, so much that he sent His Son to be born as your brother. You share this heritage with all men, rich or poor, mighty and powerless: Christ has made us all brothers, sharers in his divine life. He has removed all barriers that separate man from man; he has established a kingdom where men and women are made priests and kings. Human distinctions are no longer recognised in it: each member of it is precious in His sight; each one is sealed with His spirit, has become a prince, a royal priest. We all meet irrespective of nation or race, to herald Him as our one supreme king, to whom all allegiance, all love, total obedience is given.

Whether you are a shepherd on a karakul farm, a company director, a mine worker, housewife, contract labourer, a great scholar or illiterate, I greet you all in His love and through His grace. Human values, distinctions of class, colour, position have no place. I reach out to the Christ who is in you all and I salute you as my brothers and sisters, redeemed by Him, loved by Him, united through Him into one holy fellowship of His Catholic Church.

But there are serious and mounting divisions among us. There are massive fears in many of our hearts; there are tensions and racial problems. There is increasing polarisation, we feel afraid, estranged from each other. There are many among us who are confused; many who have lost hope, who have given up trying to love, to forgive without daring to admit it. We have sometimes looked to the Church to provide a way of comfort, of escape, from the problems of life and its agonies, but even within its walls, the pain of a divided world intrudes. What do we do: give up, retreat into our corners and let the rest of the world go by? Some of us have been victims of violence. Is there a way ahead, are we fools to go on hoping, has the Church any solutions to offer our society and country?

I write this in exile from you, separated and forbidden to be with you all. I write this conscious of the love I feel for you all, the ache I have in my heart to be near you and to minister among you; but full of hope. This poem expresses the yearnings of so many thousands of us who are exiles; composed by an African, it was included in the last issue of *Omahungi Vehi.* It says it all for me.

Shall we meet again at home
To talk and sing again
To walk and sit again
In our homes?

Shall we meet at home—
What a meeting it shall be.
Shall we meet again in the
  land of our love?
In the land of our dear hope?

Shall we meet again at home
And end the longing of home
And send the wronging home
And from sorrow over be free?

You have it all within your grasp in the church in Damaraland today. Ours is the only society left within the entire nation where men and women of different races, cultures, backgrounds, can learn to know each other, trust each other, serve each other, for Christ and in Christ. I ask you all to ponder this great mystery at this season of Christmas. The Church has the power to bring healing to the nations. This can never be done if the Church becomes muted or afraid; if it turns away its face from the world around it. The power of Christ and the love of Christ are at its disposal to heal the wounds of a divided society. Where there are divisions among us; where men hate, or exploit; when they are in our society, the Church must take the fullest blame. It is because the Church has failed in South Africa that apartheid and all its ills reign supreme. Society's failure is the Church's failure. We have missed the spirit of Christmas and its attendant message: ". . . and on earth, peace, among men with whom he is pleased."

If Christ is "risen with healing in His wings," as the Christmas hymn declares, then let the church bring this healing to the nation, "by turning the hearts of the disobedient to the wisdom of the just." We have tried our way in South Africa; it has brought suffering, confusion and death. The call at Christmas is to do it His way. Christmas speaks to me of hope, brotherhood, peace on earth, joy. He was born to grant light to them that sit in darkness and in the shadow of death and to guide our feet into the way of peace.

May He whose name is peace, who died to bring peace with God to all men, lead our nation into that peace which is His alone to give. God fill you all with joy and peace this Christmas time.

+Colin Damaraland-in-Exile

Chapter Twenty-one

Epilogue

My life nowadays is filled with speaking and preaching engagements which take me all over the world. One question I am regularly asked is, "Given hindsight, was it worth it? Could you have not been of more use to Namibia and the work of the church there by staying in and working for change from the inside?"

I am no longer on the defensive as I used to be when I come across this question. I did what I did because I believed it was right. Clearly the majority of those in my parish endorse this, because they have on two occasions reelected me as their bishop—for the first time in 1972 and again in 1975. This fact has afforded me the great strength to continue the struggle on their behalf. Exile has enabled me to develop a far greater sensitivity to the feelings and condition of my brother exiles. I think I am closer to Namibians today than ever before, because I am now sharing their suffering to a greater degree. Like them, I feel a sense of outrage at the machinations of the West. I stand appalled at the blocking devices used by the United Nations. I marvel that Christians in Europe and America can connive in South Africa's institutionalized violence on the one hand, but howl with rage at the struggle for freedom being launched by the people's army of liberation.

What I began doing nervously, almost apologetically, I am now prepared to lay down the rest of my life to obtain—the total liberation of Namibia from the jackboot of South African control. What began as an act of love and gratitude by a determined group of African peasants in a remote corner of Christendom has become the burning issue in my life. The Anglican Church in Namibia has faced much suffering from the state, endured much vicious if somewhat veiled criticism from the church in South Africa, but has made an heroic stand on the Christian gospel. The manifesto of the African strikers, "We do not believe in a system which sells people," has become the watchword for our church. The people of my church in Namibia, by supporting me as their exiled bishop, are telling that loud and clear to the rest of the world. Our church is prepared to go under fighting against an evil system of institutionalized racism which strips people of their God-given dignity as children of one heavenly Father, rather than submit or cower in acquiescence.

All twelve accused in the strike got off. Ed Morrow paid their fines on behalf of the Church, and they returned to their homes to continue the struggle. Richard and Cathy Wood returned from their honeymoon and, after consulting with black leaders of my diocese, I nominated Richard to be my suffragan bishop. At once a storm of protest erupted. A church leader in South Africa wrote an angry letter telling me to think again. It was clear that Richard was determined to follow the same course of action that I had initiated, and this frightened the church leadership in the South, who would have preferred a more cautious approach. They wanted us to back off, calm down, and become less "provocative." We were not prepared to do that.

When two hundred people were publicly flogged in Northern Namibia it was Richard Wood who took action against the government officials who had ordered this. It was he who informed the world at large of the barbarities being perpetrated under South Africa's rule. Requests were made internationally for the huge sums needed to bring a successful action against the guilty party, and the Church won in a high court appeal. When intimidation and violence were used to force African people to vote in Northern Namibia, Richard Wood initiated an investigation in which sworn statements were made to expose this blatant form of coercion aimed at convincing world opinion that African people in Namibia were at last seeing the wisdom of South Africa's Bantustan policies and were voting in increasing numbers to support its advocates. Government officials were rightly alarmed at the consequences of the bishop's inquiries; unable to refute the truth of them, they deported him and his wife under the same order which they had used against me, the Removal of Undesirables Act. So three Anglican bishops removed in the space of six years. The official authorities in the Church of England did nothing, though Richard Wood was born in Britain, educated at a British seminary and served for a period as a priest in that country before devoting the rest of his ministry to the Church of South Africa.

I am convinced that my love for and ministry to the leaders and members of Namibia's liberation group is one of the chief causes of enmity between me and my brother bishops in South Africa and also in England. It is useless for me to declare that most members of the liberation group are Christians. I am rebutted repeatedly and have been told that the church cannot identify itself with any one political group or opinion. What I feel my accusers fail to realize is that there is only one major issue in Namibia today—freedom. All other issues are secondary to that. SWAPO, to my mind, is the one group which can achieve that for my suffering fellow countrymen; I see them as one part of God's plan for the liberation of our country. I think also that those archbishops and bishops who fulminate against them would see things in a somewhat different perspective if they took the trouble to meet them collectively or individually. To dismiss them as cold-blooded killers, the dupes of communist masters, is naive and uninformed. At home they are regarded by the majority as patriots who are prepared to die that others may obtain a freedom which has eluded them for over a hundred years.

If opprobrium is to come because I have allowed priests and lay people to minister in SWAPO camps in Zambia and have answered their appeal by offering educational help to their members, I accept it. Government and church leaders will one day soon have to reassess their opinions of them, and this could be an embarrassing operation. It needs saying that for the most part the churches in South Africa, Western Europe, and America have found it difficult, if not impossible, to react sympathetically or effectively to the challenge posed by the liberation struggle in Southern Africa. When the crunch comes, Western churches think and react "white." We in Namibia have been shunned and ignored because we have tried to think and act in other dimensions.

Namibia, I believe, is entering the final stages of its struggle for freedom. Will America and the West allow it to gain truth and rightful independence or will they attempt to keep it under the South African yoke, another maimed and muted Transkei? As I write this, we hear news of a plot to pour in millions of U.S. dollars to train black Namibian troops under U.S. instructors to prop up a puppet, multi-racial government controlled by and answerable to Pretoria. Will then Namibia go the way of South Korea and Chile, or will the West realize before it is too late that such a step will certainly meet with the increased resistance of the forces of liberation as well as that of the majority of those within the church. Would other forces in the Eastern bloc be drawn in to prevent this from happening and would we then face the global racial war that Secretary General U Thant predicted?

As we witness the evolvement of the revolutionary process in Namibia, I ask myself, are we attending a birth or a funeral? So much depends on John Vorster, prime minister of South Africa. Can he free himself from his own doctrines of white domination? Much depends too on the quality and integrity of the future leadership within the United States. Can that leadership put people before profit, and can it look hard and honestly into its own past history and recognize that the overwhelming majority of the people of Namibia call out with the words of the American patriot, "Give me liberty or give me death"?

Appendix

STATEMENT BY TOIVO HERMAN JA TOIVO

My Lord,

We find ourselves here in a foreign country, convicted under laws made by people whom we have always considered as foreigners. We find ourselves tried by a Judge who is not our countryman and who has not shared our background.

When this case started, Counsel tried to show that this Court had no jurisdiction to try us. What they had to say was of a technical and legal nature. The reasons may mean little to some of us, but it is the deep feeling of all of us that we should not be tried here in Pretoria.

You, my Lord, decided that you had the right to try us, because your Parliament gave you that right. That ruling has not and could not have changed our feelings. We are Namibians and not South Africans. We do not now, and will not in the future, recognise your right to govern us; to make laws for us in which we had no say; to treat our country as if it were your property and us as if you were our masters. We have always regarded South Africa as an intruder in our country. This is how we have always felt and this is how we feel now, and it is on this basis that we have faced this trial.

I speak of "we" because I am trying to speak not only for myself, but for others as well, and especially for those of my fellow accused who have not had the benefit of any education. I think also that when I say "we", the overwhelming majority of non-white people in South West Africa would like to be included.

We are far away from our homes; not a single member of our families has come to visit us, never mind be present at our trial. The Pretoria Gaol, the Police Headquarters at Compol, where we were interrogated and where statements were extracted from us, and this Court is all we have seen of Pretoria. We have been cut off from our people and the world. We all wondered whether the headmen would have repeated some of their lies if our people had been present in Court to hear them.

The South African Government has again shown its strength by detaining us for as long as it pleased; keeping some of us in solitary confinement for 300 to 400 days and bringing us to its Capital to try us. It has shown its strength by passing an Act especially for us and having it made retrospective. It has even chosen an ugly name to call us by. One's own are called patriots, or at least rebels; your opponents are called Terrorists.

A Court can only do justice in political cases if it understands the position of those that it has in front of it. The State has not only wanted to convict us, but also to justify the policy of the South African Government. We will not even try to present the other side of the picture, because we know that a Court that has not suffered in the same way as we have, can not understand us. This is perhaps why it is said that one should be tried by one's equals. We have felt from the very time of our arrest that we were not being tried by our equals but by our masters, and that those who have brought us to trial very often do not even do us the courtesy of calling us by our surnames. Had we been tried by our equals, it would not have been necessary to have any discussion about our grievances. They would have been known to those set to judge us.

It suits the Government of South Africa to say that it is ruling South West Africa with the consent of its people. This is not true. Our organisation, S.W.A.P.O., is the largest political organisation in South West Africa. We considered ourselves a political party. We know that whites do not think of blacks as politicians—only as agitators. Many of our people, through no fault of their own, have had no education at all. This does not mean that they do not know what they want. A man does not have to be formally educated to know that he wants to live with his family where he wants to live, and not where an official chooses to tell him to live; to move about freely and not require a pass; to earn a decent wage; to be free to work for the person of his choice for as long as he wants; and finally, to be ruled by the people that he wants to be ruled by, and not those who rule him because they have more guns than he has.

Our grievances are called "so-called" grievances. We do not believe South Africa is in South West Africa in order to provide facilities and work for non-whites. It is there for its own selfish reasons. For the first forty years it did practically nothing to fulfill its "sacred trust." It only concerned itself with the welfare of the whites.

Since 1962 because of the pressure from inside by the non-whites and especially my organisation, and because of the limelight placed on our country by the world, South Africa has been trying to do a bit more. It rushed the Bantustan Report so that it would at least have something to say at the World Court.

Only one who is not white and has suffered the way we have can say whether our grievances are real or "so-called."

Those of us who have some education, together with our uneducated brethren, have always struggled to get freedom. The idea of our freedom is not liked by South Africa. It has tried in this Court to prove through the mouths of a couple of its paid Chiefs and a paid official that S.W.A.P.O. does not represent the people of South West Africa. If the Government of South Africa were sure that S.W.A.P.O. did not represent the innermost feelings of the people in South West Africa, it would not have taken the trouble to make it impossible for S.W.A.P.O. to advocate its peaceful policy.

South African officials want to believe that S.W.A.P.O. is an irresponsible organisation and that it is an organisation that resorts to the level of telling people not to get vaccinated. As much as white South Africans may want to believe this, this is not S.W.A.P.O. We sometimes feel that it is what the Government would like S.W.A.P.O. to be. It may be true that some member or even members of S.W.A.P.O. somewhere refused to do this. The reason for such refusal is that some people in our part of the world have lost confidence in the governors of our country and they are not prepared to accept even the good that they are trying to do.

Your Government, my Lord, undertook a very special responsibility when it was awarded the mandate over us after the first World War. It assumed a sacred trust to guide us towards independence and to prepare us to take our place among the nations of the world. South Africa has abused that trust because of its belief in racial supremacy (that white people have been chosen by God to rule the world) and apartheid. We believe that for fifty years South Africa has failed to promote the development of our people. Where are our trained men? The wealth of our country has been used to train your people for leadership and the sacred duty of preparing the indigenous people to take their place among the nations of the world has been ignored.

I know of no case in the last twenty years of a parent who did not want his child to go to school if the facilities were available, but even if, as it was said, a small percentage of parents wanted their children to look after cattle, I am sure that South Africa was strong enough to impose its will on this, as it has done in so many other respects. To us it has always seemed that our rulers wanted to keep us backward for their benefit.

1963 for us was to be the year of our freedom. From 1960 it looked as if South Africa could not oppose the world for ever. The world is important to us. In the same way as all laughed in Court when they heard that an old man tried to bring down a helicopter with a bow and arrow, we laughed when South Africa said that it would oppose the world. We knew that the world was divided, but as time went on it at least agreed that South Africa had no right to rule us.

I do not claim that it is easy for men of different races to live at peace with one another. I myself had no experience of this in my youth, and at first it surprised me that men of different races could live together in peace. But now I know it to be true and to be something for which we must strive. The South African Government creates hostility by separating people and emphasising their differences. We believe that by living together, people will learn to lose their fear of each other. We also believe that this fear which some of the whites have of Africans is based on their desire to be superior and privileged and that when whites see themselves as part of South West Africa, sharing with us all its hopes and troubles, then that fear will disappear. Separation is said to be a natural process. But why, then, is it imposed by force and why then is it that whites have the superiority?

Headmen are used to oppress us. This is not the first time that foreigners have tried to rule indirectly—we know that only those who are prepared to do what their masters tell them become headmen. Most of those who had some feeling for their people and who wanted independence have been intimidated into accepting the policy from above. Their guns and sticks are used to make people say they support them.

I have come to know that our people cannot expect progress as a gift from anyone, be it the United Nations or South Africa. Progress is something we shall have to struggle and work for. And I believe that the only way in which we shall be able and fit to secure that progress is to learn from our own experience and mistakes.

Your Lordship emphasised in your judgment the fact that our arms came from communist countries, and also that words commonly used by communists were to be found in our documents. But my Lord, in the documents produced by the State there is another type of language. It appears even more often than the former. Many documents finish up with an appeal to the Almighty to guide us in our struggle for freedom. It is the wish of the South African Government that we should be discredited in the Western world. That is why it calls our struggle a communist plot; but this will not be believed by the world. The world knows that we are not interested in ideologies. We feel that the world as a whole has a special responsibility towards us. This is because the land of our fathers was handed over to South Africa by a world body. It is a divided world, but it is a matter of hope for us that it at least agrees about one thing—that we are entitled to freedom and justice.

Other mandated territories have received their freedom. The judgment of the World Court was a bitter disappointment to us. We felt betrayed and we believed that South Africa would never fulfill its trust. Some felt that we would secure our freedom only by fighting for it. We knew that the power of South Africa is overwhelming, but we also knew that our case is a just one and our situation intolerable—why should we not also receive our freedom?

We are sure that the world's efforts to help us in our plight will continue, whatever South Africans may call us.

That is why we claim independence for South West Africa. We do not expect that independence will end our troubles, but we do believe that our people are entitled—as are all peoples—to rule themselves. It is not really a question of whether South Africa treats us well or badly, but that South West Africa is our country and we wish to be our own masters.

There are some who will say that they are sympathetic with our aims, but that they condemn violence. I would answer that I am not by nature a man of violence and I believe that violence is a sin against God and my fellow men. S.W.A.P.O. itself was a non-violent organisation, but the South African Government is not truly interested in whether opposition is violent or nonviolent. It does not wish to hear any opposition to apartheid. Since 1963, S.W.A.P.O. meetings have been banned. It is true that it is the Tribal Authorities who have done so, but they work with the South African Government, which has never lifted a finger in favour of political freedom. We have found ourselves voteless in our own country and deprived of the right to meet and state our own political opinions.

Is it surprising that in such times my countrymen have taken up arms? Violence is truly fearsome, but who would not defend his property and himself against a robber? And we believe that South Africa has robbed us of our country.

I have spent my life working in S.W.A.P.O., which is an ordinary political party like any other. Suddenly we in S.W.A.P.O. found that a war situation had arisen and that our colleagues and South Africa were facing each other on the field of battle. Although I had not been responsible for organising my people militarily and although I believed we were unwise to fight the might of South Africa while we were so weak, I could not refuse to help them when the time came.

My Lord, you found it necessary to brand me as a coward. During the Second World War, when it became evident that both my country and your country were threatened by the dark clouds of Nazism, I risked my life to defend both of them, wearing a uniform with orange bands on it.

But some of your countrymen when called to battle to defend civilisation resorted to sabotage against their own fatherland. I volunteered to face German bullets, and as a guard of military installations, both in South West Africa and the Republic, was prepared to be the victim of their sabotage. Today they are our masters and are considered the heroes, and I am called the coward.

When I consider my country, I am proud that my countrymen have taken up arms for their people and I believe that anyone who calls himself a man would not despise them.

In 1964 the A.N.C. and P.A.C. in South Africa were suppressed. This convinced me that we were too weak to face South Africa's force by waging battle. When some of my country's soldiers came back I foresaw the trouble there would be for S.W.A.P.O., my people and me personally. I tried to do what I could to prevent my people from going into the bush. In my attempts I became unpopular with some of my people, but this, too, I was prepared to endure. Decisions of this kind are not easy to make. My organisation could not work properly—it could not even hold meetings. I had no answer to the question "Where has your non-violence got us?" Whilst the World Court judgment was pending, I at least had that to fall back on. When we failed, after years of waiting, I had no answer to give to my people.

Even though I did not agree that people should go into the bush, I could not refuse to help them when I knew that they were hungry. I even passed on the request for dynamite. It was not an easy decision. Another man might have been able to say "I will have nothing to do with that sort of thing." I was not, and I could not remain a spectator in the struggle of my people for their freedom.

I am a loyal Namibian and I could not betray my people to their enemies. I admit that I decided to assist those who had taken up arms. I know that the struggle will be long and bitter. I also know that my people will wage that struggle, whatever the cost.

Only when we are granted our independence will the struggle stop. Only when our human dignity is restored to us, as equals of the whites, will there be peace between us.

We believe that South Africa has a choice—either to live at peace with us or to subdue us by force. If you choose to crush us and impose your will on us then you not only betray your trust, but you will live in security for only so long as your power is greater than ours. No South African will live at peace in South West Africa, for each will know that this security is based on force and that without force he will face rejection by the people of South West Africa.

My co-accused and I have suffered. We are not looking forward to our imprisonment. We do not, however, feel that our efforts and sacrifice have been wasted. We believe that human suffering has its effect even on those who impose it. We hope that what has happened will persuade the whites of South Africa that we and the world may be right and they may be wrong. Only when white South Africans realise this and act on it, will it be possible for us to stop our struggle for freedom and justice in the land of our birth.